Prime Target
Security Measures for the Executive at Home and Abroad

Bruce L. Danto, M.D.

The Charles Press, Publishers
Philadelphia

To my wife, Joan, my partner, love, and support, mother of our four children and more than a daughter to my late mother. For over 36 years we have shared excitement, adventure, and risks. She has survived my harrowing assignments and motivated me to survive. She is that rarity, a true friend, lover, and inspiration.

The Charles Press, Publishers
Post Office Box 15715
Philadelphia, Pennsylvania 19103

ISBN: 0-914783-38-6 (cloth)
ISBN: 0-914783-39-4 (paper)

Library of Congress Cataloging-in-Publication Data

Danto, Bruce L.
    Prime target: security for the executive at home and abroad / Bruce L. Danto.
      p. cm.
Includes bibliographical references.
ISBN 0-914783-38-6. –ISBN 0-914783-39-4 (pbk.)
1. Executives–Protection. 2. Terrorism–Prevention. I. Title.
HV8290.D36 1990
362.88–dc20
                                  90-33084
                                      CIP

Contents

Author's Note

Since being held hostage almost twenty-five years ago, I have been an avid reader in the fields of crime and terrorism. As my initial relief at surviving a hostage situation gave way to anger at my own ignorance, I turned to social work, medicine, and psychiatric texts, but found they offered no useful information on the psychological management of the man with a gun. It was an unexplored field.

This book addresses that issue in terms of establishing a secure program for executives and allied personnel. Offering advice to businessmen, security, and leadership personnel on all topics of import to any security program or agency, PRIME TARGET gathers together a unique group of writers of great expertise.

Jurg W. (Bill) Mattman, a veteran of both the U.S. Secret Service and the U.S. Border Patrol, served with President Richard Nixon and knows firsthand what it takes to protect the principal. Dr. Deborah Galvin, who is associated with a counterterrorist agency of national renown, presents a compelling study of women terrorists. Henry McDermott served with the CIA and spent ten years recruiting spies in Lebanon. Lawrence Redlinger, another expert on foreign intelligence gathering, studied social control, secrecy, illicit markets, and entrepreneurship. Together, they accurately describe the essentials of intelligence information necessary to the survival of the executive. Gavin de Becker is a personal protection specialist for celebrities. He offers valuable tips on handling the firing of the disgruntled employee. Philip Little is president of a detective agency with offices in London, Bonn, Paris, Tel Aviv, and Hong Kong, as well as San Francisco and Hollywood. It is operated like a mini-Secret Service. Marsha and Fred Newman, of Farmington Hills, Michigan, operate Assessment and Control International, specializing in electronic intruder-defense equipment. Jay Lubliner operates an alarm systems company in New York.

The contributions of these writers, all friends and teachers, are invaluable.

Foreword

There is nothing new about the need of those in power for protective services. Kings and princes have always had bodyguards. In our own day and age, the need of leaders for protection has not diminished. The deaths of King Khalid of Saudi Arabia, President Mohamed Anwar El-Sadat, Premier Indira Gandhi, and Prime Minister Olaf Palme are testimonies to the failure of bodyguarding. Recently, however, a new class of persons has been put at risk, and the protective services business has burgeoned beyond the narrow needs of kings and ministers to the wider field of executive protection. Not all the prospective victims are executives in the strict sense of the word; they all share risks because of their public positions, or because they are employed by a particular company, government, or military. Special measures, by specially prepared and dedicated personnel, must be taken for their protection.

Bodyguards do not grow on trees, yet the idea of professionalism is relatively new, and the useful literature is not extensive. Dr. Danto's book is sure to acquire a place of honor among these texts. It is a sharply focused professional statement on how to best serve the security needs that have arisen in our time.

The contributing authors have no need of any endorsement; their credentials speak for themselves. It is the genius of Dr. Danto to have brought them together to focus their talents upon this area of concern. The result is a book of considerable utility for all who need to train and certify the next generation of personal protection specialists.

Dr. Danto is a skilled and unusual professional. A psychiatrist whose long years of practice might have seemed rewarding enough on their own account, he refused to rest on his well-earned laurels. Dr. Danto, brimming with unusual intellectual energy, discovered in himself an investigator's flair that propelled him into areas where few mental health professionals choose to venture.

Practitioners of the forensic sciences often envy those on the law enforcement firing line. Police buffs abound and are, sometimes, less of a nuisance than might be supposed by those whose familiarity with these characters is derived largely from the pages of Agatha Christie or Conan Doyle. Dr. Danto, with no desire to play Sherlock Holmes or any character from the world of fiction, entered a law enforcement academy. He obtained certification as a peace officer, not to find some other identity, but in the belief that he might serve best by training for the part.

Dr. Danto has a real and unusual devotion to training, the very essence of the true professional. With a commitment to learning and to passing on what he has learned to others, Dr. Danto is an example to others and a credit to his own dedication. This book is a monument to the breadth of a personality ample enough to embrace successfully both roles in a new and exciting setting.

We all need to learn from each other. This is not a counsel of humility, but simple common sense. Only the moronic believe they know it all. Dr. Danto is himself the antithesis of such absurd arrogance. He does not pretend to have produced the definitive text. He has been around long enough to have eschewed such pretensions. Bodyguards are not made simply by reading a book, but this one can truly help. I commend it as a friend and a colleague.

Richard W. Kobetz, D.P.A.
Director, Executive Protection Institute
Berryville, Virginia

1

The Scope of Terrorism and Crime

Most American citizens find the idea of having to learn about terrorism almost laughable. Living and working in reasonably safe suburban or rural areas, many Americans feel that they have successfully insulated themselves against violent crime. Terrorism is something you read about happening elsewhere, something you see on television and in movies, a drama in which the heroes always triumph over the "bad guys." The same illusion applies to violence, which seems to take place only in the inner city of a large urban center, a South or Central American country or in the Middle East.

Some years ago, a stock broker from a mid-western city took his wife, son, and daughter for a winter holiday in Florida. They stayed in a condominium along the beach and enjoyed sleeping late, swimming, deep-sea fishing, sunbathing, and dining at fine restaurants. For them, life was good. Although normally kept to a strict evening curfew, when the teenage daughter begged permission to attend a New Year's Eve pool party, the mother relented, with the provision that the girl "stick like glue" to her slightly older brother. While at the party, a 17-year-old boy she had met at the tennis court asked her to accompany him on a short stroll down an unlighted beach. Her brother assumed that she was in good hands and thought that a few minutes stroll couldn't hurt.

She never returned from that brief walk down the sandy beach. The next day, the daughter was accidentally unearthed by a child digging for seashells in a small mound of sand near a volleyball court. She had been raped, beaten, and strangled with her own shorts.

I was at the scene of the crime and as a psychiatrist, I was asked to break the news to the family.

The effect on the family unit was devastating. The parents subsequently divorced and the brother was destroyed by his feeling of responsibility for this sister's death.

Such losses can occur to any of us.

It is the aim of this book to explore various types of violence especially as seen in terrorism and domestic crime and to provide insights into their prevention. My main objective here is to help the executive learn how to cope with his or her potential victimization by these two dreaded social phenomena.

That goal cannot be achieved, of course, unless we know the extent of these problems in our society and how they effect the executive.

How extensive is terrorism, and who does it affect?

Let's begin with some basic statistical information about terrorism.[1]

In 1986, terrorist incidents leveled off after having climbed more than 30% in 1984 and peaking in 1985 when 785 attacks claimed more than 2,000 casualties. Among those casualties were 38 Americans killed and 157 wounded. In Europe, international terrorism of Middle East origin actually fell 70% in 1986. For the first time in that year, Latin America became the region where the most attacks against U.S. property or personnel were carried out. Preliminary figures for 1988 indicate that the trends are continuing.

Since September, 1986, when five Palestinians hijacked a Pan American jetliner, the State Department's Operations Center became a central gathering agency. Terrorist crises are all handled through this agency.

All experts in this area seem to feel that the notion that terrorism is ebbing is not justified. Certainly the West has made significant progress in combatting terrorism but the problem is still very serious. The U.S. bombing of Libya in April, 1986, helped reduce the incidents as it suggested to nations employing terrorism that they risked retaliation. Other measures also helped:

In 1985 and 1986, more than 500 Libyan diplomats, students, and officials were expelled from Europe, or had their stays cut short. France and Italy toughened their visa policies, in effect closing what had been essentially open borders. Western intelligence networks were strengthened and Kadafi and his gang of terrorists were markedly curtailed. Terrorists were held for trial. The alleged mastermind of the Achille Lauro hijacking, Mohammad Abbas, was arrested and held for trial. The hijacker of TWA flight 847, Mohammad Ali Hamadi, was awaiting trial in Germany, and George Abdullah was serving a life sentence in France for his involvement in the murder of Americans.

Other important developments began to take place in the war against terrorism. The United States has allocated $2.4 billion over five years to improve security at 257 missions abroad and has upgraded the State Department Office of Counter-Terrorism. The FBI had increased the number of legal attaches abroad. The United States Middle East intelligence network has been strengthened.

In many ways, experts agree that terrorism today is merely symptomatic of the world's state of health. It is a world where several wars of varying intensity are being fought, and where one of every thousand people is a doctor but one of every forty-three persons is a soldier. It is a place where the United States spends $21 billion annually for security services; but the technology of death is available to anyone who can afford it. Terrorism has become a permanent part of the political landscape, and yet it hardly ever constitutes an issue as far as political candidates are concerned.

Vice-president Bush, now our President, led a task force on combatting terrorism. In its report of February, 1986, the task force revealed a list of significant 1985 terrorist incidents involving U.S. citizens. On February 2, 78 people were injured at a nightclub frequented by U.S. servicemen in Athens when it was bombed. In

1. Public Report of the President's Task Force on Combatting Terrorism, February, 1986.

Spain, on April 12, 18 people were killed and 38 wounded when a bomb destroyed a family restaurant in Madrid. Seven Americans were injured.

On June 14, in Greece, TWA flight 847 was skyjacked and 145 passengers were subjected to a hostage ordeal for 17 days, and among them were 104 Americans. It was during this incident that a U.S. Navy diver was tortured and killed, and he was the sole casualty of that episode.

On June 19, 1985, four U.S. Marines and two American businessmen were gunned down in an outdoor cafe in San Salvador.

In an Air India flight over the Atlantic Ocean, all aboard were killed, including four Americans.

In West Germany, on August 8, a car bomb exploded at the U.S. Rhein-Main air base near Frankfurt, killing one airman and the wife of another, and injuring 15 other Americans. Just minutes before that blast, the body of an American solider was discovered near Weisbaden. His identity card had been stolen and it was that ID which was used to gain access to the car-laden bomb at the air base.

A 69-year-old American tourist who was physically disabled was shot in cold-blooded murder aboard the Italian cruise ship, Achille Lauro. This was one time when the United States government was able to apprehend the four terrorists by way of an interception by U.S. Navy fighters.

An Egypt air flight 647 from Greece to Cairo was skyjacked. During this act of terrorism, an Air Force civilian employee was murdered and two other Americans were wounded. A total of 60 persons were killed during the rescue effort.

On December 27, in Rome airport, terrorists threw grenades and fired automatic weapons, wounding 73 people and killing 15, including five Americans. One of the Americans was an 11-year-old girl.

At the close of 1985, in Lebanon, six American citizens continued to be held hostage.

Such information depicts the length and breadth of international terrorism in one year, 1986, the most recent period upon which statistics have been released.

Terrorism is a problem much easier to photograph and describe than define. Briefly, however, terrorism is the unlawful use of threat of violence against persons or property to further political or social objectives. It is a process and an event which uses terror to make a political statement. Its purpose and goal is to intimidate or coerce a government, individuals, or groups to modify their behavior or policy.

The terrorists methods may include hostage-taking, aircraft piracy, sabotage, assassination, threats, hoaxes, bombings or shootings, or kidnapping.[1] Sadly, but convincingly, we have been brought to understand that most of the victims of terrorism seldom have a role in either causing or effecting the terrorists grievances.

Terrorism is a form of warfare. It has always been viewed as being unconventional aggression of low intensity. However, when you have a whole ship or a whole airplane taken over by a radical group as seen in recent terrorist activities, it becomes crystal clear that this has become a way of life over the past 10 or more years. Those of us in the field of terrorism studies and those associated with programs devoted to counter-terrorism usually agree that terrorism is a criminal activity. Criminal activity for the terrorist exposes their anti-social behavior and robs them of the kind of dignity that may be afforded those who are true freedom fighters.

According to the figures mentioned, most terrorist incidents until the mid 80s were seen in the Middle East in 46.6% of the cases, Western Europe in 25.6% of the cases, Latin America in 16.3% of the cases, Asia in 5.7%, Africa 5.1%. North America 0.5%, and Eastern Europe 0.2%.

From 1980 to 1985, terrorist incidents were directed toward 10 countries, one-third of the total being targeted directly at the United States. Thus, we see a problem that doesn't seem to want to go away and is getting worse.

In the past 10 years, terrorists have attacked U.S. officials or installations abroad approximately once every 17 days. Terrorists have killed as many U.S. diplomats in the past 20 years as were killed in the previous 180 years.

The number of servicemen killed in that bombing of the Marine barracks in Beirut almost equalled the number Britain lost in the entire Falkland campaign.

In 1988, international terrorist attacks rose by 15%.[2] State sponsored terrorism fell by the same amount according to Israel's Jaffe Center for Strategic Studies. Surprisingly, these attacks were not actions sponsored by the PLO as Yasser Arafat had renounced terrorism outside Israel's borders. The center listed 443 terrorist attacks world wide and passengers at the Pan Am Flight 103, which was bombed over Scotland, accounted for nearly half of the 626 people killed in all terrorist attacks in 1988.

The United States government has a very clear-cut policy which has evolved over the years for handling terrorism; it is an outgrowth of responses by various administration policies. It basically involves a non-concession policy to insure safety of the greatest number of people. That means that the U.S. will not give into terrorists demands.

Prevention is the first line of defense. Actions are taken designed to prevent an attack from occurring. The ability to employ this method depends on accurate intelligence information. Measures available in this approach involve altering travel routes or avoiding routine schedules.[3]

Delay is another concept that is important. It is used to delay or stall for time to position forces, keep the terrorists off balance, or to develop other responses, including the cooperation of different countries. When time can be won through international cooperation, it is possible to apply economic, diplomatic, legal, and military pressures.[4]

Third party arrangements represent another way to deal with terrorism. When terrorist incidents occur overseas, the host country has primary responsibility for situation management. Third parties may offer the best opportunity for successful

2. *Los Angeles Times*, Part I, Monday, August 28, 1989, page 2.
3. Livingstone, N.C.: *The Complete Security Guide for Executives*. Lexington, Massachusetts: Lexington Books, 1989.
4. Mullin, W.C.: *Terrorist Organizations in the United States*. Springfield, Illinois: Chares C. Thomas, Publisher, 1988.

resolution of the incident through cooperation with the host country.[5]

Negotiation is a time-honored approach to the problem of terrorism.[6] It is hoped that talk and the available resources will gain the release of Americans held hostage.

Counter-attack or force options as a way of resolving a terrorist incident can be risky. This was seen in the incident involving the Egyptian airline in Malta, where several Egyptians and other passengers were killed. On the other hand, the successful raid at Entebbe involved only the loss of one leader of the raid while all other rescuers plus passengers were returned safely to their homes.

Domestic Crime and the Executive

By no means is terrorism the only danger confronting the government leader, military person, politician, or businessman in this country. Security measures should not be limited to measures against terrorism alone. For the most part, domestic crime is a far more important problem for most citizens. Furthermore, the domestic crime reaches into almost every community in the United States and is different from terrorism in the sense that most of the attacks by terrorists are concentrated in 10 countries.

Let's take a look at the facts and figures and trends for some of the most important crimes reported in the 1986 Uniform Crime Reports.

In the U.S. Uniform Crime Reports,[7] a crime clock for 1986 revealed that there was one violent crime every 21 seconds. There was a crime index offense, i.e., murder, forcible rape, robbery, aggravated assault, burglary, larceny, theft or motor vehicle theft every 2 seconds. There was one property crime every 3 minutes.

Every 25 minutes, a murder occurred, and in every 6 minutes a rape occurred. Once every 58 seconds a robbery occurred, and every 38 seconds an aggravated assault occurred. Every 10 seconds a burglary occurred, and every 4 seconds some type of larceny-theft occurred. Every 26 seconds a motor vehicle was stolen.

During 1986, there was an estimated 20,613 murders in the United States, a figure representing 1% of the violent crimes committed. Most of the offenses occurred during July and August, and the lowest number of offenses was recorded in February.

The southern states accounted for 42% of the murders, western states reported 22%, the mid-western states 19%, and the northeastern states 17%.

In 1986, there was a 9% rise in murder compared to 1985. There was a 12% increase in the nation's cities. Rural counties registered a 4% decline.

In 1986, an average of 9 of every 100,000 persons in the United States were murder victims. The rate in metropolitan areas was 10 per 100,000 inhabitants, and in rual counties 5 per 100,000.

Seventy-five percent of the murder victims in 1986 were males and 91% were 18

5. Bell, J.B.: *A Time of Terror.* New York: Basic Books, Inc., Publishers, 1978.
6. Chapman, R.D. and Chapman, M.L.: *The Crimson Web of Terror,* 1980.
7. Crime in the United States, Uniform Crime Reports, for 1986, U.S. Department of Justice. July 25, 1987.

years of age or older. Forty-nine percent were age 20 to 34, and 53 of every 100 were white, 44 of the victims were black, and the remainder were persons of other races. Eighteen percent of the victims for whom ethnicity was reported were Hispanic.

In this year, 95% of the black murder victims were slain by black offenders, and 88% of the white murder victims were killed by white offenders. Males were more often slain by males, but 9 out of every 10 women were murdered by males.

Firearms were the weapons more commonly used: 44% for handguns, 7% for shotguns, and 4% for rifles.

Among non-firearm weapons, cutting or stabbing was employed in 21%, blunt objects (such as clubs or hammers) 6%, and poisons and explosives in 8%. Of interest is the fact that in 7%, hands, fists, feet, etc., were employed.

In the statistics on murder, three out of every five murder victims were related or acquainted with the killer. Along the female murder victims, 30% were slain by husbands or boyfriends. Six percent of the male victims were killed by wives or girlfriends.

Arguments resulted in 39% of the murders during the year, and 19% occurred as the result of feloneous activity such as robbery or arson. Four percent of the murders were committed during brawls and involved use of alcohol or narcotics.

The clearance rate for murder continued to be higher than for any other crime and this was reflected in a figure of 70% of the murderers being cleared in reporting jurisdictions. In cities of 10,000 to 25,000, the most successful rate, 81% was reported, and basically 78% of the murders in rural counties and 67% of the murders in suburban counties were cleared. For the executive living in a suburban area, these figures would seem to raise some question about security, at least from the standpoint of the success of clearing the murder case and finding out who was responsible for the murder.

Regionally, the greatest clearance rate was seen in southern states, 76%.

Forty-one percent of all those arrested for murder in 1986 were under the age of 25, and 9% were 17 or younger. The 18 to 24 year age group showed the greatest involvement in murder, accounting for 33% of the murder arrests in 1986.

Whites comprised 50% of the total arrested, and blacks made up 48%.

Rape

During 1986, there was an estimated 90,434 forcible rapes in the nation, making up 1% of the crime index total. As is the case with murder, southern states had the largest number of reported rapes, 37% followed by the west with 24% and the midwest with 23%. The northeast followed with 16%.

The month with the greatest number of rapes is August and the lowest, as is the case with murder, is February.

Forcible rape was reported with a 3% higher figure in 1986 than in 1985, involving cities and rural counties.

These figures are 15% above 1982 and 42% higher than 1977.

The Uniform Crime reporting definition makes the victims always female. It was estimated that 73 of every 100,000 females in the country were reported as rape victims.

Fifty-two percent of the forcible rapes reported to law enforcement were cleared by arrest or exceptional means. For those arrested, 45% were under the age of 25, and 30% of the total were in the 18 to 24 year age group. Fifty-two percent of those arrested were white, and 47% were black.

Robbery

Robbery accounts for 4% of all the index crimes and 36% of the violent crimes. There were 542,775 robberies reported in 1986. They occurred more frequently in August and least often in April. As is the case with the other crimes, there was a greater incidence in the southern states. The reports of robberies increased 9% over 1985 levels and 13% in suburban counties.

The national robbery rate in 1986 was 225 per 100,000.

The value of property stolen during the robberies averaged $596 per incident and the estimated national loss from robbery was $332 million.

In 1986, 43% of all robberies involved strong-arm tactics. Firearms were used in 35%, knives or cutting instruments in 13% and other weapons in 10%.

Street robbery was up 3% as was robbery of a commercial house, but robberies of gas stations, convenience stores, residences, and banks were all down by small percentages. The latter is attributable to increased security and protection at this level.

One of every four robberies was cleared by law enforcement. Persons under the age of 18 were offenders in 11% of the robbery clearances.

Sixty-two percent of all those arrested for robbery in 1986 were under the age of 25, and 92% were male. Sixty-two percent of those arrested were black, 37% were white, and the remainder were other races.

Burglary

The estimated national burglary total in 1986 was 3.2 million, and this type of crime accounted for 25% of all the Crime Index offenses.

The southern states accounted for 39% and seem to be the leading area for all types of crimes.

Burglary increased by 5% during 1986.

The rate of burglary was 1,345 per 100,000 inhabitants. Two of every three burglaries were residential in nature and 70% of all burglaries involved forcible entry.

Burglary victims suffered losses estimated at $3.1 billion in 1986.

Fourteen percent of all the burglaries were cleared, which is a rather low figure.

Adults were involved in 79% of all burglary offenses and young people under 18 were invovled in 21%. The highest degree of juvenile involvement in burglary was recorded in the nation's small cities.

During 1986, 92% of the burglary arrestees were males, and 71% were under 25 years of age. Of the total burglary arrestees, whites accounted for 69% and blacks 30%.

Motor Vehicle Theft

This type of crime increased 9% over 1985 and involved an estimated 1,224,937 offenses. The south again was the leader in this type of offense.

The incidence rate for this crime was 508 per 100,000.

In 1986, there was an estimated national loss of $6 billion due to motor vehicle theft. The average value of the vehicle stolen was $4,888.

Only 15% of all motor vehicle thefts reported were cleared.

Of persons arrested for motor vehicle theft, 91% were males. Sixty-four percent of the arrestees were white and 35% were black.

Fifty-eight percent of all persons arrested were under 21 years of age, and those under 18 made up 39%.

Arson

In 1986, there were 110,732 arson offenses which represented an increase of 6% over 1985. The rates for this type of crime range from 120 per 100,000 inhabitants in large cities, to an overall rate for all communities of 53 per 100,000. The highest arson rate was recorded in western states, with 64 offenses per 100,000 population.

Building arson comprised 55% of the reported incidents while 28% of arsons involved mobile property and vehicles.

Seventeen percent of all targeted residential property was either uninhabited or abandoned at the time the arson occurred. Residential property itself was involved in 60% of all the structural arson.

The estimated value of property damage due to reported arsons in 1986 totalled $1.2 billion with $13,198 being the average loss.

During 1986, the national arson clearance rate was 15%, which means that arson basically goes on unpunished.

By population grouping, juveniles were the offenders in 37% of the city cases and 23% of those in the rural counties.

The estimated number of arrests for arson during 1986 was 18,700, with 40% of those arrested under 18 and 63% under 25. Males comprised 86% of all arsonists arrested. Of those arrested, 24% were black and 75% were white.

Discussion

Unfortunately, crime statistics leave much to be desired in terms of providing the additional kinds of data needed. For example, nothing is on the reporting data about the killers themselves. Not one shred of information is reported about other security risks and crimes against executives, namely, kidnapping and extortion.

Thus, without relevant data, it is impossible to prepare the executive with statistical insights into the incidence of extortion and kidnapping. However, all is not lost. It is possible to discuss the qualitative aspects of kidnapping and extortion, as they usually occur together. Extortion to a lesser extent, can accompany bomb and arson threats and actions in domestic crime as well. Experience has shown that extortion is much more common when associated with kidnapping than when associated with bomb or arson threats.

Considerable material has been presented here about terrorism and those kinds of domestic crimes which could affect the average public official or executive.

It might be tempting (and human as well) to react to this material on the basis that violent crime and terrorism in the United States have not posed much of a real threat to public officials, executives, or businessmen. This argument is only partially true. The significance of the threat cannot be measured in numbers only. Suppose there was only one case, but the case happening to be you. Would it be less serious because it was a single case? Remember, a single case might be you!

What seems to be significant is that all violent crime statistics are rising, as are those for terrorism itself, nationally and internationally. Who can tell when or if he or she or they will become victims of either type of crime.

Until 1982, there were no Americans kidnapped in Lebanon. Yet that year, Dr. David Dodge, acting president of American University, Beirut, was kidnapped on July 19th by two armed men who shouted as they left with him that they were members of the paramilitary arm of Lebanon's pro-Iran Muslim Shiite sect. There was no publicity about his kidnapping, other than to say that no ransom had been paid. Through some behind-the-scenes government negotiations, he was released on July 22, 1983, a little more than a year later. The statistics on kidnapped Americans in Lebanon are almost non-existent, but for the Dodge family it has been a nightmare for a year.

In Vatican City, Italy, a rather nondescript person, one of no political or leadership significance, was placed in the role of innocent victim when his daughter, Emanuela Orlandi, aged 15, was kidnapped form a bus stop in Rome on June 22, 1983. As ransom, the kidnappers demanded the release of the man (Mehmet Ali Agca) who attempted to assassinate the Pope. The threatened deadline to take the girl's life passed. Would it be reasonable for her family to feel better because the kidnapping statistics for Papal messengers and their families have been low for Rome. Vigil from crime, and especially kidnapping, must be viewed from the standpoint of the basic concept of security rather than from some uniform crime report.

The material to be found in the following chapters will define various aspects of crime and terrorism as it has, does, and will affect the political leader and business executive, as well as those with whom he works and lives as a family. The requirements for a sound security attitude and program will be laid out in detail. The practical technology of security, including material on weapons, will be provided to the reader.

Although the primary focus on these problems will center on those persons who live and travel in the United States, an ample amount of material will be made available to cover the international scene so that Americans traveling abroad will learn how to view security needs and programs for that setting away from home.

This book has been written to make its contribution to fellow Americans and others so that security, safety, and—above all—life can be protected, both before and after an event of domestic crime or terrorism. What follows should constitute the practical side of what has been considered to be too technical for the public until now.

2

Self-defensive Measures for the Executive

There are schools in the U.S. that teach executive protection to security specialists desiring basic and advanced training. Executives themselves will often go through the training in order to develop a greater sensitivity to, and appreciation of, the work that they hire security staff to do.

No school can hope to achieve more than to teach the basic principles to any student during the training period. The art of the trade of executive protection can only be found in the combination of training and the judgment and wisdom that come from years of experience in the field.

In my experience, the first most difficult aspect of executive protection is to convince the executive he is endangered — whether because of his company's public image or his position of power within the company. This chapter contains basic security measures that might be used by the executive who is not yet convinced he needs a protection specialist, but wants guidelines for security-conscious behavior. Neal C. Livingstone has very effectively outlined a security guide for executives. Much of the material that follows is based on his discussion and recommendations.

The executive must at all times in all places be alert. You should be familiar with the neighborhoods in which you live. You must watch for things out of the ordinary: cars strange to the area; people who seem to be studying your house or trying to gain access to your business without proper identification. Household staff should be trained to watch for the out of the ordinary: strange delivery people; unfamiliar cars parked in front of the house; dog walkers who don't live in the neighborhood, and so forth. All of these things should be reported to the executive so that arrangements can be made for proper inquiries.

Be careful about how you carry your briefcase or purse, at home or abroad. These items should be kept under control by you or members of your family. The purse should have a long strap so that it may be worn military fashion (slung diagonally across the body). Purses and briefcases should never be left unattended anywhere and should never be carried in an open position. Not only could property be removed by someone walking alongside, but items could be dropped into the bag in an effort to smuggle or to get you into a compromising position.

Money distributed in several different pockets will discourage pickpockets. In some European cities, groups of child thieves may approach a tourist, each grabbing at different items, such as cameras, watches, or wallets. Or the children may be used to distract the victim while an adult thief approaches from behind.

Subways are always dangerous, particularly at night. Don't focus all your attention on the approaching train, but be aware of the people around you, some of whom might be looking for game to rob. Be aware that a drunk or any individual who accosts you may be a terrorist in disguise. Walk away from them — do not try to act like John Wayne and take them on. You may be killed.

Avoid sitting in the back of a bus where contact with the bus driver is almost impossible. This can be particularly important when in a foreign country where you do not speak the language and so run the risk of being isolated in a (hostile) crowd.

Do not be afraid to turn down any taxi that appears to you to be unsafe. If the driver seems to be nervous or treating you oddly, take a different cab. If taxis are lined up in rank, it may be preferable to push your way into the first taxi in order to avoid one that has been specifically assigned to you (as part of a kidnap plan). If you are visiting a city where taxi fees are negotiable, try to avoid hailing passing cabs. Have the doorman of your hotel do the negotiations; this can help protect you from robbery (even if it means being over-charged because you are a wealthy visitor in unfamiliar surroundings).

Avoid trouble by detecting surveillance. Watch for people following you or lingering on your street corner as you drive or walk to and from destinations. Be alert at home as well as abroad. Remember that terrorists, kidnappers, assassins, etc., will dress to look like anybody else in the environment so as not to call attention to themselves.

There may be teams with members conducting the surveillance from vans, bicycles, motorcycles, or on foot. Terrorist groups trying to establish the routine of a possible target are likely to work in this fashion.

The fact that you are aware of the possibility of a tail may help you because you have a mental set to be on guard. Tails can be difficult for the inexperienced to detect. They may use wigs, glasses, snap-on ties, and reversible jackets to alter their appearance several times during the tail. They may push a food cart and so look like a respectable street businessman. They may even wear military or police uniforms. In general, it is fair to say that if you see, or are followed by two or three people wearing long coats on a hot summer day, you should consider the possibility that weapons are concealed under those coats.

Inspect the tail lights of your car for small holes introduced to either the right or left light. The telltale bright white spot would make it easy for a surveillance crew to follow you even on a super highway at night. Light-reflecting tape stuck to your car bumper would serve the same purpose. (For more detailed information on vehicle security see the relevent chapter in this book).

To impair surveillance try alternating speeds and watch whether or not the car behind seems to be following the same pattern. The same advice can be followed while walking.

If you are walking and suspect you are being tailed you might try one of the following tactics:

- Walking into a building, stop and turn abruptly, causing the tail to bump into you and inadvertantly reveal his face.
- Drop something and look back to see who picks it up.
- Board subways, busses, or trains at the last possible moment.
- Look into a shop window for the reflection of your tail (who might stop when you do).
- Alter your appearance by ducking into a store and removing your coat, carry it lining out over your arm.
- Walk into a building and take an elevator up, then immediately take another elevator down a few flights, staggering your journey to the ground floor in several elevators if possible.

If you suspect you are being followed by a car, try to get the full license-plate number and note anything that will help identify the vehicle, i.e., color and manufacturer. It may be necessary to intentionally walk or drive by surveillance personnel to take careful note of their distinguishing characteristics. Then you can proceed to a police station and report the suspect.

A physical assault requires management on the spot. If you are alone, then you should approach an unarmed assailant as if you are fighting for your life. Fight as savagely as possible; the amount of aggression may catch the assailant by surprise. You can employ items that you normally carry, such as fountain pens, as weapons. I would recommend the use of a Kubaton stick. This is a stick approximately three to four inches in length, is made of a hard wood like ebony, and has a key ring. If you carry keys on the ring, its purpose as a defense weapon may be totally disguised. A fountain pen or a Kubaton stick can be applied quickly and adroitly to the supersternal notch located at the top of the breast bone where it meets the throat, thus cutting off the assailant's wind. It can induce great pain if directed toward the genitals or abdomen. Sometimes a single blow with a Kubaton stick is enough to allow you to escape.

Regardless of whether you have a stick or pen, any blow or force should be aimed at the attackers neck. A chopping motion on the side of the neck could incapacitate the assailant. A blow to the Adam's apple in the neck or the front of the throat would also be effective in immobilizing him. The assailant should be struck, kicked, or punched in any area of his spinal cord, the back of his neck, under the arm, between the legs, or in the stomach.

Even a small woman can immobilize a large assailant by cupping her hands and slapping them over the openings to this ears. This produces tremendous pain and ringing in the ears and will deter the assailant by stunning him. Biting the assailant on his ear or fingers, jamming his eyes with a finger, and pinching and twisting his nose closed so he has to open his mouth, which can then be smacked with a fist, are all effective fighting techniques.

If you are grabbed from behind, bend your knees and hurl the assailant over your head, or stand upright and stamp on his feet. If the assailant's pelvis is in contact with the victim's hands, genitals can be grabbed and squeezed. If the assailant is a female, breasts can be grabbed and squeezed. Remember that if you direct your elbow backward it serves almost like hitting the assailant in the abdomen or ribs with a two-by-four. If the abdomen is struck forcefully enough it can knock the wind out of the assailant. Canes, umbrellas, purses, and briefcases can be swung at the assailant and aimed at the neck or the throat or the head.

A note of caution must be expressed in regard to firearms. The executive who plans on using a weapon as a form of self-defense should be aware of the fact that in the United States a concealed weapons permit is required. It is limited to the jurisdiction of the state that issues it. Some states, like Michigan, will honor out-of-state concealed weapons permits—check with the office of the prosecuting attorney in the state to which you are traveling. If you are traveling abroad remember there are very strong laws in Europe prohibiting Americans, even police officials, from carrying weapons. Foreign countries permit American soldiers to carry weapons only under very limited and well-defined circumstances.

Most of us in security work frown upon the use of firearms unless there is no other alternative because assailants are armed and shooting. I have carried a gun since 1962 but have pulled it only once—during a break-in with the police on a suspected barricaded gunman. On the other hand, I was on the SWAT team with the Wayne County Sheriffs' Department and rode in tanks to where snipers and barricaded gunmen were shooting, and never found it necessary to pull a weapon. Notwithstanding its lack of application, I have maintained a weekly shooting schedule to retain my skill with shot gun, rifle, and handgun.

Using a firearm should be a question of last resort. Carrying a gun with the idea of scaring a possible assailant is a big risk because the assailant may take the gun and use it on you. Or, if you panic, an unnecessary shooting may take place. The unarmed assailant then becomes the martyr and you may become the criminal. As a criminal, you can be sued in civil court for big money.

If you decide to carry a weapon in the United States, you had best be licensed, and maintain your proficiency with consistent practice. Attend a shooting school where you will be taught to recognize the most effective time to employ firearm defense. You may learn other methods of assailant management, such as hand-to-hand combat. This may allow you to save your life by thwarting an assault without running afoul of the law.

The executive who travels at home or abroad need not feel that he is a defenseless target for a criminal or political terrorist. You should learn what to do when under various types of surveillance or when undergoing actual assault.

The best defense is knowledge of and skill in avoiding those areas of threat and danger that are fundamentally situational, i.e. dark places, unfamiliar surroundings, being alone anywhere, and places where one can be easily recognized as an American.

You should update yourself on current preventative and defensive measures against terrorists and criminals, and be informed about the latest intelligence information on groups of such persons operating in the pathways of your activities. If necessary, you should avail yourself of professional consultation with those who are recognized specialists in the security field.

3

Secure Vehicle Transportation

For most of us the use of an automobile is part of daily life. Security simply means parking in a well-lit, well-trafficked neighborhood and locking doors and trunk. When the issue of extra security becomes important in an executive's life, he must systematically and in a disciplined fashion retrain himself to a new set of defensive habits. The presence of a driver or personal protection specialist cannot alone ensure the safety of the executive.

- The governor of one of the most violent states in Colombia, was assassinated by a car bomb. As his car came near a booby-trapped vehicle, the bomb was detonated by a remote control device later found nearby. The governor's car was hurled about ten yards: the governor, three bodyguards, and at least two bystanders were killed.

What this tells me (or any security specialist) is that he had been under surveillance for some period of time. His travel routes and times of day for traveling had become so routine that the terrorist group was able to predict when his car would pass a particular point. It would not have mattered if the governor was accompanied by 40 bodyguards, each one holding two machine guns. Given this type of poor security design, where his daily routine was predictable, his assassination was equally predictable.

Livingstone[1] states that 80 percent of all assassinations and kidnapping attacks involve the victim being targeted while entering into, exiting from, or riding in his car. Illustrations of this tragic fact include the assassinations of President John F. Kennedy, Rafael Trujillo of the Dominican Republic, and U.N. mediator Folke Bernadotte. In 1914, the Austrian Archduke Francis Ferdinand was assassinated while riding in an open vehicle. Hans Martin Schleyer of Germany and Aldo Moro of Italy were kidnapped from cars. President Ronald Reagan was only a few steps from entering his limousine when he was shot by John Hinckley, Jr. Thus, as many executives view their car as being almost like a second office, they must attend to the special security requirements of that important setting, which is a vital aspect of their professional and business life.

1. Livingston, N.C. *The Complete Security Guide for Executives*. Lexington, Mass: Lexington Books, 1989.

The Secure Vehicle

At all costs, the executive, particularly when driving alone, should avoid driving flashy sports cars or land cruisers like Cadillac, Lincoln, or Mercedes Benz. These cars call attention to the economic status of the executive and are easy to follow. A large four-wheel drive vehicle such as a jeep, Blazer, Bronco, or Ranger has excellent ground clearance and traction. Such vehicles can easily circumvent obstacles and ram through barricades.

Vanity license plates should never be used.

Part and parcel of the automobile should be a heavy duty reinforced front bumper with skid plates to protect the oil pan and differential. The gas tank should be reinforced with armor or should be self-sealing with anti-explosive baffles inside. A second fuel tank is important as it will add weight to an already heavy vehicle. The gas cap should have a lock.

The transmission should be beefed up. Limited slip differentials will help a car get out of a rut.

The electrical system should be provided with a second battery in case the first one is tampered with or simply breaks down.

Remote-control starters are useful, so no one need be inside the car when it is started — in the event that a bomb has been rigged to the ignition system. (However, in Northern Ireland, according to Livingstone, terrorists are familiar with this ploy and can create bombs that are not activated until the car is in motion).

Bolts should be installed through the end of the vehicle's exhaust pipe to prevent anybody from inserting an explosive device there.

Livingstone advises fire retardant systems. He also advises the installation of a fire suppression system that will flood the exterior with various fire retardants. Air intakes should be installed so that passengers are not vulnerable to fumes.

While visiting GSG9 in Bonn, West Germany, I attended a demonstration of tear gas dispensers that can be placed in the trunk. These are useful in preventing hostile crowds from tipping the car over or generally coming close to assault it. If gas equipment is used, there must be enough gas masks available for those inside the car.

Tires must be of top quality to avoid their collapsing during stress, i.e., on an aggressive reverse 180-degree turn.

High-intensity lights should be mounted on the front bumper to give additional visibility at night. A pulsating, high-intensity light mounted on top of the car will provide a glare that will interfere with the ability of a sniper to get a clear shot at night. Night vision equipment can be useful because it allows you to turn out the lights and escape pursuit.

Car alarms can be useful, but most citizens simply tune out the sound of an alarm because there are so many accidental discharges. To me, these are of doubtful value. Sirens or air horns are useful for confusing, frightening, and disorienting attackers. Such noise also attracts much more attention than alarm system noise. A loud-speaker can be useful to permit communication with persons outside the car without having to open the windows or doors.

It is important that a telephone or communication radio be located in the vehicle. There are some two-way antennas that can be disguised to look like an ordinary A.M./F.M. radio antenna.

Door locks should be automatic and child-proof.

LeRoy Thompson[2] recommends over 35 protection-related items that should be carried in the VIP vehicle. Not all these items need be in the average executive's car, but if the threat of terrorism or crime increases, more of these items may be added. For government personnel or those living in Third World countries, these items may be made necessary because of inadequate police protection.

I recommend each vehicle carry the following regardless of the risk.

1. Spare tire.
2. Jack.
3. Fire extinguisher.
4. Radio: vehicle mounted or hand-held.
5. Medical kits.
6. Flashlights.
7. Maps of the area.
8. Containers of clean water: remember to change them periodically.
9. Local currency and coins: in some foreign countries, a few gold coins might come in useful.
10. Gas masks: enough for all passengers.
11. Spare batteries: or rechargable batteries for the radio.
12. Tow chain or rope.
13. Smoke grenades.
14. Sledge hammer.
15. Hacksaw.
16. Heavy crowbar.
17. Bolt cutters.
18. Coveralls.
19. Jumper cables.
20. Portable oxygen equipment.
21. Portable spotlights.
22. Blankets.
23. Compact survival blankets.
24. Hand-held metal detectors.
25. Explosive recce kit.
26. Explosive detection kit.

The reader should remember that the availability and presence of weapons should be consistent with local laws for license and possession of firearms. Weapons should never be stored in open view, but should be secured in racks under the dash or in the doors or on the person of the passengers or driver. Automatic weapons can be mounted below the front passenger seat. There should be spare armament and

2. Thompson, L. Legal Equipment Check List. *Guns & Ammo*. July 1989, pp. 30 and 64.

ammunition in the vehicle. Most small automatic weapons use 9-mm ammunition; this makes using 9-mm semiautomatic firearms practical because the ammunition is interchangeable. But the best possible protection is a 12-gauge pump riot gun loaded with .00 buckshot. Submachine guns and automatic weapons are useful for close assault contact, but carbines, assault rifles, and sniper rifles are of no value whatever for close encounters of this type.

The protection specialist usually carries on his person two spare magazines for his hand gun or machine gun.

Thompson recommends the car be provided with four additional pistol magazines and four machine-gun magazines, fully loaded. He feels heavy armament is important to reduce the lethal effect of sniper fire. He favors countersniper capacity for some member of the team if there are follow-up cars and the executive is a high security risk. A sniper's rifle should be carried in the trunk of the follow-up car.

Armored Vehicles

Armament of the car is a very expensive project, but the executive would be well-advised to use an armored vehicle if he is in a high-risk situation — such as an overseas placement where Americans are known targets of terrorists. It may thwart injury from small arms and some rocket-propelled grenades, but will not defend against many weapons used by terrorists today, including RPG-7 rockets, land mines, or cache bombs buried in the road.

If the decision is made to purchase an armored car, then an established dealer should be consulted. Most experienced armorers will build a vehicle to exact needs and specifications.

The vehicle should have well-fitted windows and the best quality bullet-resistant glass. All brake and fuel lines should be moved behind the armor, and care should be exercised to insure that the engine, steering, brakes, and suspension system are reinforced to accommodate the extra weight of the armor.

The purchaser should have the right to inspect the vehicle during its construction and to verify the quality of workmanship. Livingstone advises that there should be a test firing of the armor plate done at close range before the contract to purchase that vehicle is signed.

Vehicle Security Check

The executive should always be on his guard when entering or exiting a vehicle. There should be a survey of the surroundings to make sure there is no one loitering around. If possible, the entrance or exit should take place in a sheltered area or an underground garage.

If the executive has a driver, that driver should remain near the car at all times. Should the executive arrive at the car and find the driver is not present, the executive should not wait at the car. The driver himself may have been kidnapped.

All security agencies recommend a check list inspection of the vehicle. Such a list would include — but not be limited to — the following areas of concern. There should be a survey of the outside of the car for anything unusual, such as loose wires underneath the car.

- Check for a flat or slashed tire. Somebody may plan to jump the executive while he is changing the tire.
- A security conscious executive may put Scotch tape between the doors; broken Scotch tape would be a tip off that the car may have been tampered with.
- Wheel wells should be checked for possible explosives.
- The contact point of the tire with the ground should be checked for pressure-release firing devices.
- Check the exhaust pipe.
- The underside of the vehicle should be inspected for foreign objects.
- The trunk should be opened and the contents checked. I find that putting a strip of Scotch tape along the outer periphery of the trunk (away from the lock) is an excellent way to determine whether or not the trunk has been opened.
- The spare tire should be checked — explosives might be hidden inside it.
- The gas-tank cap and the grill on the bumpers should be checked. The hood should be lifted and checked, then the engine compartment should be examined. Some security people advise taking polaroid photographs of the contents of the trunk and the engine compartment. The photographs can be carried by the executive or driver, or be pulled out of the glove compartment and used for comparison when checking those areas.
- The doors should be opened and inspected carefully, then the interior of the vehicle. A search should be made beneath the seats, under the floor, under the dash, and even under the floor mats of the car, as well as behind the visors, the head rests, and in the glove compartment. (The glove box should be locked at all times, even if nothing is in it).

The Strategy of Automotive Travel Security

Common sense is the rule of thumb in limiting your vulnerability to both terrorism and ordinary street crime. People flagging you down for assistance, hitchhikers, even traffic accidents, an injured person in the road, or children approaching the car might be staged distractions designed to take your attention away from your own security. A call from the car phone or radio will bring appropriate help and does not require that you endanger yourself by stopping.

Travel routes should avoid narrow or congested streets. Try to stay on main streets or highways where the traffic generally moves in a smooth manner. Whenever areas that restrict mobility are unavoidable — congested areas, steep hills, intersections, traffic signals, or railroad tracks — remember to be particularly on your guard. Such areas make you especially vulnerable to assassination or kidnapping because a slowed or stopped vehicle is easier for an assailant to approach unobserved. Assassins will frequently use bicycles or motorcycles so the executive and/or his driver should be especially aware of their presence. When on a freeway, the driver should use the inside lane near the center of the road, as it is more difficult to force a car off the road in that position.

When pulling up to a traffic light, never stop parallel to the car in the next lane but slightly behind it. Avoid pulling up to the bumper of the car in front, because there is no escape if there is an assault on your car.

In rural areas (especially in foreign countries) extra caution must be exercised when traveling at night. You could be a victim of domestic crime, attacked and murdered simply for your money and your car.

The driver and passenger should always wear seat belts with shoulder harnesses. Doors should be kept locked while traveling. In all kinds of weather, the windows should be kept closed and locked.

The executive and/or his driver would be well-advised to take an aggressive driving course. You will learn, among other useful driving techniques, to perform a reverse 180-degree turn, to ram obstacles out of the way, or to make a 90-degree turn by slowing down and stepping on the emergency brake.

When ramming through a barricade, the driver and passenger should be prepared for a shock. When ramming a car, aim your vehicle toward its taillight or rear tire; the collision will force the car out of your path.

If an attack occurs, every effort should be made to avoid stopping your vehicle. Even if some nail-embedded board or other object has been planted in the road to puncture tires, you should proceed at full speed, whether or not you have a flat tire.

If your vehicle is pulled over by a police agency, obtain identification from the police officer before the doors and windows are opened or anyone exits the car. Use of a police uniform is a favorite trick of assassins and kidnappers.

Parking spots should be varied. The vehicle should never be parked in a spot personalized with the executive's name. When using valet parking, only the ignition key should be given to the valet.

4

Making the Home Secure

Aside from automobiles, the next most vulnerable place is the executive's private residence. An Israeli attache in Washington was killed in his own driveway. Israeli commandos killed a top member of the PLO, Abu Jihad, in his own home in Tunis. The Lindberg kidnapping involved a child taken from his own bedroom.

Choose a residence with clearly visible approaches, off-street parking, and multiple access routes. Efforts should be made to establish good relationships with neighbors; you can reinforce each other's safety measures by reporting strangers and pooling resources like exterior lighting, block patrols, alarm systems, and a common security force.

Particular attention should be paid to terrain; the grounds should be easily observable from various points within the house. A careful check should be made for drainage ditches and other areas that might provide concealment for a kidnapper or sniper. These areas could be filled in, brightly lit, or a sensor system installed to enhance security.

It is a good idea to encircle the property with fencing. It could be a chain-linked fence supplemented with intruder defense equipment such as motion detectors and pressure pads embedded in the ground below the fence. If there is a high wall, concertina wire, broken glass, or sensors can be embedded in the wall to help afford better protection. A strong gate should be installed — one that cannot be rammed through. If a security guard is stationed at the gate, he should be housed in a bulletproof guardhouse.

Guard dogs are always useful, particularly if they are attack-trained. Even the posting of a sign reading "Beware of the Dog" contributes to security.

Doors should be made of steel or solid wood. They should be closed by door bolts, and if they open inward, the jamb of the door frame should protect the bolt. If the doors open outward, hinges should be nonremovable, perhaps even welded into the metal door. If these hinges are only screwed into the door, then an additional screw between the door and its frame should be installed to keep the door in place in case the hinge is undone.

Strong locks that require a key on both sides to enter as well as to exit are advisable. A mortise lock should have a dead bolt that protrudes at least half an inch. Secondary locks can be useful as a form of back up in the event something goes wrong with the primary lock. However, most locks can be picked. That is why alarm systems and door chains are important.

Sliding French doors should be fitted with shatterproof glass. Windows should be protected with bars or decorative wrought iron. Steel shutters that can be locked from the inside are even better (the beauty of the glass can be viewed from the outside). Shatterproof panes should be installed in a frame that cannot be knocked out. Pay particular attention to fortifying all ground floor windows and all windows facing the street. Windows covered with Mylar offer some protection against small arms or the blast effect from bombs. (Mylar reduces the light coming through the windows.) At night, before turning on the lights, the shades should be drawn.

Phone numbers should be unlisted; they should be handed out with a great deal of caution, and perhaps even changed periodically. The person who answers the phone should never identify himself personally, and should never reveal his address or phone number. A clever enemy might pretend to have dialed a wrong number or to be making an emergency call, and ask for the number in order to check whether or not he has called the right one. He should be told to redial the call. A telephone recorder is a valuable piece of security equipment, not only to keep track of messages and suspicious calls, but because it records the nuances of the callers voice.

The phone should never be located in front of a window, because this would make it possible for an assassin to call and then set up his cross hairs on the person answering the phone.

Bugs should be searched for periodically. (They can be inserted in the telephone handset or inside stereo or television speakers. Government agencies have very sophisticated eavesdropping equipment that can be operated from a vehicle close to the target area. Very little can be done to prevent this type of spying.). The most reliable method of insuring privacy in phone conversations is the installation of scramblers.

The family should construct a system of code words so that subtle hints about trouble can be communicated without alerting wrong-doers to the fact that a code is in operation. Emergency numbers for fire stations, police, ambulance service, and hospitals should be clearly posted by all telephones.

Alarms are essential: external alarms that operate from doors and windows and possibly a back-up alarm system employing motion or infrared detectors or pressure-sensitive mats. The system should have automatic dial-out capability to alert the alarm company or police directly. It should have a battery or generator back up. Naturally, it should be installed by a reputable company.

Each person should have an evacuation plan.

There should be a safe room that can be secured with heavy dead-bolt locks and it should have a flashlight, batteries, food, water, emergency supplies, and firearms (if the family feels safe having them available). A world-band radio is useful if the executive is living in a Third World country, so that news will be available regarding civil strife or revolution. Fire extinguishers should be placed at strategic points around the house. They should be of the ABC type, capable of handling wood, grease, or electrical fires.

Mail should be handled with extreme care. It should be a reflex action to check for plastic explosives, which are easily molded into many shapes or rolled out in flat sheets and slipped into envelopes. (The explosive devices will sometimes melt, particularly in hot weather, and a greasy discharge will be found coming out of the envelope. Sometimes the electrical circuit wires can be felt through the envelope). If a package or envelope is suspected of being explosive, it should not be handled: the room should be cleared and the police called immediately. There should be no attempt to handle any package that is left on a doorstep. Remember that mailboxes have been booby trapped with everything from bombs to rattlesnakes.

Children

Children should be educated about the basic rules of self-protection. They can be given whistles or horns to carry in the event that an assailant makes an attack upon their person.

Children should be driven to school. Special care should be taken to choose schools whose personnel respect and comply with the unusual security needs of the children of executives. The names of those authorized to pick up the children should be given to the school: Children should not be released to anybody without that prespecified identification.

Household Staff

The household staff should be screened with great care: References should be closely checked.

Household workers can engage in valuable surveillance by listening for local gossip, watching for suspicious cars, or reporting repairmen who appear to take an inordinately long time to do their jobs.

They should be instructed not to discuss the layout of the house, security procedures, family life, or business matters with anyone outside the family.

Every delivery person and utility inspector should be treated with suspicion. No one should be admitted to the house without prior clearance by the executive or his security personnel: No one should be admitted without a proper identification card that includes a picture. Household members should be given training in first aid.

Apartment Buildings

The apartment building must have a 24-hour doorman or receptionist. It should be an apartment with closed-circuit television and locked underground garages.

An apartment above the second floor will reduce the likelihood of a burglar opening windows or balcony doors with ease. On the other hand, the apartment should not be so high up that fire fighters cannot reach it easily in an emergency.

Caution should be exercised when getting onto an elevator with a stranger. All strangers should be viewed with suspicion in an apartment building.

The most vulnerable site for the apartment complex is the parking garage. It should be well-lit, preferably patrolled, and accessible only with a key, access card, or remote control device.

Make certain that the management company carefully screens all maintenance workers, desk workers, doormen, and other apartment personnel before they are hired. Ask about security procedures. For example, all movers, carpenters, decorators, painters, and repairmen should be required to sign in and out and to wear identification badges while in the apartment building.

5

Security Alarm Systems

Jay Lubliner, C.S.C.

The purpose of an alarm system is frequently misunderstood by the general public. In theory, alarms are designed to alert the intruder (with or without criminal intentions) that he or she has violated the premises or vehicle, with the hope that the intruder will be frightened away as they realize that (true or false) the alarm will be swiftly answered by the authorities or some other respondant. However, many owners perceive the alarm (siren, bell, tape recording, etc.) as a signaling device for them to hear and personally respond to. This can be a dangerous misconception. Frequently, people complain that they can't hear their alarm ringing from their house to their car or from a particular distance away from their home or business. The alarm is not for the owner, manager, or client to hear but rather, to scare off the thief and alert those trained to deal with intruders to respond to the alarm. Some people shy away from purchasing an alarm when informed of their purpose. Yet, when educated in total security strategies and procedures, they begin to view the alarm as one more tool that will protect their life and property in times of emergency. Although many have said that a dog is the best means of security and others state a security force with bodyguards is best, the alarm serves as a significant factor in any holistic security system.

Local and Monitored Alarms

Basically, there are two types of alarms. A local alarm sounds a horn, siren, or bell in the premise or vehicle only at that specific location. A monitored alarm alerts an outside source trained in security (public or private) that the alarm has been set off. The local alarm is typically less expensive and is a weaker system as it relies on the surrounding environment for response. It assumes that the perpetrator will be frightened by the alarm and cease his intrusion into the alarmed location or that some outsider (neighbor or passerby), fellow employee, or family member will alert the authorities of the intrusion. If the location is a home and it is in a concerned neighborhood, the chances are that someone will respond to the alarm by calling the police. If the alarmed location is a business, and there are few inhabitants in the environment when the alarm sounds, there is a lower probability someone will alert the authorities. If the alarm is placed in a car, a boat, or an airplane, the location the vehicle is placed is a major determinant as to whether anyone will even hear the alarm, much less respond by calling the police. The time of day can greatly influence the usefulness of a local alarm. If the majority of people in a neighborhood are at work during the day, a sounding alarm will meet deaf ears. In areas where there are a large number of alarms that have a tendency to alarm falsely at some frequency, the local alarm may be ignored. In neighborhoods with large numbers of alarmed cars, it is difficult to determine which is ringing unless the car has flashing lights or a strobe inside. It is also important to consider the time it takes for the police or authorities to respond to the call.

Police response-time studies (Kansas City and Police Executive Research Forum) indicate the longest response time is not due to the police responding to the call, but the time it takes the individual to decide to call the police. People often cannot make up their minds whether they should call—they may call a family member or other neighbor before deciding to phone the police. These precious minutes spent on "to call" or "not to call" can override the positive features of the local alarm.

There are several methods of monitoring an alarm. In a home or business, the most common method of monitoring is with a tape or digital dialer. Once an alarm occurs, a pair of contacts in the alarm panel closes, this in turn powers a tape recorder or a digital communicator that transmits data over the telephone line. In most cities, the use of the local phone company's wires must be leased and an FCC approved connection (a RJ31X) must be installed. The RJ31X seizes control of the phone line to transmit the data concerning the alarm condition to the monitoring station or police. If the phone was off the hook, for whatever reason, the data would be prevented from leaving the premise (along with the phone line being tied up). If the phone lines are down or cut, the data cannot be sent, creating at best a local alarm condition. Following the transmittal of data, the RJ31X restores the dial tone and normal phone use. As long as the perpetrator is unaware of the monitoring alarm, the data typically reaches its destination in several seconds. Tape dialers are becoming obsolete because it takes too long to send the data, allowing the intruder enough time to disable it.

A recent development for cars is an interface, connected to a cellular phone, which will dial up to four different telephone numbers in case of an emergency. This type of device almost guarantees that someone will be able to receive the reported intrusion. The weak link of the device is its reliance on the car's battery, which is easily accessible or which might go dead. One solution is to add a hood lock to prevent the opening of the hood, thus protecting the battery.

Radio transmissions serve as a popular form of monitoring alarm. Often a business or vehicle (car, airplane, or boat) will contain a backup two-way radio that transmits a signal to the owner or a monitoring station or both. Their use is limited because of their relatively short sending range. However, new technologies are establishing links between satellite networks and newly available higher frequencies to enhance the range of radio monitoring alarm systems. Pagers are available for cars, boats, and airplanes that alert the vehicle owner to an intruder by sounding a personal device (usually a beeping noise), indicating that alarm conditions were met. There are several weaknesses of the pager: the range the pager can be from the location of the alarmed object, and the potency of the batteries in the pager. If the batteries are weak or dead, the pager cannot operate. The owner must constantly recharge the pager batteries or remember to replace them as they weaken. Some pagers have indicator lights warning the owner of the need to change or recharge the batteries.

One of the most overlooked problems is protecting the alarm components. Too often the alarm module or panel is easily damaged because it is plainly visible to the intruder. Not enough planning is done prior to installing the alarm to hide and protect the equipment from tampering by outsiders or by employees with easy access to the vehicle or building. Drivers commonly leave their keys with garage attendants or mechanics who can easily duplicate the keys to use at a later date, the address of the driver having been found on an insurance card, car registration, charge card receipt, or other identification left in the glove box or car. In my business, we have installed alarms and components in spots impossible to detect without tearing the car's interior and exterior apart (which we have done to install the parts). Each vehicle is different, each need varied. All installed alarms have custom-designed details based on the particular life-style and needs of the client and the vehicle's unique layout.

The Physical State

Alarms are comprised of a combination of several components. Each individualized combination creates a distinct system for the business, home, car, boat or airplane. Even single items such as data disk files, safes, and firearms can be alarmed.

The brain of the alarm system is the microprocessor. It controls timing functions like exit and entry delay, alarm duration, reset and re-arm. Often there are local noise abatement laws that limit the length of time a siren can sound. For business and commercial use, usually 15 minutes is a maximum and for cars, up to 7 minutes is typical. The microprocessor also can control communicators, lights, radio equipment, fire controls, and locks to doors, etc.

Attached to the microprocessor are switch sensors and contacts that make or break circuits. They tell the brain that a door or window, fire or other form of environmental change, or intrusion has occurred. The switch sensors and contacts are made of metal wires or magnets. There are also shock detectors and glass detectors in case a window or wall is broken or hit. On retail store fronts and windows, thin silver foil is frequently used. When the glass breaks, so does the foil, opening the circuit to sound the alarm. All of these devices protect only the exterior of the vehicle or premise.

For the interior there are more elaborate devices. Roofs, skylights, exit doors, and common walls are prime targets because the perpetrator knows that the doors and the windows are alarmed. Breaking through a roof is common, as well as breaking into an adjacent or adjoining store or building that is not alarmed to achieve entry into the targeted location through an interior wall, crawl space, or attic. Devices for indoor protection include ultrasonic, infrared, and microwave alarms. Basically, all of these alarms emit a series of invisible beams. If an intruder enters through the alarmed roof, the pattern of beams is disturbed, and the alarm is triggered and sounds. Infrareds and ultrasonics suffer from wind drafts and heating ducts that may upset the beam's patterns resulting in a false alarm. The placement of these alarms is critical. On the other hand, microwave can sometimes pass through walls and detect movement in someone else's place.

The most reliable detector currently available, is a combination detector. It uses powerful microwave and infrared or ultrasonic waves to detect body movement and heat. Only when both sensors are tripped together would an alarm occur. This eliminates false alarms.

The next major component is the communicator or radio transmitter that sends the data to a police monitoring station. Too many false alarms can produce the well known reaction of "never cry wolf." If the alarm falsifies on a regular basis, it is unreliable. Police are called more frequently for false alarms than for the "real thing." In some neighborhoods this has affected their response time to alarms. In many communities police will fine a business if three or more false alarms occur in a month. In addition, if there is slow police response time, the owner of the alarm will be uneasy, never quite knowing if the police will respond and if it will be fast enough to catch the perpetrator. We hear many of our customers who have been victims of burglaries complain that the alarm worked, but no one responded fast enough.

The final component is the bell, siren, or other sounding device that one hopes will ward off the intruder. The sounding device must be controlled in some fashion. It must be turned on and off daily or as required. The simplest method is a key switch. However, the key switch is vulnerable to lockpicking or plain attack. A keypad offers the security of a secret code number that can be reprogrammed in the event someone finds out the code number. A little more sophisticated is the hand-held remote control that sometimes has several channels to operate different functions. Also, there are magnetic cards that are inserted into a reader that controls the alarm and doors. If a card or remote is stolen or lost, it can be changed any number of times. This is especially useful in situations where there is large employee turn over or frequent break-ins.

With the cost of goods constantly rising along with the cost of doing business, and with the increasing crime rate and white-collar crime, it is easy to see why the alarm justifies the expense of trying to protect and keep what is ours. Almost anything can be alarmed. Buildings, cars, boats, airplanes, floppy disks, art objects, or your pet cat. There are as many types of alarms as we can imagine. With high technologies entering into the alarm business, the number of variations on a theme has increased exponentially. Some of these include a car alarm that can tell you if you've left your keys in the ignition; it can roll up the windows if it rains or open your electric garage door and turn on your living room lights before you even enter the house. Suppose you were on vacation and wanted to know if an attempt was made on the vehicle at home? Some alarm panels can tell you exactly what occurred in the past: How many attempts were made to enter the location, what time of day the attempts were made, etc. I have installed alarms in cars and boats that were connected to a personal computer that printed out the condition of the vehicle and what occurred to it while the owner was away. Alarms can be useful for monitoring other environmental conditions besides intrusion such as smoke detection, fires, flooding, leaking gas pipes, and even explosives (in case someone plants a bomb in your car).

Alarms can be offensive as well as defensive devices. There are high frequency sounders called "pain generators" that can cause the intruder permanent ear damage and make it impossible to stay in the car or building. There are dye bombs that can stain the merchandise or intruder with purple dye to aid police in apprehending the perpetrator. The legality of these and other alarm systems should be checked in each particular geographical location.

Alarm systems have been here since before the telephone; they have a history of success in crime prevention techniques, and with the new and growing age of high technology, their possibilities are numerous. Alarms can be designed to incorporate microchips to work in a variety of environmental conditions responding in a wide range of patterns for specific circumstances. If an intruder comes within so many feet of a premise or alarmed location, a light can come on; within a few more feet, a tape recording of people talking; within a few more feet, music or television. If the intruder continues to come forward, a siren can be sounded; step further and an outside source can be alerted to the intrusion.

When purchasing an alarm or alarm system, one must be aware that the alarm is only one part of a holistic approach to security. Other forms of protection are as important — or more important — than the alarm system. The owner should be aware of all environmental factors that can influence the performance of the alarm system selected, and know of its weaknesses as well as its strengths. Depending upon the complexity of the system, owners should be well versed in all aspects of the system and should have back-up plans should some function fail.

6

Firearms, Body Armor, and Electronic Equipment

The formula for most movies about terrorism is action plus weapons equals excitement. The mainstay of executive protection, namely, prevention of difficulty, is never emphasized perhaps because it is not understood or because it simply is not sexy. Most of us in executive protection are very happy to miss the drama of a kidnapping attempt or a shoot-out. A combination of luck and intelligent advanced planning should result in a routine and uneventful day for the executive, whether at home, driving to work, or traveling abroad. But if an assault does come from a distance, from a passing car, or from behind a barricade, the security specialist must be equipped with the proper response weapons to armed assault in case a situation arises in which a confrontation is unavoidable.

I must emphasize that shoot-outs should be avoided at all costs. In the event an ambush does occur, the primary goal should be to remove oneself from danger as quickly as possible. Your adversary has the advantage of surprise; terrorists in particular usually have the advantage of overwhelming fire power and more than likely will have automatic weapons. Trying to escape and establish resistance simultaneously might result only in confusion and the protection specialist may be deterred from his primary mission, protection of the principal. If this is a one or two-man detail, it could be catastrophic because the executive may be placed in greater danger, even injured by the frantic shooting that is brought about as a result of the agent returning fire. Heroics should be abandoned and reaching safe shelter should be the first course of action.

Firearms

The primary weapon of the personal protection specialist is the firearm. The specialist should be aware of local laws that govern owning and carrying guns.

Firearms should never be used to impress people. All efforts should be made to achieve total concealment. It is for this reason that I prefer automatics that are flat. They can be worn on the side, hip, or under the arm in a shoulder holster and concealed under a coat. I prefer a stainless steel weapon because, with a coat on in the summertime, body perspiration can easily ruin the bluing on a standard automatic.

My preference for side arms has been the automatic. I prefer a stainless steel Smith and Wesson, model 5609, 14-shot with an extra round in the chamber. I prefer the 9-mm pistol because it carries a maximum number of rounds — 14 with one in the chamber, if it is the model just referred to. Another model, the Browning high power, has a 13-round magazine, is reliable, effective, and basically maintenance free. It dates back to World War II, and was used by both the Nazis and the Allies. However, there are three reasons that keep it from being my weapon of choice: it has a problem with its sight: it can be difficult to find replacement parts; and, most important, it is single action. I prefer a double-action weapon; when I draw down, I like to have the capacity to fire without rocking the weapon.

Heckler and Koch makes an excellent 9-mm pistol known as the P-7, probably the flattest gun made. However, it has the disadvantage of holding just about seven rounds, and it also takes a long time to get parts for repair. Other 9-mm favorites include model 226, made by Sig-Sauer, and Glock 17 or 19, an Austrian product that carries the advantage of 18 rounds of 9-mm ammunition. The latter model almost never requires repair and is one of the most serviceable handguns currently available. An enlarged magazine adds two more rounds.

The 45-mm weapon is an excellent old standby. The major problem is that you are limited to seven or eight shots. The 1911A-1 model 45, is large, bulky, and limited to single action. If you use the Smith and Wesson stainless 645, you are limited to eight shots, but have the advantage of double action. The Sig-Sauer 220 model 45 is also excellent.

For the practical purpose of carrying additional ammunition, I also prefer the 9 mm. I usually have my tailor make a small pocket, which is a part of the seam, on the left side of my trousers. If measured back seven inches from the zipper line, then a pocket that is four inches long and four inches deep can be inserted along the running edge of the belt line of the trouser. This will hold two full magazines of 14 rounds each and is much less perceptible than the wearing of a bulky magazine pouch. The ammunition is within easy reach should reloading be required. This gives the bearer of the 9-mm handgun an extra 28 rounds, in addition to the 15 he carries in his weapon.

There are many who prefer revolvers. I would like to point out that you only get five or six rounds per firing load. Trying to reload bullets into the wheel during the excitement phase of a gun fight can be extremely difficult. Sometimes while unloading the weapon, even though it is held upright and the extractor rod is pushed downward, one or two shells may hang up in a smaller, sub-nosed revolver. This can cost precious seconds and might even mean the life of the agent.

Regardless of which side arm the agent prefers, it is of paramount importance that he maintain the cleanliness and smooth operation of his weapon as if it were part of himself. It should be fired frequently, as much as 25 to 50 rounds a week at a time. It is ever so easy to get out of practice. In my judgment, when shots begin to land outside of black circles, there is a critical loss of control of the weapon that needs to be immediately corrected with practice.

Sometimes shotguns are safer than handguns. They rarely, if ever, malfunction. They can be used with buckshot or solid slugs. Racking the weapon, meaning advancing a shell into the chamber, is a very frightening sound—just hearing the noise and seeing the weapon is sometimes enough to deter assailants. It has the advantage of not requiring precise aim; if it is pointed in the appropriate direction it can hit just about anything, particularly at close range. Also, shotguns are legal almost everywhere.

The big disadvantage of a shotgun is that it is not easily concealed on the person. It must be kept in a vehicle, either in a shotgun rack or, for greater concealment, in a specially built rack in back of the front seats or on the floorboard (which is where I prefer to carry it).

A short barrel skeet-type pump gun like a model 870 Remington is probably the most effective one for self-defense. Again, when employing such a weapon, there should be a check with local police to find out the legal limits for barrel length.

The LEO striker 12-gauge, 12-shot shotgun can be used with any combination of 12-gauge, 2 3/4" shell, as well as the unique 12-gauge subcaliber inserts that this company markets in 9-mm, 44 mag, 38 special and 357 sizes. This weapon comes with a lifetime warranty. It is very effective for large crowd confrontation and has the advantage of carrying two-and-a-half times the normal load that the average shotgun permits (four or five shells). LEO Striker 126A operates with a two-stage trigger; its major safety value is that it operates on a battery. Thus, it cannot discharge accidentally. Finally, it offers the advantage of allowing you to alternate any combination of projectiles, i.e., tear gas, 12-gauge standard, Avon loads, and 00 ammunition. It is ideal in any situation where an executive vehicle, residence, or office might be surrounded or confronted by a large group of terrorists.

Not only are the Remington 870 and the LEO Striker 12-gauge excellent, but many other companies make excellent shotguns. Beretta has produced a new A-303 youth model with a 20-gauge and they offer many different 12-gauge models. They are chambered for 2-3/4" shells and have a folding stock. Browning is an all-time favorite shotgun, pump design, but tends to be a little heavier than the other makes.

For the average personal protection specialist guarding an executive in the United States the use of a machine gun is unnecessary. In foreign countries, where the risk of terrorism may be greater, host governments may supply armed protection or armed protection may be available for hire. In either event, as the risk of terrorism increases, and particularly if armored cars are not available, it may be necessary to carry an automatic weapon. One of the favorites of security details, (both civilian and government) in many countries, is the Heckler and Koch MP-5 submachine gun, which fires a 9- mm bullet. It has a collapsible butt, making it easy to conceal, and is a highly accurate weapon. The Uzi submachine gun, manufactured by Israeli defense forces, has been used by terrorist groups since its inception in 1952. (It is also a favorite in the armory of the Secret Service.) It is easy to obtain, easily concealed, very light, highly accurate and simple to use. It can be left in mud, filled with sand, and will still fire just as accurately at a high rate of 600 rounds a minute.

If fired fully automatic, clip after clip of ammunition will be used. Thus, it is important to carry extra magazines of ammunition. But it should not be fired fully automatic unless one is in a high-level combat fire fight. Even then, wisdom would dictate that blind firing Rambo-style is inappropriate for the effective use of any weapon, including the machine gun. Terrorists may be using a Kalashnikov AK-47, a highly accurate and deadly weapon, whose ammunition can penetrate automobiles. Other weapons favored by terrorists include M-1 carbines, submachine guns, and the Skorpion VC-62, a 32-caliber or 9-mm Czechoslovakian submachine gun that fires 700 rounds a minute and is easy to conceal. The M-26 grenade launcher, RPG-7 portable rocket launchers, RPG-5 antipersonnel hand grenades, and SAM missiles have all been used by terrorists. When the possibility of coming up against such weapons exists, then it is obvious that it will be necessary to have machine guns close at hand. Magazines, fully loaded, should be ready in the event that extra ammunition is required during an assault.

One final note about firearms used for protection. It is important when chosing your caliber and type of weapon to avoid heavy calibers such as the 44-magnum handguns or the 30-caliber range, 7-mm or the like military-type rifle. These weapons are not in any sense defensive. They are assault or offensive in their design and their presence can cause the protective detail to go well beyond the mission of defense. Indeed, they may endanger the lives of innocent bystanders. The disadvantage of high-caliber weapons, even for handguns, is that unless the bullet hits skull or bone or causes some body part to explode, the bullet can go clean through a body and hit another person. Both adversaries, although wounded, would be able to continue their assault. The silver-tipped round of ammunition fired from a 45, a 9-mm, or even a 380, is designed to stay in the body and expand. The incapacitating power of any ammunition rests on its ability to stay in the body and fragment, causing massive hemorrhage. The more hemorrhage it produces, the more effective the ammunition round will be.

Remember that explosive devices and hand grenades are illegal in most countries and have no place in the arms cache of the executive protection specialist.

Body Armor

If armed protection is deemed necessary, then it is important for all members of the security team, plus the executive, to wear body armor. Protection vests can be purchased at police uniform and supply stores. Most are effective against 38, 9-mm and 32-caliber ammunition and offer considerable protection against a shotgun blast coming from a distance. However, when it comes to 44-mag, 357, or military ammunition (such as the 7.62 x 39-mm ammunition or 223-caliber rifles), there is nothing, in my judgment, that is going to stop such high-powered ammunition. There is no vest that will stop explosive or Teflon-coated ammunition.

Bear in mind that these garments do not offer protection from head shots or injuries to the legs or the genitals. Some forms of body armor used by SWAT teams are manufactured with protective coverage for the genitals, but they are of no value to the personal protection specialist because they cannot be concealed.

Electronic Equipment

There are do-it-yourself devices on the market that will detect voltage variations in a telephone line when a bug is competently installed.

If the executive wishes to be reasonably certain that all lines are clean, then a reliable company should be retained to do the work. But even the best equipment may fail. This comes under the heading of do what you can, but do not expect miracles from any of the phone-sweeping equipment.

Part of the problem in debugging a room is that there are so many places where sensors that pick up conversation can be planted. The walls have to be examined almost inch by inch. A nonlinear junction detector, which emits a signal revealing the presence of microphones or electronic components in the wall, can be employed by a trained technician. These can pick up most microphones. Remember that FAX and Telex machines also have to be protected.

Scramblers can assist in providing improved telephone security. It is most effective to have them installed not only on your telephones, but on those of people with whom you frequently speak. To anyone listening, scrambled conversations are unintelligible; it takes time and sophisticated computers to reconstruct the intercepted conversation.

The best security measure for telephone, Telefax, or Telex communications is to always exercise discretion in the choice of information being transmitted, perhaps employing a code for sensitive material and never discussing specific travel plans.

7

The Executive Travels Abroad

The ordinary American's chances of being killed or injured in a terrorist attack are slim; in fact, the chances are far lower than accidental death due to fall, being struck by lightning, poisoning, or some natural disaster. Certainly, with the number of automobile fatalities that occur in the United States, the chances of being killed in a terrorist attack are almost ridiculously small by comparison. Most air and ship travel is far safer than automobile transportation, making the threat of terrorism almost remote for the average citizen.

Furthermore, some foreign countries are safer than the communities we live in; we may run less risk of becoming a victim of crime or terrorism than we do in our own backyards.

The executive is not, however, an "ordinary" citizen and he should take extra security precautions when planning a trip abroad. In his book *Complete Security Guide for Executives*, Neil C. Livingstone offers some practical suggestions regarding preparation for a trip.

Only a travel agency with which the executive is familiar should be used to make travel arrangements. The agency must respect the executives need for privacy and secrecy. Reservations might be booked under a different name to preserve anonymity. The agency should have knowledge of the security arrangements of possible hotels so that the executive can make an informed decision about accommodations.

An effort should be made to book travel arrangements with an airline that has an established record of safety, like Israel's El Al, or Germany's Lufthansa Airlines. Some airlines, such as Kuwait, have been singled out for attack by Shiite terrorists. Scandanavian airlines are safest when traveling to Third World destinations.

It is important to check the travel route of an aircraft to insure that it is not scheduled to stop at a particular hot spot, like Beirut Airport. It is advisable to pay the difference for a direct flight rather than one involving a number of stop-overs; this will help minimize the possibility of explosives being planted along the way at each or any of several stops.

Travel plans should exclude visits to countries with permissive attitudes toward terrorism. At one time, this would have eliminated France because terrorists groups were offered safe sanctuary in the city of Paris. A director of antiterrorist services with the Sureté (the French police agency) has assured me that terrorists are no longer welcome in France.

If the travel plan involves an airplane, flying coach is preferable because it is safer. Terrorists generally turn to the first class section as their command post. In the event that a rescue is necessary, there will be less risk of being caught in the crossfire if the executive is placed in the coach section.

Even on the airplane expensive clothing and jewelry that calls attention to the economic status of the executive should be avoided. Aisle seats should be avoided as well; if there is a terrorist attack, those occupying the aisle seats will be subjected to the greatest physical abuse.

Bookings on a large aircraft are preferable. Terrorist assault teams usually operate in groups of five; they may hesitate to pick small aircraft.

The State Department has a service known as the Citizens Emergency Center, (phone number 202-647-5225) for warnings regarding destinations dangerous to Americans.

An itinerary or trip plan should be filed with a relative or trusted fellow executive who can be relied upon to keep the information confidential.

Special attention should be paid to the passport that will be used for the trip, as well as any entry visas that may be necessary. A check should be made by the executive's staff to insure that the passport and entry visa are properly filled out.

Check with the travel agent as to whether health or immunization records are required by the country to be visited. Make certain any necessary immunization vaccines are arranged for in a timely fashion so the executive is not physically weakened or his concentration impaired by a reaction to the vaccine during his trip. Remember to check if the destination country has any restrictions on prescribed medication — some sort of extra documentation from your physician may be necessary.

It is important that the executive avoid open identification with any religious or ethnic group, by wearing of medallions or carrying identification, of membership in organizations.

The possession of political literature should be avoided at all costs as it may help establish national identity.

There should be no loose talk about the purpose of the trip while in transit.

One should leave a supply of necessary medications in the carry-on luggage, (remember some countries have restrictions on the importation of drugs, even during visiting periods). A card indicating blood type, allergies, vaccinations, home physician, and other vital medical information such as heart disease or diabetes should be available for each member of the traveling party. Extra diapers and formula should be carried for children particularly when visiting Third World or certain Asiatic countries.

Avoid drinking excessively while flying.

Procedure Upon Arrival in the Terminal
Spend as little time as possible in the airport, especially in unsecured areas. Airline club membership should be taken out by the executive or corporation for any of its

personnel who travel internationally or to large urban centers so that the traveler can use the lounge (a more restricted area).

While waiting, the executive should keep his back to the wall so he can see what's going on around him. Avoid sitting at windows and so reduce the possibility of flying glass injuries if there are shots or bombs exploded in the terminal. The executive should try to position himself near pillars that will help provide cover during a crisis.

Exposure as a group should be kept to a minimum; have one member of the group check in for everybody else.

Bags should be checked at the counter and not at the curbside where one is a perfect target for drive-by terrorists.

Avoid standing near physically unattended bags as they could contain a bomb.

Any suspicious person or activity that does not look like it fits within the travel scene should be reported to authorities.

If some commotion occurs, it is best not to gawk or rubber-neck as it is easy to become an innocent victim if whatever is transpiring involves gunplay.

If an explosion does occur or gunfire can be heard, the executive should immediately drop to the ground and place his arms or hands over his head for additional protection.

Survival During a Skyjacking

The traveling executive should be aware that many airlines employ armed guards as sky marshals. If they find it necessary to intervene during an effort to take over a flight, passengers should be encouraged to drop down as low as possible toward the floor. This is particularly important if gunfire is exchanged. The passengers should remain on the floor until ordered to get up; curiosity about what is happening can result in a bullet in the head.

If there is an explosion that rips a hole in the plane, there may be a decompression, with objects and passengers being sucked toward the hole. Enhance safety by maintaining a fixed position with the seatbelt locked in place.

Follow the instructions of the flight crew, and again, as in all travel situations, as much effort as possible should be extended to avoid calling attention to oneself.

If terrorists do succeed in taking over control of the plane, the executive should not try to negotiate with them. Prepare for the worst. Many terrorists are unpredictable and react to the slightest provocation. There should be no effort to plead, negotiate, or in any way strike up a relationship with the terrorists.

As planes may be skyjacked in extremely hot climates, every effort should be made by the executive and his family to eat and drink in order to maintain nutrition, strength, and adequately functioning kidneys. Water balance is essential; under the stress of anxiety and heat, valuable amounts of water will be lost and have to be replaced. Be prepared to suffer extreme physical discomfort: shortage of water and food; toilets overflowing; shortage of toilet paper; and the odor of menstrual discharge by female passengers. Many women begin to menstruate under stress, even those who have entered menopause.

Without being obvious try to take note of the number of terrorists, description of weapons, routines the skyjackers have established, their locations — as well as location of hostages — and any clues as to their nationality, identity, and language capabilities.

When the time comes for the plane to be vacated, it should be done as quickly as possible. At all times be prepared for possible rescue attempts, in which case drop into the seat and cover your head or shield family members or children.

Remain aloof from any rescue effort — be prepared even to be handcuffed and treated roughly following the end of the skyjacking, until police officers can establish proper identity. This is not the time to become offended by rough treatment by the police or military. The mental notes about the appearance of the terrorists can be useful following a successful rescue as they may attempt to blend in with passengers or others in the area.

Be prepared to have a rough time after release. The executive may withdraw socially from people, not want to talk about the experiences, have nightmares, or require professional assistance from a psychiatrist, psychologist, or social worker to help work through the emotionally traumatic events.

Special Instructions for Visits to Third World Countries
The executive would be well advised to carry a world-band radio to monitor both international news and local developments in the country he is currently visiting.

Carry a flashlight and a multilingual card with blood type and medicines to which he may be allergic.

Learn how to use local telephones.

Travel Measures at the Hotel
Consider checking in under an assumed name, be on guard for eavesdroppers, and avoid rooms at the ground level (more vulnerable to attack than those at upper levels). Particular attention should be paid to those who occupy surrounding rooms; if there is a security force traveling with the executive, part of their risk assessment will include such surveillance. Rooms with balconies should be avoided. Assume that rooms in communist countries are being bugged.

Preparations should be made in the event of a fire as many hotels in other countries are without sprinkler systems. Carry a small rope or ladder in the luggage in the event that it is necessary to escape through a window. Polyester garments should be avoided — during a fire they may melt to the skin and provide less protection.

The room should be left in such a condition that upon return the executive can identify any tampering or rearrangement of property. Be prepared to look for loiterers outside of the room, in the same way you would look for strangers at your own business or home.

When Visiting a Foreign Country

Executives traveling abroad (or in this country) should try to go in pairs. This will reduce the risk, particularly for women, of being subjected to sexually explicit insults, as well as bodily injuries.

In general, the executive should try to maintain a low profile by keeping your travel plans out of the newspaper. Avoid having photographs published in the media of your own country and particularly in the countries you plan on visiting. Do not allow photographs to be published during your visit.

T-shirts bearing slogans, excessive jewelry, and any form of conspicuous or inappropriate clothing should be discarded for trips to foreign countries. The wearing of American buttons, flag pins, or patches should be avoided.

Inquire about security arrangements at special functions to which you have been invited. A low profile should be maintained. Selection of restaurants and clubs should be handled carefully, always avoiding popular tourist haunts and places where American citizens are known to congregate. These areas are vulnerable to the indiscriminate type of terrorist attack. Remember the tragedy of the American soldiers in Germany, slaughtered in explosions at their clubs.

Great care should be taken in exchanging money. In the Soviet Union, it is a serious crime to be caught dealing in black market money exchange; prominent Americans have been arrested for dealing with black marketeers (who may be members of the KGB).

In certain countries it is an accepted part of the culture to pay a bribe in order to pass through military checkpoints, or to pay soldiers for allowing their pictures. In Mexico, if peasants are to be photographed, be prepared to pay for that privilege.

Graft is common in many countries; sometimes the official who is greeted with a passport from which a $20 bill is protruding may be offended, while another may suddenly discover a way of expediting the executive's business. Graft can be particularly useful when trying to obtain a hotel room.

Make every effort to avoid any kind of rampaging mob or riot.

Adult Entertainment Districts

The executive should exercise care in how he goes about finding adult entertainment. Never go anywhere alone and always dress in casual clothing. It would be wise to hire a car with a driver who is familiar with the area and, in Third World countries in particular, be accompanied by a bodyguard. As a security agent, I would advise the protectee to avoid areas where trouble is highly probable.

Robbery, venereal disease, and other problems are often found where drinking, sex, and drugs are easily available. Avoid gambling except in large, well-established casinos like those in Monte Carlo, the Carribbean, Las Vegas, or Reno. The executive who gambles makes himself a potential robbery victim.

The executive should make sure that he knows something about the cultural ways of the country he is visiting and should at all times be appreciative and respectful of the values of the host country. (Livingstone suggests the executive learn common phrases in the national language such as "It is a pleasure to meet you" and "Thank you" and "Where is the bathroom?" Learn how to say "police", "help" and "hospital."

He should carry himself as if he is a formal diplomat for the United States and be as uncomplaining as possible; roll with the punches and do not complain about service, cleanliness, accommodations, or food. Absolutely avoid any comments regarding how much better life is in the United States

Neil Livingstone advises that travel be avoided around certain terrorist holidays when demonstrations can be expected. The following is a selected calendar of terrorist dates organized by geographical region.

Cuba and South America

January 1: the date of the Cuban revolution that brought Fidel Castro to power.

January 23: the date when dictator Marcos Perez Jimenez of Venezuela was overthrown.

February 5: the date of the founding of the National Liberation Army in Columbia.

February 20: the date of the death of Cesar Augusto Sandino of Nicaragua.

March 13: the date of the death of M-19 leader Alvardo Fayad of Columbia.

March 20: the date of the death of M-19 leader Carmenza of Columbia.

March 24: the date of the assassination of Bishop Romero of El Salvador.

March 31: the date of the overthrow of the leftist president Goulart of Brazil.

March 31: the date of the killing of three communist leaders in Chile.

April 9: the date of the Bolivian bloodbath.

April 17: the date of the Bay of Pigs invasion in Cuba.

April 19: the date of the founding of the M-19 terrorist group in Columbia, and the Day of Victory in Cuba.

May 18: the date of the founding of the Shining path in Peru.

May 20: Cuban Independence Day.

June 19: the date of the founding of the National Revolutionary Movement in Bolivia.

July 1: the date of the death of Juan Peron of Argentina.

July 5: Venezuela Independence Day.

July 9: Argentine Independence Day.

July 18: the date of death of Benito Juarez.

July 19: the date of the Sandanista revolution in Nicaragua.

July 28: Peruvian Independence Day.

July 31: the date of the kidnapping of Dan Mitrione by Tupamaro guerillas in Uruguay.

August 13: the birthdate of Fidel Castro in Cuba.

August 25: Uruguayan Independence Day.

September 7: Brazilian Independence Day.

September 11: the date of the coup which overthrew and led to the death of President Salvador Allende of Chile.

September 15: Independence Day in El Salvador, Honduras, Nicaragua, and Guatamala.
September 16: Mexican Independence Day.
September 18: Chilean Independence Day.
October 7: the date of the death of Che Guevara (Cuban guerilla executed in Bolivia).
October 8: the birthdate of Juan Peron of Argentina.
October 10: the date of the founding of the FMLN of El Salvador.
October 11: the date of the founding of the MIR of Chile.

Middle East

January 9: Palestinian Memorial Day.
January 15: the birth date of Gamal Abdel Nasser of Egypt.
March 21: International Solidarity Day for Palestinians.
April 4: the date of the founding of Syria's Baath Party.
April 8: the date of the founding of Iraq's Baath Party.
April 9: the date of the Israeli raid on Beirut, Lebanon.
April 15: the date of the U.S. air raid on Tripoli, Libya.
April 17: Syria Independence Day.
June 5: the date of the revolution and a national day of mourning in Iran.
July 4: the date of the Entebbe Raid by Israel to liberate aircraft hostages in Uganda.
September 5: the date of the attack of the Munich Olympic Games by Black September, a Palestinian terrorist group.
September 20: the date of the bombing of the U.S. Embassy in Beirut, Lebanon.
September 22: the date of the Iraq declaration of war on Iran.
September 23: Saudi Arabia National Day.
September 28: the date of the death of Gamal Abdel Nasser of Egypt.
October 6: the date of the Yom Kippur War in Israel.
October 23: the date of the bombing of the U.S. Marine Headquarters in Beirut, Lebanon.
November 4: the date of the seizure of the U.S. Embassy in Tehran, Iran.
November 29: the date of the Proclamation of the State of Israel in terms of its independence and formation.
December 12: the date of bombing of the U.S. Embassy and other targets in Kuwait by the al-Dawa party.

Great Britian and Ireland

January 30: the date of Bloody Sunday in Northern Ireland.
March 17: St. Patrick's Day.
March 24: the date of the beginning of the British Direct Rule in Northern Ireland.
May 5: the date of the death of the IRA hunger striker Bobby Sands of Northern Ireland.
July 21: the date of Bloody Friday in Northern Ireland.

August 11: Internment Day in Northern Ireland.
August 12: the date when British troops arrived in Northern Ireland.
November 15: the date of the Anglo-Irish Accord.
December 21: date of the bombing of PAN AM flight 103 over Scotland.

Turkey and Armenia

February 27: the date of the death of Yanik Yanikian of Turkey; leader of the Secret Army for the Liberation of Armenia.
The month of April; the Armenian Month of Revenge, commemorating genocide by the Turks.
April 24: the National Day of Sorrow for Armenians.

India, Pakistan, and Sri Lanka

January 20: the date of the assassination of Mahatma Ghandi of India.
March 23: Pakistan Republic Day.
April 4: the date of the execution of former President Zulfikar Ali Bhutto of Pakistan.
April 13: the date of the founding of the Sikh religion in India.
May 22: Sri Lanka Republic Day.
June 6: the date of the government attack on the Sikh Golden Temple in India.
July 5: the date of the overthrow of President Zulfikar Ali Bhutto.
August 14: Pakistani Independence Day and the anniversary of President Mohammed Zia ul-Hag seizing power in Pakistan.
August 15: Indian Independence Day.
October 31: the date of the assassination of Prime Minister Indira Gandhi of India.

Philippines and Southeast Asia

March 29: the date of the founding of the New Peoples Army (NPA) in the Philippines.
August 21: the date of the assassination of Benigno Aquino of the Philippines.
November 27: the birthday of Benigno Aquino of the Philippines.
December 10: Constitution Day in Thailand.
December 31: the date of the founding of the Philippine Communist Party.

Japan, China, and Korea

April 15: birthday of North Korean President Kim Il-Sung.
April 19: the date of the Student Revolt in South Korea.
May 3: Constitution Day in Japan.
July 1: Communist Party Day in China.
August 15: South Korea Independence Day.
September 9: the date of the death of Mao Tse-Tung of China.
October 1: National Day in China.
October 9: the date of the North Korean-sponsored bombing of the South Korean

cabinet delegation in Burma.

October 26: the date of the assassination of President Chung Ha Park of South Korea.

December 26: the birthday of Mao Tse-Tung of China.

Africa

March 15: the National Front for Liberation of Angola Day.

May 31: Republic Day in South Africa.

June 16: the date of the Soweto Riots in South Africa.

October 10: Kruger Day in South Africa.

December 10: the Popular Movement for the Liberation of Angola Day.

December 27: Kenyas Independence Day.

Europe

May 13: the date of the attack on Pope John II.

July 31: the date of the founding of the Basque ETA of Spain.

September 27: the Basque Nationalist Party Day.

October 18: the date of the death of the Baader-Meinhof leaders in West Germany.

November 25: the date of the unsuccessful leftist coup in Portugal.

8

The Personal Protection Specialist: Requirements and Duties

Increasing crime and terrorism have forced most corporations to realize that protection of the corporate leadership and facilities is of paramount importance. In a competitive market for both civilian and military goods, the secrecy and safe storage of product development information is essential. If thefts or breaches of security occur, or if an executive is kidnapped or killed, a company's performance and even its stock value can be negatively affected. In many ways, protecting the executive is a way of protecting the company, much as protecting the President protects the country.

As executive protection has evolved as a profession, a cadre of executive protection specialists has developed. Corporate in their image and thinking, well-trained and highly committed, these individuals focus on a single mission, the protection of the executive and his family. Executive protection specialists must blend in with the background, looking as indistinguishable from the executive as anyone or perhaps passing as an administrative assistant. Although many are armed, their last option will be an armed response to impending danger. Their first response will be to protect the principal—the executive.

Personal protection specialists should be selected on the basis of intelligence, training, agility, wisdom, and appearance. They should be versatile, know CPR as well as the martial arts, though not necessarily needing the skills of Bruce Lee. Personal protection specialists should be able to deal with the stress of the long hours of service required by the job. They should be well-mannered and able to relate well not only to the business or political associates of the executive, but also to children and other members of the executive's family.

In addition to protecting the executive, the protection professional must be orientated toward resolving conflicts. They must be able to anticipate problems and to conduct an effective risk assessment. They should be people managers, and exude confidence and professionalism in all they do. They should know how to maintain the proper distance from the executive, neither too close nor too far away, so that they can respond in the blink of an eye to do whatever necessary to protect the principal. They must be able to make crucial judgments, committing themselves to save the life of the principal, while knowing that such a decision may readily involve

45

the sacrifice of their own lives. This is a tough choice to make, and requires the utmost discipline of the personal protection specialist.

Each assignment undertaken with the principal must include advanced planning at the site, and a review of the equipment needed for the task. In much the same way airplane pilots run through pre-flight checks before take-off, protection specialists follow accepted professional procedures to ensure the safety of the executive through pre-assignment planning. Experts at executive protection must be able to maintain a low profile, and avoid a show of force, unless the situation demands it. When well-trained, two protection specialists are worth 14 gorilla-sized strong-arm men. The skills necessary to professional protection are not the same as those used in barroom brawls. Truly professional personal protection specialists will want to avoid a brawl in the first place.

Personal protection specialists should be experienced. Many come from military or police backgrounds, having served with Delta Force, the Seal Team Six, or law enforcement executive protection details. There also are a number of private academies that turn out capable bodyguards.

The executive undertaking the development of an executive protection service should know that police or investigative experience alone is not sufficient qualification for this job. Applicants for security details should be interviewed closely about their life experiences and sensitivity as well as their relevant personal protection experience. All military records, including medals and awards, should be verified. Former CIA, FBI, or Secret Service agents are not automatically qualified to handle the job. FBI agents spend most of their time chasing criminals and many CIA employees just collect and analyze data, often concentrating their efforts on countries and activities that may have nothing to do with, for example, the life duties of an executive in a Southern state in this country.

Similarly, former law enforcement officers are not necessarily qualified to be personal protection specialists. They may lack the polished dress and manners that are necessary to look like extensions of the executive rather than an obvious copy. The run-of-the-mill policemen who have been on the streets most of their lives may have developed a cynicism that would interfere with their performance as personal protection specialists. One of the key skills is the ability to anticipate problems without being given explicit orders. In this respect, military men and police officers often run into problems because most are not trained to think for themselves. To take care of the executive, personal protection specialists must be able to act upon their own initiative.

I recall a personal protection specialist with a Federal Reserve Bank assigned to be the driver for the chairman of the board. Once, while driving the chairman and his wife to the airport, he overheard them arguing over getting their children pumpkins for Halloween. The chairman said that his business trip was more important than pumpkins, which angered his wife. When the man returned from his business trip two days later, he found two large pumpkins in the trunk of his car. Nothing was said between the chairman and the driver, but the security supervisor received a letter from the man, stating that the driver had saved his life. It's obvious that the driver was a self-starter, and that his attention to detail in fact might save the executive's life in a more serious circumstance.

As well as an ability to anticipate needs, good communication skills and self-direction are essential. Fluency in a foreign language is useful if protecting executives who travel out of the country. As their behavior and speaking ability reflect on the image of the company, protection specialists should be reasonably well-educated, preferably with a college background, and be sophisticated in matters of travel, dining, dress, and manners. They should be free of arrogance and the need to exert power over others. Since a nervous guard will unnerve anyone he is suppose to protect, personal protection specialists should be able to maintain their cool.

Personal protection specialists must be self-disciplined, free from the kinds of behavior associated with drinking, drug abuse, and sexual acting-out. They should be able to control their bodily needs to ensure that the principal is not left alone when he may need assistance.

A case in point involves a minister for whom I did a risk assessment that included a psycholinguistic analysis of a number of notes to him mailed by one of his parishioners. Making references to rifles, these notes revealed an increasingly frustrated and violent personality. Because of these threats, the minister hired a bodyguard. During one of the Sunday services as the plate was being passed, this guard stepped out of the main sanctuary for a few moments. During this brief lapse of security, the psychotic parishioner approached the minister, striking him, gesturing wildly, and reciting prayers and accusations. If this parishioner had been armed the minister might have died, though his security guard deserted him for such a short time. Public appearances do not permit leaving the principal alone for even a minute. At times of public exposure, the function of the guard is to be with the principal always.

Protection is a 24-hour mission. If their replacements do not arrive, protection professionals cannot refuse to stay with the principal. This is one of the reasons why they must be in good physical condition. Personal protection specialists may need great endurance, as they must do without sleep, eat irregularly, and push their bodies to the upper limits of stress when the job demands it.

Personal protection specialists should choose the weapon with which they are most comfortable. Many prefer snub-nose 38s and other revolvers; others, automatics or 45s. I prefer a 9-mm semiautomatic, 14-round pistol, preferably the Smith and Wesson stainless steel model. As most shootings occur at between seven and twenty feet, larger calibers such as the 44 magnum are rarely necessary.

The choice of ammunition is also important. I prefer a hollow-point bullet that does not mushroom in more than 50 percent of the cases, but is more reliable than the standard load. In addition, jacketed ammunition offers better penetration power.

Whatever weapon is chosen, it should be carried in one particular spot, so that it may be retrieved without hesitation. The weapon should be scrupulously serviced and practiced with often: I usually shoot once a week to keep my timing good. As well as frequent target practice, personal protection specialists should periodically refresh their skills by attending security training schools. Security for the executive is serious business. Attention to detail is essential. Those who specialize in personal protection must make the protection of the executive, his family and property their highest priority.

Advanced planning makes up the majority of any good executive protection service. When the executive plans to attend any function, the site should be visited first by a personal protection specialist. The site must be swept for explosives and entrances must be secured. In addition, the stage equipment in auditoriums contains many potential locations for snipers, and should be examined thoroughly. The location of exits, the availability of fire extinguishers, proximity of hospitals and heliports or landing fields, and the security of vehicle storage areas are just a few of the details which must be investigated. If the facility has its own security detail, the specialist must discuss ways they can work together.

The more publicized the event, the greater the risk to the executive. The guest lists for all social functions must be checked for the presence of terrorists and their sympathizers, and for criminals and members of radical political groups. If the executive is a featured speaker at a function, he should be provided, where possible, with a bullet-proof lectern.

The security detail must plan all trips well before departure time. Arrangements should be reviewed with the executive. Whether traveling by car or plane, an advance list of emergency numbers, including police, hospital, and fire department should be compiled. Local law enforcement agencies should be contacted to determine if there are any criminal or terrorist groups in the area that may pose a security problem for the executive.

Attacks on vehicles frequently come from the driver's side. Most assailants try to stop the vehicle by incapacitating the driver, so the driver must be good at evasive driving manuevers. As with any skill, driving evasively requires practice. Some practice runs should include the executive so that he will be familiar with the procedure should the occasion arise when it must be employed.

Upon arrival the executive should not get out of the car until the security detail is satisfied that there is no danger. The driver should remain on duty with that car, prepared to leave quickly. This is particularly necessary if the executive has a history of ill health or if his life has been threatened.

Personal protection specialists should not dine out with the principal while on duty unless other members of the security detail are elsewhere in the room watching for them. Members of the security detail should not interact with other guests in the restaurant, nor should they drink while on duty.

Where a corporate security office exists, the protective detail should always stay in contact with it. Communication may be by walkie-talkies or a beeper or paging system. Portable scramblers that prevent eavesdropping may be strapped to any telephone for private contact with the command post.

If a hotel stay is required, the hotel staff must be informed of the need to handle a possible crisis. If necessary, the executive may be registered under an assumed name. The executive's account card should state clearly who is to have access to the room and what phone calls are to be put through. Separate phone lines can be installed to ensure privacy. The protection specialist should be alert to possible security breaches when maid service and room service are used. Food and service carts should be checked thoroughly for hidden weapons or bombs. After the service personnel have left, the protection specialist should ensure that the window and door latches are tight and that no one is hiding in the room. Valuables should be kept in the safety deposit box of the hotel, as the security of the executive is more important than guarding his jewelry. Door alarms are available for hotel rooms. I found it necessary to use one when I testified in the execution phase of the trial of a bomber in Wyoming. Because he threatened to kill anyone associated with the prosecution, I took with me two pistols for which I had received concealed weapons permits, as well as body armor. I registered at a hotel under an assumed name. No one knew my whereabouts except my wife, whom I would not permit to call me. Having a door alarm at the entrance to my hotel room gave me the additional security I needed.

Security professionals must be able to analyze threats to determine whether terrorists or criminals are attempting to harm the executive. The security staff must weigh the possible motivations for an attack and how it might occur, determine which weapons might be used, and whether this individual or group has acted similarly toward others. It may be necessary when lethal threats have been made for both the personal protection specialist and executive to wear protective body armor.

Aside from planning and determining the security needs of the executive, it should go without saying that personal protection specialists must protect the executive from danger. When confronted by hecklers or those shouting threats, the executive must be moved out of the path of trouble. Protection specialists must not be distracted into responding to the hecklers.

When the executive gives a press conference or attends a social function, the eyes of the security agents should be upon the crowd. If the security detail is large, then each one should be assigned a small area from which their eyes must never rove. Some years ago, the actor Sylvester Stallone was accompanied by two tough looking bodyguards to an interview. At no time did the bodyguards take their eyes off Mr. Stallone, whom they obviously admired. Anyone could have slipped past their bulky bodies to harm the man they were hired to protect.

The executive needs to evaluate the performance of his personal protection specialists to ensure that they are not distracted by rubbing elbows with a prominent person. This is a major problem in the protection of movie stars. The security detail should never try to become on a first-name basis with the principal, as friendship is not the aim of their service. Prevention of harm is the only mission befitting a personal protection specialist.

The protection specialist detail must exercise critical judgment and self-control so that when danger is perceived, the executive can be removed from the scene as quickly as possible. The executive might be pushed into a car or to the ground, covered by a protection specialist. Fire should not be returned until the executive is safely out of range. Because disabling the attackers is a secondary concern, the security detail may jeopardize their own lives while saving the principal. A hasty retreat is neither surrender nor weakness, but is often the most sensible course available.

If the executive is injured, advance planning proves its worth. Security personnel should know immediately where to take him for medical care. Planning for an emergency should include naming a replacement for the executive in the event that he is unable to perform his duties. The protection specialist should have a list of people to call and should know what to do if the executive is incapacitated.

The executive should keep in mind that he is mortal. Because he has a security detail, it does not mean that his death can be prevented. All that personal protection specialists can do is minimize the risks. By having such protection, assaults may be discouraged because the executive will not be considered a safe target.

Robert Kennedy disregarded the advice of police agencies in Los Angeles that he needed trained and armed security. He rejected offers of protection by the sheriff's department and the city police departments. He felt that two brawny friends, one of whom was a football player, would be enough to protect him. All they were able to do was to mourn the death of their friend.

Personal protection specialists have responsibilities and talents that go beyond physical prowess. Experience, intelligence, alertness, and the ability to commit oneself to absolute responsibility are the qualities that make up those who serve on a security detail. Because security concerns and planning are never complete, personal protection must become a way of life, both for the executive and for those who serve him.

9

Protection: The People and the Process

Jurg W. Mattman

It is difficult to isolate protectees and their role in protection from those who provide the protection. The interpersonal relationship, the interaction and personal dynamics between the two are integral to the effectiveness and efficiency of a quality protection program.

One cannot escape from the fact that the protectee and bodyguard are human beings, with the full range of human emotions, reactions, capabilities and failings that make each of us unique individuals. We are not dealing with inanimate objects relating in a static environment. This alliance between at least two, and sometimes several, individuals takes place within a volatile, ever changing environment with inherent tensions, stress, and fears.

To better understand the dynamics involved in this kind of an association, one must define the primary relationship that exists. Here, the first elements of confusion surface. The protectee will either personally contract for the services of a body guard or is provided these services by an employer or agent. In either case, it appears that an employer/employee relationship is present. However, a scenario emerges that is not typical of the usual employer/employee relationships.

The mere presence of a bodyguard will not guarantee the aversion of an attack. It is the employee or bodyguard who will be called on to direct the employer's or protectee's physical movements through crowds, streets, hotels, airline and train terminals, as well as other public places. Car and airline routes are open to scrutiny and may be revised at any time for the sake of safety. The protectee's routine visits to relatives, friends, doctors, hairdressers, and shops may be altered by the bodyguard, sometimes at a moment's notice, all in the attempt to avoid routines that might be observed by a criminal. Should round-the-clock protection be required, the movements of the protectee could be severely constrained even within his own home and office.

The extent to which the protectee allows the bodyguard to direct movements and change schedules and travel routes as deemed necessary can be integral to the success or failure of a protection program. A well-trained, professional bodyguard will do his or her best to be as unobtrusive as possible, and will provide what I refer

51

to as "transparent security." In other words, the quality bodyguard will provide a service that is invisibly ubiquitous yet still reduces the vulnerability of the protectee to a threat.

In the beginning of the working relationship, the bodyguard must become intimately familiar with the protectee's personal, business and travel schedules, habits, personal and professional acquaintances, as well as the home and work environments. He must be aware of every movement made by the protectee, sometimes from sun-up to sundown. Looking at the potential for threat to the protectee, there are three kinds of individuals that pose a danger; the criminals, the crusaders (including terrorists), and the mentally disturbed. It is difficult to identify and define any one set of recognizable characteristic traits of one specific group. A terrorist with political motives involved in the kidnapping of a government official may exhibit psychotic behavior. A street criminal may take on a cause and commit violent acts, all in the name of the crusade. Then there are the occasions when an individual with a serious mental illness will exhibit delusions of grandeur and take on a cause such as saving the nation from a politician who, in his mind, has not adequately responded to the needs of the people.

When selecting a target, terrorists and other criminals have been known to evaluate their chances of success on the following criteria:

Apparent Wealth: The potential gain from a burglary or robbery and the apparent ability of the executive or his company to pay a ransom or extortion demand are important considerations in the target selection.

Media Value: Individual or corporate name recognition, product or service identification, and controversy in business, government, entertainment industry or social circles, all add to the media value.

Family: Spouses and children of targeted executives are particularly valuable as kidnapping victims. Because of the strong emotional considerations, concessions often exceed prudent limits.

Accessibility: the paradigm of the path of least resistance applies. A "hard" or protected target executive is less likely to be a victim than a "soft" or vulnerable target.

It is the bodyguards job to "harden" his client. It is by becoming intimately familiar with a range of personal details concerning the client, that the bodyguard can be effective at his task.

It might be appropriate in the early stages of the working relationship to establish a kidnap file for the protectee and immediate family members. This requires the collection of full sets of finger and voice prints, current photos, dental and medical records, and handwriting samples for each individual. This information will be collected, tabulated, and maintained either by the bodyguard or the firm he or she represents.

If there exists a history of attacks or attempts to harm the protectee in any way, the bodyguard or the firm they represent must investigate and assess what, if any, dangers continue to exist.

If there were past incidents there must be open discussions about the attacks with the protectee, his family, and critical staff. These discussions will most assuredly invoke unpleasant memories and must be handled in a sensitive manner.

Any past or recent publicity concerning the activities of the protectee must be reviewed by the bodygaurd. Even incidental reports and seemingly benign mentions in the press concerning the protectee should be noted. Any necessary changes in routine or precautions should be instigated as soon as possible in response.

As an example, there is often a tremendous amount of publicity given to corporate takeovers, hostile and friendly, in which the assets of the "corporate raider" are mentioned. These figures may or may not be accurate. Remember, it is the perceived value of the target or victim that a potential terrorist or criminal will consider in his attempt to weigh the advantages and rewards of a successful kidnapping or extortion effort.

In order to reach the intended target, a terrorist or criminal will observe the personnel closest to the intended victim sometimes during weeks of surveillance, to discern patterns in movement and travel to and from the office, home and elsewhere. The criminal will try to identify any existing security hardware or personnel with the obvious intention of outwitting them.

Bear in mind that a terrorist or criminal will attack a protectee in any number of places; at home, the office, while traveling, in the street, or during religious or leisure activities. It is with this knowledge that a bodyguard may advise the protectee to tone down obvious appearances of wealth and affluence, such as expensive automobiles, jewelry or furs in public places. The suggestion of driving an understated car and leaving the diamonds at home when the protectee wants to enjoy signs of his hard-earned wealth, may not be well received, even if they are given with all good intentions.

What can be done when the executive, anxious for publicity, does not appreciate the precautions taken by his bodyguard to bring him out of the corporate headquarters via a back exit to a waiting car. After all, there may be a waiting press corps hungry for news in front of the building, providing a fine opportunity for the executive to pontificate on the merits of his latest corporate takeover. That executive may still choose to exit from the front of the building thereby creating an unnecessary risk.

My point is that rarely, if ever, is an employer so closely and intimately managed by an employee as in the case of a personal bodyguard directing the movements of a protectee. It is simply the nature of the security business and the process involved in providing for quality services that necessitate certain constraints.

In my own observations of the personalities of successful people I find that they tend to share a high degree of independence, self-sufficiency, and confidence which in some cases, certainly not all, borders on arrogance. Couple these personality traits with at least one or even several bodyguards attempting to direct, manage, and control the movements of a protectee and there exists a potentially difficult situation.

Chauffeured limousines, private jets and yachts are among the marks of success in this country. Each of these perks also provides an environment where the protectee can be in command and control of his own movements as well as the personnel around him. Executives in stressful positions require a certain amount of isolation from the distractions of co-workers and others to rejuvenate themselves. These isolated means of transportation also provide valuable private time for an executive to read reports and newspapers or to peruse confidential material.

So there exists a situation where the protectee may, for his own sense of gratification, or for the sake of efficency and time, require these outward symbols of affluence.

I must, at this point, refer to my previous comments about the dangers of ostentatious displays of wealth. Remember, it will be the bodyguard or protection firm employed by the protectee that may be in the position to recommend curtailing the use of such luxuries. Yet it may be the protectee who, for whatever reasons, may request or even require them.

Joseph Pulitzer, the multimillionaire newspaper publisher purchased a yacht so that he would not have to depend on the existing commercial lines to transport him around the world. In addition to having greater control over his own travel arrangements, the yacht provided an environment that Pulitzer could command. W.A. Swamberg in his book, described it this way:

> In this luxurious craft, he was uncontaminated by influences, regulations or persons beyond his jurisdiction and command, out of reach of church bells, trolleys and drill sergeants, surrounded only by things he desired and by some 75 employees, every one of them trained to cater to his whims. It gave him complete control. It was an absolute monarchy, he was king and the 75 employees were his subjects.

Yet, it is a bodyguard who should be in command, not only of the movements of the protectee, but to some extent over the movements of those surrounding the client, i.e., critical staff members, family members, and others who interact with him.

Let us now look at several scenarios that actually occurred, resulting in the deaths of publicly known individuals. I suggest that in each of these instances, death could have been avoided.

The murder of John Lennon in 1980 illustrates a fatal decision by the protected individual to exit his limousine in the street in front of his apartment building rather than within the protected interior courtyard. Lennon's mentally deranged killer was waiting for him on the sidewalk with a revolver.

A bodyguard or bodyguard/driver might insist that the protectee exit within a more protected area. It is not known if Lennon's driver did try to insist on this course, or whether he even had Lennon's authority to do so. If Lennon wanted to leave his vehicle from the front sidewalk, who could stop him.

How can we quantify those times when preventive measures insisted upon by a bodyguard have saved a protectee from injury or death? Certainly there may be times when a perpetrator is caught fleeing with gun in hand and it can be proven that the presence of a bodyguard or other preventive measures kept the criminal at a safe distance. But what about the times when the criminal moves quickly enough or is clever enough to completely evade being seen by protection staff or security cameras?

Another scenario, this time in the corporate environment. In 1985, the chairman of Deak-Perera (the foreign exchange company) and a receptionist were both killed by a deranged woman. The woman simply walked into the company headquarters with a gun. The firm had been aware of her delusion that she was a part owner of the firm but dismissed her as a "crank."

Had there been an effective protection program with the support and backing of top management, this tragedy may have been prevented. I state that it "may" have been prevented. Even the most diligently prepared and executed programs are still open to attack by a determined enough individual or group.

In 1982, in Laporte, Indiana, a disgruntled employee named Harold Lang decided to take his problems to Mayor A.J. Rumely. He went to the mayor's home without an appointment and was ordered to leave and not return. During the night of May 31, 1982, Lang returned to the mayor's home and killed both the mayor and his wife.

Each of these cases point to varying degress of independent thought and action taken on the part of the protectee. In all cases there seems to be a willingness to minimize the potential threat to the protectee and those surrounding him. It may be difficult at this time to determine who was responsible for making the decision to either ignore standard safety procedures or to ignore known threats. But clearly, the independent thinking on the part of one or several individuals, without regard for consequences, resulted in tragedy.

One of the long standing problems in the protection industry is in measuring the effectiveness of personnel and hardware. When no attacks occur, is this the result of an effective bodyguard or is it simply that no risks exist for the protectee? What CEO or independently employed individual will not question the funding of a service when the effectiveness is difficult to determine.

The costs for a comprehensive security program are great. Providing one protectee with one well-trained bodyguard, seven days a week, 24-hours a day, can cost as high as $250,000 per year. This cost excludes travel, lodging, meals, and other expenses that may be incurred while performing necessary duties for the client.

Security devices and hardware will add to the cost of protection. Armoring a car with plates, bulletproof glass, and other devices may run from $20,000 to $200,000. Closed-circuit television surveillance systems can easily reach $50,000 for an executive mansion. Protecting private yachts, aircraft, additional residences, and offices with electronic security systems can run into additional six figure amounts.

Expensive precautionary measures such as these should be integrated with an established crisis management program to be implemented in the event of a kidnapping or attack. The cooperation of the protectee and his family and staff, is vital to the development and implementation of such a program.

The program has as its purpose the establishment of a definite plan of action, agreed upon by all participating parties, to be implemented in case of a major crisis involving designated individuals, groups, or facilities.

A crisis management program may cover any range of emergencies from illness and accidents involving the protectee to natural disasters, kidnapping, extortion, hijacking, political crisis with economic consequences, and any other incident of a newsworthy nature.

The structure of the crisis management team will vary somewhat for each organization. In most cases the team will include a team leader and alternate, a banker or financial advisor, a media spokesperson, an attorney, and the security consultant.

In the corporate environment the executive protectee is not only partially responsible for his own safety, but is responsible for employees and visitors to the corporate facilities.

As demonstrated in the case of the Deak-Perera shooting, the vulnerability of receptionists and front-line staff can be as great or greater than the vulnerability of the executive. This is particularly true in corporate offices where the public has direct access to service areas.

Often executives are lulled into a feeling of security when a large number of uniformed and/or armed guards are visible within the facility. Yet the presence of guards, without the support of appropriate hardware and security procedures, will be inadequate. An overabundance of guards can create an unpleasant, oppressive working environment not conducive to creativity and productivity.

Everyone within the organization must be made security aware. Once procedures are established it is most important that they be maintained and monitored on a continuing basis. The convenience of executives or staff must never take precedence over these procedures. Allowing known staff members to bypass regulations such as wearing I.D.s or using normally prohibited entrances as a convenience will only increase potential for attack. As with any management system, the tendency to bend established rules over a period of time is pervasive. Yet the cost of slackened security may be the loss of life or injury to executives or staff, sabotaged utilities or computer systems, or damaged inventory or facilities. Ultimately, in the corporate setting the organization's life is at stake. The issue goes beyond the economics of the cost and staff, hardware, and software to the potential for loss. The death or temporary incapacitation of a chief executive officer or other top executive, or the loss of computer files or inventory can put a small company out of business overnight and can easily create havoc for a larger firm. With publicly held organizations, media coverage of violent incidents will play an important role in the volatility of stock prices.

The legal aspects of corporate responsibility for the safety of employees while on the job is an additional issue that cannot be ignored. A recent incident in northern

California involved a female employee of a city police department who was attacked in the parking lot while leaving her office. The employee is now suing the city and the police department for negligence.

Organizations of all kinds now maintain operating hours beyond the standard nine-to-five. The value of equipment, computer software, proprietary documents, and sensitive materials is greater than at any time in our economic history.

The role of the protectee in the protection process, at least within a corporate environment, expands beyond concern for himself, the immediate family, and staff all the way to any corporate association and, at times, to the public.

This is not to say that private individuals with protection programs do not have responsibilities to their staff, but within the corporate setting the issues are further reaching and in most instances carry greater financial implications.

Consider the cost and effort required for recovery from an attack. This final response to an incident should initially be developed as part of the crisis management program. Establishing ransom demand levels and securing insurance coverage when available and if deemed appropriate will be the responsibility of the protectee, his staff, and security consultant. Contingency planning for the continuing operation of any corporate activities under emergency conditions must also be addressed.

So it is not simply a passive, reactive role that the individuals involved in the protection program face, but an active, participatory, and ever changing role that must be responsive to, and responsible for, the safety of a wide range of people and property.

10

Development of a Security Program
for the Business

If anything is true about corporate security today, whether it concerns a business in a national or international location, it is that the executive, his staff, and their company are on their own. The image and military advantage of the United States is such that it can no longer present an international appearance of supremacy. Small groups of terrorists have taken us on and shown that fundamentally, despite our B-2 bomber and exquisitely complicated weaponry systems, we cannot protect our businesses or citizens abroad.

On a national and local basis, police departments are rarely in a position to help a business maintain security because crime is too big a problem and there is not enough staff to give any semblance of personal service to the local businessman. Thus in his own community, the businessman is also on his own.

What can the business man do to protect his assets at home and abroad? No place is safe for his business or himself or members on his board. Livingstone[1] covers the essentials of how to establish a security program; much of this material will follow his guidelines.

Multinational corporations and local businesses have to accommodate to this change. In 1990 one percent of U.S. gross national product, according to Livingstone, will be devoted to home and industrial security.

Thus, no senior corporate manager or executive can overlook the necessity to involve himself in his company's overall strategic planning, regarding security matters. This is something that cannot simply be delegated to specialists and forgotten. It is becoming more complicated and high tech all the time, and requires profound attention and highly professional staff to develop and maintain.

An important part of any corporate security program is the development of a corporate intelligence service, a program which gathers information about what is going on in the corporate community, in terms of high tech research or defense production and what is being done within the company itself in these areas that may make it a target for foreign intelligence services.

The protection of corporate staff and property, as well as secrets, is an important area for security concern.

---

1 Livingstone, N.C. *The Complete Security Guide for Executives*. Lexington, MA: Lexington Books, 1989.

Corporate Security Digest[2] reports a story of a Pittman-Moore employee who embezzled millions of dollars. Darrell A. McConchie was held on a two million dollar bond. Some $300,000.00 was located in seven banks and frozen by authorities and three million dollars in investments and purchases were traced.

Had there been better and more frequent audits as a part of a security program, this man's deeds would have been thwarted or kept to a lower amount before discovery.

In the same report Sherwin-Williams Co. was ordered by the court to pay $31.1 million dollars to the Glidden Co. for hiring workers to obtain industrial secrets. Five former Glidden employees had been hired to obtain information on plastic pigment technology and cost reduction methods. Sherwin-Williams planned an appeal of the verdict and vigorously denied any wrong-doing.

It was apparent that Glidden Co.'s security was good and caught the former employees in an act of industrial espionage. This case serves as a warning about such activities and shows how costly such a practice can be because of the fines and tarnished reputation. Without a security program and staff, important technological advancements could have been stolen.

In the same issue of *Corporate Security Digest,* there is a report about an unidentified group of computer pirates who stole the technological blue print for the Apple Computer Company's Macintosh. This opened the door to the production of cheap copies of Apple's product. The group called itself Prometheus League (Software Artists for Information Dissemination) and sent letters to various industry observers with portions of the Macintosh source software code. Copyright registration will protect Apple but, in countries without adequate laws, such theft becomes profitable for the thief.

Without an effective security program such incidents cannot be prevented or properly investigated.

Risk assessment is an important procedure regarding the operations of a multinational company overseas or locally. The political climate of the host country, in which that oversees division is located, must be very clearly determined. Terrorist activities and undercurrents for political change through revolution must be known by the corporate board in order to determine whether or not operation should continue or be switched to another company.

The corporation should establish a country Risk Management Group, which will monitor political and economic change, instability and violence, and will be prepared to intervene by negotiations should members of the overseas groups be taken hostage.

In the event the corporation does not have such a group, there are companies that specialize in providing such services, like the Miami based Ackerman and Palumbo, Londons Controlled Risks Limited and Risks International in Washington, D.C.

The Risk Management Group or any corporate administrative groups assigned to this task must determine the stability of the host countries political system, how long

---

2. *Corporate Security Digest,* Vol. II, (26):2-6, July 3, 1989.

it's likely to remain in power and whether or not there's been active political violence in the country. If there has been, it should be determined who is the primary target of that violence and what groups are involved and what is their attitude toward foreign companies.

It should be determined how closely the United States is related to that host government, and what effect a violent change in government would have on the business climate.

Companies both locally and internationally have to keep tabs on inventory control because pilferage and theft represent a major problem for every company both nationally and internationally.

A considerable number of terrorist threats are hoaxes and such pressure can be disruptive to the company and produce a negative morale for the employees. The hoax calls, threatening bombings or kidnappings, also can lower profits.

Constant surveillance must be maintained regarding the possibility of sabotage. Cars and machinery can all be affected by various gumming agents and abrasives. The computer system can be tampered with and can literally bring about system shut-downs. Files can be destroyed and tight control over these areas must be maintained by the corporate administration.

It is apparent that industrial espionage mentioned earlier in this chapter, is an important area because secrets may be stolen. By the same token, corporations may have staff which steal the secrets of others, and when detected can bring about great embarrassment and fines for the company sponsoring such activities.

Arson, assaults on employees by terrorists, and disgruntled employees and product tampering are all frightening realities with which the corporation must deal, in terms of its security program.

One of the major problems facing business security programs is the difficulty that exists in hiring employees who take their jobs seriously and want to be professional in their work. They have to feel a sense of commitment to the company and through their work need to develop the kind of pride and discipline that goes along with an effective security service.

Security staff needs to check security badges, ensure complete control over access to the corporation and equipment, scan bags and lunch buckets to ensure that drugs, alcohol and weapons are not smuggled into the plant and products are not smuggled out.

One of the major problems in developing a security program is to recruit, train and supervise security guards to be polite and tactful as they invade the property of employees. Some of them tend to become surly and overimpressed with their power, and can provoke poor morale in workers who might want to retaliate and sabotage the employer.

Employees should always be informed in advance of changes in the security system. This will help them feel that changes are not arbitrary, as they have been prepared for the addition of different screening programs.

One of the biggest failures of the security programs in business in the lack of training of personnel.

Staff needs to learn to deal with problems in a courteous and professional manner. There has to be professional use and management of a firearm or night stick. They need to be trained in the laws of the state and, fortunately, in states like California, security guards are required to take a training course and pass a test before they can serve in that capacity.

They need to know something about crisis management and how to take initiative in handling a crisis. They need to know about first aid and fire fighting procedures and how to be observant. They also need to know how to do a bomb search.

Good people in the security field can succumb to boredom and routine. The same problem plagues the police who patrol the streets at an average of 30 miles per hour and who have to fill out endless paperwork.

The security system needs to be tested constantly by people who will attempt to break through the security system, or to alter identification badges. If infiltrators are successful in gaining access to classified document storage areas or critical machinery, then the security program is worthless. Unless the administration is prepared to test the adequacy of the security system, there's no way of knowing whether it will hold up when a real threat materializes.

The corporation needs to make its security staff feel important. There should be various promotional opportunities within the security system and the staff should be made to feel they are a part of the corporate family. They should understand, and those who are not a part of the security program should appreciate, the fact that profits for the company are as much due to good security as they are to product development and marketing.

A corporate officer should regularly establish contact with security staff to get the reaction to the security program and the measures that need to be taken for a more effective program.

Security guards should not be exposed to unnecessary risks. Those in outside posts should be in bullet-proof vests and should have armor to protect them from drive-by shootings or efforts to crash into the corporate yard.

In addition to an effective security guard human patrol program, there also has to be other security measures.

Fences are very important and there should be some type of access control and perimeter warnings such as motion detectors on the fences. The fences should be embedded in concrete. They should be designed so that an intruder must cross the area without benefit of any cover, and thus be in plain view of a guard's line of vision. The fence, in and of itself, is not enough to deter those who would like to gain access to the facility.

There should be a patrol available to respond to a signal given off by a sensor.

A building has to be designed so that it provides greater resistance to grenades and other explosives, as a fence may not be tall enough to repel such assaults.

There should be security access roads, and brush and trees should be cut back on both sides of the road to reduce the risk of ambush.

Efforts should be made to reduce gaps in the defense system. Fences should be marked so that persons cannot be accidentally injured or electrocuted, in the event the fence is electrified. Signs should be posted indicating that there is an electrified fence that could subject someone coming into contact to injury and electrical burns.

There are instances where the product of a corporation is so explicitly sensitive, such as classified military material, that guards may have to be furnished with special night vision equipment. The lighting should be such that the guards are not silhouetted, and it must be located comfortably within the cross hairs of the snipers rifle.

The overall affect of lights can be enhanced further by painting buildings a light color so that intruders wearing dark clothing stick out all the more, and are much easier to identify.

There should be alarms passing a current through a wire or strip of metallic foil, so that when a window or door is opened contact is broken and the alarm is triggered.

Other systems can be used involving an infra-red beam of light which, when broken sounds the alert and, in a highly classified or sensitive area, it should be located on the inside of the building while the conventional alarm is found on the outside.

There are alarms utilizing ultrasonic or microwave broadcasts of a signal into the room, triggering an alarm with a pattern of returning echoes.

There are other kinds of alarms like electromagnetic ones which create an electronic field around non-ground and metallic objects that will sound if the field is disturbed.

There should be a power back up with any alarm system to prevent its failure in the event the power lines are cut.

Both precautions and guards should be posted to prevent an interloper or intruder from cutting cables to the alarm or from the alarm system to the guard station, and there should be a strict accounting of all keys, particularly duplicates.

The screening of employees is particularly important, even for top management. A good deal of successful industrial espionage involves the cooperation from the inside of both workers and/or management.

Backgrounds and references should be checked very thoroughly, if at all possible, through the security agency. If there's a good relationship with the police, there should be a routine record check with serious efforts to record information about drugs, alcohol and psychiatric problems.

The personnel officers should maintain histories of short term employment and the reasons for those employment problems, particularly if these are potentially disgruntled employees who are rebellious toward the authority of a company.

Wherever legally possible, polygraphs may be of some help in screening, and a particular caution and supervision should be extended to temporary help. Their I.D. badges should be different from regular staff, and they should not have access to sensitive areas, where classified designs and test information is located.

As is the case with the executive at home who educates his house staff, the employees of the company should similarly be educated in matters of good security. They should report all strange and suspicious behavior of employees, as well as strangers, and should have an idea of who belongs in what section of the company.

Employees who violate security procedures should be instantly terminated.

Files should be locked and stored in fireproof cabinets. Locks on these units should be the combination type.

Desks should be cleared at the end of each work day to ensure that no sensitive documents will be left out.

Computer security should be very strict, and unauthorized employees should be prevented from obtaining access to sensitive files.

11

The Importance of Intelligence

Henry J. McDermott and
Lawrence J. Redlinger

Does the executive need intelligence and if so why? The answer to this question is Yes. Otherwise the executive and the company are operating in a vacuum, giving all the advantages to their opponents. This is true whether we are discussing business strategy and tactics, product and client information, or information necessary to protect life and property. For executives (and their families) traveling and living abroad, the importance of accurate intelligence and information control cannot be overestimated. In addition to issues such as foreign competition and employee theft, the contemporary scene raises the spector of international terrorism and kidnapping.

Intelligence, good intelligence, is made up of information that reduces uncertainties and raises the probability of making the best decision(s) under the circumstances. Intelligence is always aimed at providing information key to making decisions and involves continuous scanning of the environment.

The Functions of Security

The gathering of intelligence is a security function different from the actual protection of life and physical property and so requires a different perspective. Intelligence gathering is aimed at proving protection through knowledge as opposed to, for example, establishing an obvious security presence. Intelligence makes one more aware of the environment and the choices and options available. The goal of this understanding is to make the executive such a difficult target to approach that opponents will decide to look for another target.

Intelligence gathering differs from crisis management because it is a continuous process. For many security directors and security consultants, emphasis on intelligence gathering means a dramatic change in mind set. Intelligence must ultimately lead to a more flexible security net, to adaptive procedures as opposed to "normal" routines. It means thinking in terms of prevention by knowledge as opposed to prevention by presence; it means becoming a personal advisor to the executive staff and CEO. Security directors and consultants must be able to become the "silent" and "hidden" fixers without alienating others or disrupting normal organizational procedures. Security personnel are frequently thought of as threatening by employees: in fact they are not. Their overall goal is to reduce divisiveness in the company and raise the level of cooperation in information gathering and information control. Areas of divisiveness within the company and executive boardroom create tactically weak points for outsiders to penetrate. It is our opinion that a nonvisible, nonthreatening style reduces blocks to cooperation by other staff who can thwart intelligence gathering and processing attempts. The opposite style of operation provides numerous (and visible) signals to those on the outside trying to gather insider information. The disruption of routine organizational procedures signals those who might be watching that something is amiss, and allows them to hide their actions and modify their plans all too easily.

It must always be remembered that the goal is prevention—prevention of hostile actions against the company and the executive and his/her family; prevention of information loss; and prevention of property loss. We are collecting information for use in developing and maintaining competitive advantages, not simply for busting the bad guys.

From the executives point of view, what is the true function of the security consultant or director of security? As mentioned above, the answer focuses on two objectives. The first is to provide physical protection; the second is to provide knowledge of the environment sufficient to allow the executive to move about with a high degree of confidence, security awareness, and assurance. The first objective involves defensive and passive thinking that can culminate in what we call the "wall theory" of security. Embracing the wall theory means simply that valuables are encased within a wall or walls and the perimeter is defended. For assets that remain in place, there are sound reasons for "walls," e.g., access codes, security clearances, and the like. However, in the modern era of high speed communication and interactive systems, walls have become much more difficult to construct and defend. In terms of protecting human assets that must as a matter of course move about, the wall theory is sorely tested and very often comes up lacking. Walls, whether built of bricks and mortar or a covey of bodyguards, are very often obtrusive. They call attention to that which we want protected and in this sense alone are counterproductive. Walls sometimes lead to passive thinking; all the personnel (bricks) are in place. Finally, for the executive the wall can take on a life of its own such that it disrupts personal and professional operations, subverts the authority structure, and interferes with the real purpose of the company.

The second objective, knowledge of environment sufficient to move about with security awareness, confidence, and assurance involves a much more active approach to security, particularly the security of human assets. Obviously, it actively involves monitoring the external and internal environments through which the executive must pass and in which he or she must do business and live. This monitoring is intelligence gathering. Executives should be able to obtain from their security up-to-date, detailed intelligence on the major social and structural strains in the societies in which they do business, work and live that might lead to hostile situations toward the company or its personnel. This involves environmental scanning of political parties, religious groups, ideologies, and fringe groups. These must be placed in the context of the cultural milieu of the society; an understanding of the major habits of the people is necessary. Some common rules of thumb for environmental scanning and development of a flexible security net include the use of extensive background checks on both foreign and domestic employees working for the company overseas to locate and prevent leaks and to locate loyal employees who can "spot" and provide information on local communities; the setting up and use of contingency plans having alternative living arrangements, communication systems, and modes of transportation in place; and the use of tightly linked internal communication systems for travel planning and other activities.

With an understanding of the socioeconomic, political, and cultural conditions, a good security director can greatly reduce the chances of an incidence occurring. The security director should have a crisis management program in place and be prepared to respond appropriately if an incident does occur. Good, timely, and accurate intelligence about national and localized conditions is critical both for prevention and for the development of crisis planning. It is simply impossible to effectively plan responses to situations without the relevant information. Where situations are changing, what is known this month may be out-of-date and inaccurate next month. Planning based on static assumptions in a changing world rarely is adequate. Therefore, we believe that emphasis must be placed on intelligence and particularly on strategic prevention rather than tactical response. After all, why wait until a dangerous situation develops and occurs when one can, with a bit of prevention, avoid the situation altogether?

Analyses of recent assassinations, kidnappings, and other attacks demonstrates that in most cases, the executives and the security directors became complacent. For example, taking the same routes to and from work allows those who would like to intervene to be able to do so with accuracy. Many executives and their protectors become lulled into believing that nothing will happen to them, that they are not targets. Often executives and their security consultants rely on armored cars and bodyguards, believing that they are "in their castles and therefore safe." This is an example of the "wall theory" mentality that ignores any number of factors. And when it becomes a set of numbing routines, that outcome is virtually certain to be bad.

With the above perspective in mind let us examine the travel of a CEO to a number of cities in Europe. The principles presented below may actually be in conflict with the routine procedures in any number of companies: we assume a modern security director is present.

1. The security director must be completely aware of the travel plans of the CEO and major executives even to the point of his personally arranging the flights and reservations (as opposed to secretaries). At the very least, the flights should be screened from their point of origin to their final destination. Consider, for example, the flight that goes from New York to Paris, but then continues on to Athens and Cairo or vice versa.

2. The security director should also have personal knowledge of the cities and contact points to be visited. Ideally the security director or his staff should have performed reconnaissance on the cities. This should include, but not be

limited to: hotels, possible meeting sites and their strengths and weaknesses; means of transport within cities; problems with transportation both technical (do the trains run on time?) and people-related problems (see below).
3. The security director must have made social and political surveys of the cities and region and kept up with the political and social events in the area especially those of active radical groups.
4. Finally, the executive with the advice of the security director must decide who needs information on the strict basis of need to know: those who don't, shouldn't; those who should, must, and be held responsible. Limit those who have access to information concerning travel and other plans of senior executives.

In contrast to the above discussion, consider the following example distilled from the activities of an actual company that we will call Company X. Personnel of Company X always fly the same commercial carrier and always book flights through a local well-known reliable travel agent. The same agent has always booked not only flights but hotel reservations. (Applying our principles we can see security problems.)

In this company it is not uncommon to find office memoranda circulating with details of the CEO's travel plans, hotel reservations, and numbers where he can be reached in an emergency. This information is copied routinely any number of times, left on desk tops, and, in some cases, deposited in wastebaskets. Even the cleaning force has access to the information. In this instance, there should be a reconsideration of the need to know, the handling of the information, and the need for security. There must be a balance between the need to know and the need for security.

What we are in fact discussing is counter intelligence procedures to control information within so as to limit the degree to which those without can pose a threat to us. We are using our intelligence resources to counter before a threat occurs and any hostile actions are taken against the firm. If the company can be made difficult to attack, there is a greater likelihood that other targets will be chosen.

Two other companies with which we are familiar provide useful examples. The first provides the visiting CEO with a car and driver when he is in the city. The driver is a young junior executive "grunt" with no security experience and no defensive driving training. The executive always stays in the same hotel and frequents the same restaurants with all the reservations made well in advance. The CEO's spouse, when she travels with him, is left in the custody of the junior executive grunt to sightsee and shop. In the second company, a car and driver are hired from a local firm with, in our opinion, perfunctory checks ("They performed well last time, so theres no reason not to use them again"). The drivers loyalties, beliefs, and past are unknown to the company. The company is relying on what we call the "logic of confidence;" they confidently assume that the company they have hired is doing what they ought to do and therefore fail to check it out. The company drivers use established routes (efficiency) and are thus predictable. Such patterns make it easier to be followed and harder to tell if one is being followed. Such predictability has lead to kidnapping and assassination. Both of these companies have disregarded the principles we discussed above. They have given control of the environment and information as well as physical control over to unknown people, and established known patterns of action. This might appear to be efficient management of a busy CEO's time but this style of management assumes that no one in the immediate or wider environment has hostile intentions. It further assumes that random violent actions will not fall in the path of the CEO. In these times, both assumptions are foolish and court tragedy.

Hidden Areas of Vulnerability
One critical area of vulnerability is the family of the executive particularly when the family is traveling or living with the executive overseas.

While the executive is doing business with "all proper security " (as we noted in one example above) spouses and children are often left to sightsee and shop, or go about their daily rounds with, at best, a driver. Or the spouse may be seen with the spouse of an executive from the company with which the visiting executive is doing business. In either case, the spouse is vulnerable and so, indirectly, the company is vulnerable and it is directly liable. Often nothing is done to provide the simplest security procedures. One key area of vulnerability is kidnapping for ransom and/ or political ends.

Why does this situation exist? First, the company does not consider the family an asset. Thus, the family is not included under its umbrella of protection. Such protection is rarely provided for in the security budget and furthermore, security directors often do not see such protection as a priority. There are two reasons why security directors may not view such protection as a priority. First, the family is "indirectly" attached to the company and thus cannot "directly" influence the outcome evaluations of the security directors performance. Protecting a key executive is perceived to have more direct benefits for the security director and the security staff. Secondly, the security director and staff are quite often not properly trained to provide services to families. By this we mean that there are qualitative and quantitative differences in the services provided to executives and those provided to spouses and families. This is because the rounds of activities are quite different; locales vary and situations are often unpredictable and uncontrollable. It is one thing to protect an executive having a liaison under relatively controlled conditions: it is quite another to protect a 17-year-old and her boyfriend as they move around an area.

Given the number of times executives, spouses or family members have been kidnapped for ransom, we believe this is a critical area of vulnerability for the company. Security for the entire family is, in fact, holistic security. Security for the executive is a family affair and must be treated as such by security directors. This is true not only when executives and their familes are overseas, but domestically as well.

Another area of vulnerability from a security point of view are employees in key positions. Consider the personnel who drive CEO's about in light of the following account. A particular firm had employed a driver for many years. He had always demonstrated total loyalty and was a model employee. Unfortunately, thugs kidnapped his wife and only daughter and told him that he must do exactly what they wished him to do. To back up their point, they sent him the first two digits of his teenage daughter's little finger. They also sent him instructions for cooperating in the kidnapping of the executive he was scheduled to be driving around and made very clear what would happen to his daughter if he did not cooperate. What was he to do? He carried out the instructions. In this particular case, the security director and his staff, through sluggishness and inertia, ceased years ago to keep tabs on such a loyal employee. Caught in the routines of their jobs, they neglected this area of vulnerability. While the reader may think this is farfetched, a real case similar to the above scenario happened to an American in Beirut, Lebanon.

A third area of vulnerability concerns corporate or industrial espionage. Why kidnap the executive when you can steal his information and not have him know you have done so? Companies with new information, processes, and products are extremely vulnerable because they generally do not have the funds necessary to pay for adquate protection or intelligence. Security, after all, is often seen as being an administrative cost rather than a production cost, an add-on cost rather than a necessary cost to be factored into the price of a product. Security in this sense is treated rather like employee programs to raise motivation and loyalty. Yet anytime a company is going to make a new product or send a new marked signal it is vulnerable. Vulnerability takes two forms: internal, from disgruntled or greedy employees, etc.; or external, from other companies. Without adequate environmental intelligence, the company is at a severe disadvantage.

Scenario of Business Trip

In the following example, we provide a scenario of an executive who is planning to travel to Germany from the United States on business. The example is designed to demonstrate a standard set of procedures and a critique of their weaknesses.

George Folly, CEO of Apex Chemicals, must travel to Frankfurt, Germany, to negotiate a business contract. Folly calls in his executive secretary and dictates a confidential memo to all senior management on his travel plans. The memo includes the dates he will travel, the airline, the hotel, who he will meet in Frankfurt, when, where, and why. The secretary is also instructed to make the necessary arrangements. She does so through the travel agency always used by the company. As a matter of procedure the German office is called and a copy of the memo is telexed to the EVP. The telex indicates that Mrs. Folly will also be traveling and assistance with shopping, sight-seeing, etc., is requested. A limo is to meet them at the airport.

The telex request that the Frankfurt office make arrangements within a given window of time for a one-day trip to Bonn. No specifics are given except as to time frame and the fact that the executive has an appointment with another company there. His wife will not accompany him to Bonn, but will need her own transport and driver to be available.

The Folly's teenage daughter and son will remain at home and the servants have been instructed to arrive at the usual times and perform their regular duties. The cook, (who has been with the Follys for several years) has been given all of the information concerning dates, places, etc., in case of emergency. The son and daughter also have this information and with parental approval, plan a pool party to be held during their absence. While inviting six to eight couples to come over they mention that their parents will be in Europe.

Folly's Follies
1. Made travel plans indiscriminately public which breaks the rule of need to know.
2. Gave control of his critical environment to others.
3. Used local and public travel agencies.
4. Put wife in a vulnerable position (she is under local office control).
5. The German office information is not contained and therefore must be assumed to be widely available.
6. Limos draw attention and exposure.

Folly's Lessons
1. Travel plans should be made using internal resources with maximization of information control.
2. The German office should only be notified of living arrangements after arrival.
3. Security consultant should coordinate travel with German officer to reduce links in the information chain of those who know plans.
4. Security consultant should review all aspects of trip, transport, entertainment, etc. and attach a benefit-risk analysis to each activity.

When a CEO is traveling abroad there are several major areas of vulnerability that arise simply from the position itself and can be exacerbated by the person in the (CEO) position; that is, by the personnal style of the executive. Some of the major areas of potential vulnerability include:
1. Perquisites of the position:
    a. prearranged shelter accommodations;
    b. personal chauffered transport;
    c. prearranged business schedule;
    d. prearranged entertainment schedule;
    e. information distribution concerning each of the above prior to departure.
2. The above problems are complicated when they involve, for example, a board of directors and their spouses.
    a. prearranged shelter for a group perhaps in different cities at different phases of the trip;
    b. prearranged meeting places for business purposes that put the entire

corporate brain in a single place/time;

c. planned sight-seeing excursions that are prearranged;

d. excursions that necessitate the hiring of local firms and individuals for each segment of the trip;

e. planned social events for an entire group, plus, given their status, the arrangements of suitable local aristocrats for them to mingle with. This inadvertently, at worst and consciously at best, involves the board, CEO, and company in the internal political problems of the locals, which in some countries, like Spain, can also mean involvement with groups such as ETA.

f. separate site excursions for spouses using locals, which also necessitates additional security that often is also local and therefore inadequate.

g. finally, the staging of large public social events or the fact that such events are already scheduled (e.g., national holidays).

h. all of above planned through local public relations company who frequently handles other Fortune 500 companies. The PR firm is thus a major information node to be penetrated.

Some Important Rules of Thumb

We believe the following seven items are important for information control and intelligence gathering both in the United States and especially abroad.

1. *Make a habit of controlling information about and the need to know about:* (a) travel plans; (b) corporate decisions; and (c) market information. This should involve a periodic and thorough review of the design and operations in each area as well as the distribution of information. One key question concerns what is essential information and who must know it; another concerns the time of the release of the information.

2. *Reduce reliance on outsiders for scheduling plans. If outside agencies must be used, complete a thorough background check of the agency and the specific personnel to be assigned to the contracted functions.* Particularly for companies dealing with sensitive information and for executives who because of the nature of their companies business may be at risk, a thorough check of those outside is essential. This must include complete back-grounding of the personnel who will be utilized; one cannot assume that the outside agency has done an adequate job. In addition, company security staff must be able to immediately recognize all outside staff that have been assigned to contracted functions.

3. *Control personal and work environment; structure access.* Just as a good financial accounting system provides adequate controls for inventory and embezzlement, a good information control system must limit access and reduce areas of vulnerability. Just as a company must decide what needs to be accounted for, it must also decide what information needs to be protected.

Without such a decision any security measures are meaningless. Information concerning the executive's personal environment must be screened and protected.

4. *Do not establish routines.* Routines are numbing and blind us to the numerous possibilities of untimely and unwanted intervention. Insofar as it is possible, routines should be limited. Where routines for executives must be established, security for the executive must never be routine; all situations however repetitive must be considered novel by security.

5. *Maintain current background files.* Realize that many employees may not agree with company policies and politics. Realize that many employees including senior management have personal (and hidden) agendas and vulnerabilities that provide seedbeds for hostile action.

6. *Know your environment.* Realize that cultural, political, and social environments differ from locale to locale. Briefings, risk assessments, cultural/social analyses must be complete and include knowledge of those variations. A key question concerns what elements in the environment directly or indirectly pose security and personal threats to the executive, the family, and the company.

7. *Do not rely on the company security to provide indepth and responsive cultural analysis.* Normally, they will not have the in-house capability of doing so because it was not included as a function in the design of the company's security system. This is especially true when the security staff is made up of ex-law enforcement personnel with only (and often limited) domestic experience. An executive must know the bounds and limitations of the company's security staff.

8. *Anybody who touches information or is one handshake away from the information is considered a key person and must be checked.* This includes a secretary's boyfriend even if he is not a company employee. While this might be seen as an invasion of privacy the option is one of naive belief about the trust in the world as it is currently constructed.

9. *The employee's (including executives) family must be considered as a unit.* One must understand the chain of affiliation and obligation that family members have to each other and how it appears to outsiders.

Conclusion

Executives need accurate and timely intelligence not only to make good decisions generally, but in particular to make good decisions about security and protection of themselves, their familes, and their companies. Intelligence needs add a new dimension to the functional areas of corporate security and security for the executive.

We are in an Information Age that will revolutionize security and the manner in which it is undertaken. Security directors of the new age will be flexible and imaginative and will understand the use of information as an essential and valued tool in the protection of the corporation, its critical knowledge, products, and executives. Providing physical protection is not enough, for such protection must be environmentally relevant. To make it so, security must be well informed, and must actively seek intelligence. The Information Age has thrust uses of security beyond the essentially passive and static "fortress to be defended" mentality and into "real time," in which events are changing and dynamic.

Security must be realistically integrated into the corporate structure; in particular into the thinking of senior executives who may be for two reasons, the most difficult to convince. First, they usually are the ones who have hired the security people already in place; often, they did so without thinking through what it was the company actually needed. In many instances, there isn't a well thought out security plan. The result is covey of retired law enforcement officers who rely on their good-old-boy networks. Further, their relative lack of savvy about the corporate culture seals them off from where security would be most valuable. Secondly, senior executives enamored with the bottom line often fail to see how security can be cost effective. Part of this difficulty is due to the fact that they have previously constructed security as a piece of the physical structure or as unessential overhead and part is due to the fact that security is not seen as essential to the production process. Conceived as just badges, passes, uniformed gate guards and the like, security is passive and defensive. Moreover, some of the worst offenders in breaching even these types of security are senior executives! Viewing security as part of the information process, both the protection and generation thereof, changes the conception of what security is supposed to do and what its real value is: to protect information and provide intelligence. It must be kept in mind that, unlike other property, information can be stolen and the owner never knows it because duplication does not require removal. Security becomes essential to the production process when the process, including pricing, can be stolen and the company may not know it until too late.

Intelligence gathering is of vital importance to those in charge because we live in a multicultural and multinational world, a world in which plants and products, executives and their families are dispersed across the globe. Security in the new age must be able to provide information that is situationally relevant and from it be able to generate security procedures for executives that work. Ultimately, executives who have the intelligence they need will be better able to effectively function in complicated domestic and foreign environments, with freedom from concern about their own and their family's security. They can devote their total energies toward corporate goals which is critical in maintaining a competitive edge. It is the task of security as intelligence in the New Age to provide what is necessary and it is the task of the executive to design a corporate security plan with intelligence as its centerpiece.

12

Security Management:
Coming to Terms with Budget

Marsha J. Newman
Frederick M. Newman

Before man developed the deadbolt lock or digital keyboard entry system, he erected fences. Building fences is a primal territorial instinct shared by both humans and animals. The dog marks his territory by scent. Even the domesticated poodle compulsively marks every vertical surface in the neighborhood to define and possess his turf. Man has marked, defined, and possessed territory using a variety of elements from rocks to electronics to create what we now define as a fence.

The settlement of the American West was virtually an expansion of fence lines. Before settlers would build a house, they would mark their territory, delineate their turf, and claim their stake. The benefits of delineating a perimeter even before a home was erected were multifold. Fencing a homestead fulfilled the need of every settler to own a personal space, provide a safeguard against unauthorized entry, and gain control of an unknown and potentially hostile environment. Thus, the history of access control began not with a door but a fence.

The concentric theory of physical protection starts with an outside circle of protection providing delay and enunciation and ends with an innermost circle of response and control. Although the management and interaction of the concentric circles varies from site to site, it all begins with the outermost circle functioning as the early warning system.

The physical protection industry today often suffers a myopic view of front line security, particularly in the United States where large oceans and friendly countries serve as national borders. Case in point is the FAA regulation mandating the installation of door access technology and staff badging at most airports in the U.S. by the year 1991. The FAA security amendment is a response, in part, to the Pacific Southwest flight that crashed near Paso Robles, 175 miles northwest of Los Angeles on December 7, 1987 as a result of a vengeful former employee's gunshot. Authorities believe he gained unauthorized entry into the aircraft with a handgun. Many airport managers, security directors and contracted aviation security consultants were aware of the vulnerability of their airports perimeter as well as their doors long before the PSA incident. The PSA incident focused the government's attention on door access vulnerability even though hands-on aviation security managers have been dealing simultaneously with security problems on many fronts on a continual basis.

From a criminal viewpoint, violating an airport perimeter, entering the airport operations area, planting a bomb, or stealing costly avionics from an aircraft and escaping without any evidence of intrusion could be a simple procedure at most U.S. airports right now. In fact, tightening entrance and egress security may very well drive the committed intruder out the door and into the backyard where miles of unguarded perimeter lay waiting.

Many airport and security professionals are left to define for themselves what kind of access points need controlling; their decisions may be based upon budget restraints rather than proven security technologies, theories, and procedures that save both life and property.

Although the FAA began to review and assess the security needs for the U.S. civil aviation industry at least two years before the PSA tragedy as a response to growing global terrorism aimed at airlines, it took a catastrophic incident involving the loss of human lives to warrant swift and comprehensive security upgrades. Even so, the FAA has mandated the upgrade through a multi-leveled bureaucratic decision-making process. Airport security directors, working in conjunction with contracted security consultants, define and analyze the security needs at each airport. The proposals are submitted to regional FAA offices, which in turn submit them to officials in Washington, D.C., for review.

At the onset, the FAA "guesstimated" funding levels for the purchase and installation of the security gear necessary to fulfill the mandate needs. However, vendors and installers were basically not involved in the cost estimation process. Therefore real dollar funding for security upgrades is unrealisitic. Furthermore, the FAA is unsure from where the funding dollars will come. Although billions of dollars have accrued from surcharges on airline tickets, ostensibly for security upgrades, politicans are eyeing this fund to help balance the budget instead of putting it back into the aviation industry.

The reality of budget managers ultimately taking responsibility for the protection of life and property is a hot issue in today's security profession, not only for the protected people and property but for vendors of security equipment, security mangers, and security designers. Again, we are drawn back to the myopic view of American security in general, "What cannot be seen as a threat, cannot be acted on as a threat." The expense necessary to provide appropriate physical security in a civilian environment is not yet viewed as a capital expenditure but as an extraneous and often superficial expense. When the protection of lives and property is seen as important as climate control, then the security profession will have the same clout as the air conditioning and heating profession in the vast civilian construction marketplace.

Budget considerations are a paramount aspect of security management. In order to implement the correct level of security, funds must be available to support the security manager's plan. This, of course, in many instances is not the case. Under these adverse budget circumstances, the security manager must not forget his responsibilities, for it is these responsibilities that can literally mean the difference between life and death, injury and safety, and serious loss of assets.

The executive protection market, a direct offshoot of the civilian construction market, suffers greatly from nearsightedness. A brief analysis of a fictional case illustrates this point. The initial reaction of an executive perceiving threats to his life, family, and/or property is to harden all door entries and install an interior intrusion detection system with some kind of monitoring capability. In reality, this approach provides no delay or early warning for the executive and his/her family. Once an intruder has entered the property and approached the residence, response will almost always be too late or insufficient if the intruder is committed to his crime. Security theorists argue in favor of tightening the perimeter first and subsequently focusing in on the residence, thereby providing early warning, delay, and protection.

The industrial marketplace reflects the same insufficient attitude as the executive protection industry. For the most part, real and perceived threats to a commercial entity are ultimately dealt with by managers who balance dollars of damage over an extended period of time over initial up-front security purchases. Budget managers often prefer paying direct damages resulting from criminal intrusion. A useful example is the parking industry, where at any time millions of dollars of automobiles are contained within a single perimeter. Does the sign outside the parking area saying "Not Responsible for Loss or Theft" also include the irresponsibility of the owners to provide basic protection against rape and murder? What is the purpose of an attendant or guard at a parking lot? Does the parking lot owner have a basic responsibility to vehicle owners beyond simply providing a parking space? Although this is not meant to be a liability exercise, the authors believe that management can no longer regard physical security purchases as superfluous.

The issue of personal responsibility rides strong for the security manager. If a successful breach of security takes place, ultimate responsibility will be assigned. These issues must never be forgotten. Regardless of the attitude of nonsecurity personnel, including top management, security management must always know and understand all potential threats. The establishment of a budget must include plans to protect from all evaluated potential threats. Realistically, this may not be accepted.

However, there are two reasons for initially submitting an all encompassing security budget. The first is that the professional security manager has the ethical responsibility to inform those around him of any and all potential threats and the means to properly protect from these threats. The initial budget reflects the thoroughness of this evaluation. The second reason is to protect the security managers reputation and, inevitably, his or her career. Hiding issues in order to placate one's superiors can lead to disastrous personal consequences. For example, take the security budget submitted for a medium to large airport which does not include a request for an electronic perimeter detection system. In due time, a criminal easily climbs unnoticed over the fence along the length of the airport perimeter and steals $500,000 in avionics from a parked, unattended aircraft. In the ensuing investigation, the question is asked of the security manager, "Why wasn't the perimeter protected?" At this time the security manager cannot say, "We had no money for a perimeter," because the response from budget decision makers can be easily anticipated—"The security director did not inform us of this need. Had we known, we would have seriously investigated a fiscal source to fulfill this need."

After the fact it is unimportant whether the budgeting manager would have actually followed through as he had assured the investigators. Responsibility is being focused on the security manager, who, in this case, did not fulfill professional ethical responsibility by informing top airport decision makers of all possible threats and practical ways to protect from them. If this had been done, a decision to veto this request for whatever reasons would, in effect, protect the security manager from blame in the event of future criminal actions that may have been prevented if the warning was heard. Careers can rise and fall on this issue.

Realistically, a "comprehensive" security budget proposal is sizeable in dollars and will not be accepted in its entirety. Traditionally, security has not been prioritized in the business sector. But with ever increasing crime, the possibility of injury and/or loss of life and assets is growing, and so is the exposure of security managers to professionalism. Someone will be made responsible for security failures and that individual must live with this failure, particularly if it is significant, such as a rape or loss of sizeable assets.

Perhaps the segment of society most aware of the intrinsic need for physical protection starting from the perimeter inward is the military and corrections industry. Prisons have always protected their perimeter. Human beings provided a plentiful and cheap resource to provide early warning and delay tactics as guards and patrol officers. In the early twentieth century, federal prison guards could be hired for less than $900 per year to live and work on site, every day all year, strictly to patrol and guard the facility. Although it is almost impossible to track the competence and ethical nature of these guards, it is reasonable to assume there was a large amount of indifference and graft in the security staff of 80 years ago.

The construction of a prison or military facility often included officer towers that were fully manned 24-hours a day to provide or assist in perimeter protection. Even today, many facilities still depend upon towers for such protection. Corrections and military managers fully concur on the importance of perimeter protection. The issue that exists today is the reliance upon people and guard towers versus the reliance upon technology to guard a perimeter.

The cost of human personnel to protect a perimeter has skyrocketed. Gone are the days of $900 per year employees who live and work on site. Today's prison guards are well paid civil servants with handsome benefit and compensation packages. Correctional managers are concerned with optimal staffing and budget resources. Meanwhile, tower construction and maintenance costs are dramatically escalating as well.

Officials at the Michigan Department of Corrections estimate that the purchase and installation of electronic perimeter security equipment results in construction costs savings of $250,000 to $400,000 per facility. The cost of staffing a tower 24-hours per day, throughout the year, runs from $150,000 to $175,000. Construction costs of each tower are approximately $50,000 to $75,000. Electronic perimeter equipment results in total savings of $750,000–$1 million per institution by the elimination of guard towers in this state.

In the past, corrections managers were reluctant to depend upon electronic detection systems for many reasons, including a historical tie and reliance on towers, poor technology, and the expense of installation and maintenance. System failures, numerous false alarms, and prohibitive maintenance costs often gave perimeter systems a bad name.

However, major advances in field-tested technology now provide cost-effective and reliable systems acceptable to even the most committed skeptics. Some systems are so user friendly in both appearance and operation that their application in the commercial sector, both industrial and residential, is enormous. For example, systems exist that have the capability to mount on any axis on any fence including concertina and razor coil, under water and on walls. There is virtually no "tuning" of the sensors in the field.

Installation and maintenance are simple, labor-saving, and cost efficient. Zone lengths can be as short or long as desired without the need for dedicated processor units for each zone length change. Gates and individual zones have the option for separate zoning either on automatic or manual instruction. There is no need to patchwork several systems to cover gate protection as one continuous system can cover all.

Each zone can be adjusted for sensitivity from a computer keyboard with custom supervisory software/hardware that includes any number of ID code levels and pathways for entry into the system as specified. The computer has the capability to supervise thousands of alarm points in the field as well as the ability to "talk out" to thousands of field points. Digital voice alarm announcements, which keep the security staff alerted, can include voice announcements of tampering with field equipment or invalid ID code entry attempts.

Customized computer graphics generating from a PC-AT are able to show all alarm zones as well as detailed layouts of buildings, and terrain. It is possible to include in the supervisory software any number of ID code levels, assignments, pathways, color tablet screen with system and event adjustments, and detailed, customized help screens.

To combat the persistent problem of false alarm and false alarm response, meteorological data are constantly entered into the system that distinguish environmental factors from actual intrusions, thereby virtually eliminating the major cause of false and nuisance alarms. This feature alone propels perimeter technology into a multi-segmented marketplace where digital dialers can report to a central monitoring station, as is the case in most residences and in many commercial sites.

There is full detection of fence climbing and cutting even on decorative wrought iron mediums. System bypassing and sensor line cutting and tampering is fully detected as well. Finally, the system can be expanded on a modular basis, which allows for future control of added security devices as well as additional fence sensor line.

The trend in the corrections and military market is toward electronically supervised perimeters. This attitude is reflected in the purchasing and specifying trends of corrections professionals today. The civilian sector can learn a great lesson from corrections and military personnel. In terms of human resources, depending on a completely reliable electronic sentinel eliminates the critical issue of guard stress and accountability. Architecturally, electronic surveillance allows for greater design flexibility and community acceptance. Prison officials frequently must deal with community pressure to build an aesthetically pleasing, nonthreatening, but safe, correctional facility.

However, the problem of communicating actual security needs as ascertained by a security manager to a business manager still remains a difficult one in both the private and public sectors. The problem is by no means insurmountable and, within a reasonably short period of time, can be remedied. First, the security manager can no longer regard his professionalism as strictly an offshoot of the law enforcement industry. Security managers are business managers; they must learn to speak the same language as the people who approve the programs they recommend. That language includes a fundamental, although not necessarily comprehensive, knowledge of business policies and practices. The security manager must have a firm understanding of the corporate business structure in which his/her security entity exists. A security manager must gain respect as both a security professional and a solid business person. If this is achieved, then comprehensive security programs will be taken seriously and budgeted appropriately.

Too many times the security manager is networking exclusively within the security industry. If a security program ultimately emerges from the hands of fiscal managers, then security professionals must develop close and enduring ties with that group. Professional organizations can assist by providing training and information seminars specifically focused on these issues.

There are quite a few professional security organizations that do a successful job of keeping the security professional updated in the field. These same organizations can offer an added service to its members by offering programs such as business education, improved communication skills, presenting security needs to nonsecurity decision makers, and influencing fiscal managers through powerful and understandable presentations.

Gone are the days when tall tales of heroic deeds in the law enforcement field alone garner the respect necessary for a security manager to get what is wanted. Today's security manager must be able to comfortably justify large dollar purchases using the concepts budget managers are fluent in, such as: bottom line; long term product depreciation; initial capital expenditure outlay versus long range crisis dollars expenditure; lease/purchase agreements; liability and accountability, to name a few.

Some kind of general business background would greatly enhance a security manager's skill. In almost any American city there are community colleges and adult education programs that offer business education. Selling a security program is not unlike selling any large ticket commodity where presentation, preparedness, confidence and knowledge go hand in hand. Lack of business skills leaves a gaping hole in the security professional's tool kit.

Ideally, a well-trained security manager should have extensive security review and analysis capability, strong management skills, technical fluency, and basic business skills. Of course, communication and presentation abilities greatly enhance the probability of the security manager's programs to be understood and approved. Also, the security manager must make himself known as the sole mover and shaker of security decisions within the organization. Like all issues, the security manager must realize that budgets are fluid. When budget people are taught to see the necessity of appropriate security funding they are comfortable in reestablishing bottom line figures and setting new standards for the security program in general. Instead of approaching budget requirements and restrictions as problems, the security manager must create a vision for the organization that can be shared by all. It is futile for a security manager to be an expert on access control, if the budget counterparts are totally unaware of their own personal vulnerability without it. Like all leaders, the security manager must no longer consider himself as a policeman responding to problems as they arise or anticipating them based upon past experience but rather as a builder of an organization that has the intrinsic skills necessary to create the success that everyone aspires within that organization.

Essentially, this implies that the security manager break out of the mold created years ago by ex-law enforcement and military personnel. That mold, or image, is one of an isolated expert belonging to a closed club of similar professionals, with little or no knowledge of anything else in the world. A strong curriculum vitae in security no longer guarantees success as a security manager. The "old boys club" is not the place to develop and nurture contacts for successful project making.

Hospitals offer an interesting parallel on this issue. Squeezed by skyrocketing costs and increased competition, they began to appeal to their direct source of revenue—patients. They appealed through an understandable language and an appropriate medium—advertising. Hospital administrators became business managers and as revenues increased, the medical professionals were able to obtain the equipment and personnel to keep the hospital, and themselves, competitive.

The parallel lies in that a group of professionals, whose responsibilities are basically different from one another, learn to focus their interests as one. As that is achieved, each group begins to fulfill their personal goals as well as moving the entire organization forward.

Again, taking the parallel further, as the cost of managing security programs becomes more expensive and technical, security managers must appeal to the source of revenue, the budget department, with understandable language and an appropriate medium and prove that their program, without a doubt, benefits the whole organization.

The security field, in our opinion, is still in its infancy precisely because of the isolated and short-sighted views shared by the security manager and budget decision makers at this time. Professions leap to adulthood when they are regarded as necessary to the well being of all. However, the future is rosy and as more and more business managers are forced to deal with security, in both the public and private sector, then security managers will be forced to deal with business managers to get what they want. In this case, the giant leap from infancy to adulthood comes with planning, education, and vision—not with a whimper and a sigh.

13

Employee Management

Gavin de Becker

- ESL Company in the Silicon Valley of California is a well-run subsidiary of TRW. As at all big companies, managers make decisions on policy, procedure, and personnel. They draw upon training, ability, and experience, and they are well prepared for most challenges. They were not prepared for the Tuesday afternoon in February, 1987, when an employee they had fired the year before came back with a vengeance. Richard Farley, carrying a rifle, two shotguns, and several handguns blasted his way through a locked door and furiously fired at employees, many of whom were former co-workers. He killed seven people and injured four others, including Laura Black, whom he had been obsessed with for four years. It was for harassing her that he had been fired.
- In December of 1987, a PSA airliner crashed after gunfire erupted at 22,000 feet. It was a disgruntled employee, recently fired for stealing $69, who had smuggled the gun on board to kill his former boss and 42 other passengers in the process.
- In 1986, Pat Sherill, a 44-year-old Oklahoma mailman known to co-workers as "Crazy Pat," was threatened with dismissal. Soon after, he came to work with three pistols. He killed 14 co-workers, injured six, and finally killed himself.
- Robert Jimenez, a steelworker at USS-POSCO in California, was injured at work when a grinding wheel fell on his foot and crushed it. The severe injury caused him to miss work frequently. Eventually, the company doctor, John Irion, recommended him for a medical retirement. Plant officials met to discuss whether they might keep him in a light job, but decided against it and accepted the doctors recommendation. Robert Jimenez did not accept it. He walked into Dr. Irion's office with a shotgun, and killed him.
- A Los Angeles bank employee, feeling that he was unappreciated at work, threatened to blow up the bank.
- A frustrated aerospace executive began inputting false data into a project computer.

- In April of 1987, a former employee of a telephone company took several hostages and destroyed nearly $10 million in equipment. He was in a rage over the loss of retirement benefits.

Destructive acts against companies and co-workers are not isolated incidents in today's high-stress, short fuse business environment. In an age of takeovers, mergers, and down-sizing, where employees are frequently laid off, fired, or experience a loss in power or status, employee emotion must be seen as a force to consider during the hiring and firing process. Loss of a job can be as traumatic as loss of a loved one, so the strategies applied must be reasoned, particularly with problem employees. And all companies have had them.

This chapter will discuss suggestions on how to avoid these problems, along with some strategies to apply when faced with a difficult employee. It will not present solutions. These situations defy complete solution once they have escalated to the crisis stage. There is rarely an action to take or a decision to make that resolves the problem happily for all parties. Management is faced with damage control, limiting the impact on the company, and cutting losses. The question is not, how can we solve this problem? The question is, how can we best lessen the harm and the likelihood of harm to the company and its personnel?

The first step is to better understand the type of employee and circumstance likely to cause hazard.

The Scriptwriter

This employee has several characteristics that are detectable early in his employment. One of these is inflexibility. He is not receptive to hearing new ideas or suggestions because he takes them as an affront or criticism of his way of doing things. Another is that he expects the worst from people. On entering a discussion about a discrepancy on his pay check, for example, he says or thinks, "You'd better not try to screw me out of any money." He invests others with the worst possible motives and character. It is as if he expects people to slight him or harm him. In this regard, he writes the script for his interaction with co-workers and management. In his script, he is a reasonable and good worker who must be constantly on guard against the ambushes of co-workers and supervisors. The things that go wrong are never his fault; even accidental, mistakes are the work of someone who will try to blame him. Others are out to get him; the company does nothing about and does not appreciate his contribution.

When you try to manage or reason with such a person, you find that he is not reacting to what you say, but rather to his script, to what he expects you to say. His is a personality that is self-defeating. The "Jack Joke" demonstrates this dynamic at work.

A man driving along a remote stretch of highway gets a flat tire. On preparing to put on the spare, he realizes he does not have a jack to raise up the car. Far in the distance, he sees the lights of some small farmhouses, and begins the long walk to borrow a jack. It is getting dark, and as he walks on, he worries that the people will be reluctant to help him: "They'll probably refuse to even answer the door, or worse still, pretend they're not home. I'll have to walk another mile to the next house, and they'll say they don't want to open the door, and that they don't have a jack anyway. When I finally get somebody to talk to me, they'll want me to convince them I'm not some criminal, and if they agree to help me, which is doubtful, they'll want to keep my wallet so I don't run off with their stupid jack. What's wrong with these people anyway? Are they so untrusting that they can't even help a fellow citizen? Would they have me freeze to death out here!"

By this point, he has reached the first house. In a virtual state of rage, he bangs loudly on the door, thinking to himself, "They better not try to pretend there is nobody home, because I can hear the television." After a few seconds, a pleasant woman opens the door wide and asks with a smile, "Can I help you?" He yells back at her, "I don't want your help and I wouldn't take your lousy jack if you giftwrapped it for me!"

The Scriptwriter gives no credit when people are helpful, and this causes alienation from co-workers. This kind of interaction eventually causes people to treat him as he expects. His script begins to come true, and that validates all his worst expectations. By the time you encounter him, he has likely been through these problems at other jobs or in other relationships.

The Scriptwriter issues warnings, such as "You'd better not try to blame me for what happened," or "I'd better get that promotion." Even if he gets the promotion, he believes it's only because he forced the company to give it to him. He thinks management was trying to get out of elevating him, but couldn't find a way, and that intimidation worked for him.

Because this dynamic feeds on itself and gets worse, and because the longer he is there, the more he feels entitled to be there and to advance, the key is to get rid of him early. You should terminate this person the moment you have cause to do so. Be sure the cause is sufficient, and that your determination is unshakable. If you try to fire this person and fail, you are setting the stage for the T.I.M.E. Syndrome.

The T.I.M.E. Syndrome or "We Should Have Fired Him Long Ago"

The T.I.M.E. Syndrome occurs when management allows a situation to include Threats, Intimidations, Manipulations, and Escalation. T.I.M.E. is on the side of the difficult and violently inclined employee, unless management acts quickly. Management may have good reason to expect that such an employee "won't go quietly," but the sooner he is fired, the easier it will be because of less emotional investment on his part and fewer perceived "unfairnesses" on your part. This is often someone who has had many, usually too many, chances to conform to policies and has not. He might be someone people fear or are suspicious of; someone who has little in common with co-workers, and he will most likely feel he hasn't been given a fair shake. This person has successfully used guilt and intimidation in the past and he expects such tactics to work again. He has talked himself out of being fired in the past as his superiors feared that getting rid of him might be more difficult in the long run than keeping him.

Now management has taken the bold step of firing him, and they are faced with a person who acts shocked and feels he is being treated unfairly. He may be partly right because compared to all the things he's done that he didn't get fired for, the cited reason may appear petty. He is angry, threatening, and cannot be appeased. These manipulations have worked for him before, when they appear not to be working now, he escalates them. Management must consider the various sorts of harm this person could do to the company or its personnel. On previous occasions, management had retreated before his threats. This time they stood their ground and he has upped the ante by saying or doing things that make clear the obvious: They should have fired him long ago.

The Dignity Domino
To judge the likelihood of violence and to better understand the dynamics in play, we must draw on the behavioral sciences.

Inhibitors are factors that lessen the likelihood of violence. When these factors are not present or dominant, and one is sufficiently provoked, there is little to inhibit an adverse reaction. A calm and reasoned disposition might serve as an inhibitor. Likewise, an aggressive and bullying disposition might weigh more heavily than inhibitors. For most of us, even at the height of provocation, the things we could lose as a result of committing violence serve as inhibitors against the violence. Family, home, career, self-esteem, control, freedom, are all things at risk if one uses intimidation or violence as a tool of survival.

When faced with a challenge, alternatives can act as inhibitors. The fewer alternatives available, the more likely it is that violence might be used. Fear of retribution can be an effective inhibitor if it is perceived as an immediate result of violent action. For example, if you swing at the big muscular streetfighter, he will hit you back right away and with injurious impact. You know this without much analysis. In this regard, fear is a better inhibitor when it is an emotional process, rather than an intellectual one. (In the larger social context, this is called deterrence, but it is rarely swift enough or sure enough to inhibit criminal violence.) In dealing with the threatening employee, seeking to instill fear in him to control his conduct rarely works.

Counter-threats by the employer usually bring about escalation rather than retreat. The problem employee may himself succeed by using threat and intimidation because management knows that he, having little to lose, might act recklessly. Conversely, he intuitively knows that management won't. Other thought processes that might affect violent action are called appraisals and expectations. In his excellent monograph, *Predicting Violent Behavior*, [1] Dr. John Monahan describes these processes:

1. Beverly Hills, CA: Sage Publications, 1981.

Appraisals refer to the manner in which an individual interprets an event as a provocation, and therefore experiences it as aversive. Perceived intentionality is perhaps the clearest example of an antagonistic appraisal (e.g., "You didn't just bump into me, you meant to hit me."). How a person cognitively appraises an event may have a great influence on whether he or she ultimately responds to it in a violent manner. Some persons may be prone to interpret seemingly innocuous interactions as intentional slights. The chips on their shoulders may be precariously balanced.

Expectations are seen as cognitive processes that may influence the occurrence of violence in several ways. If one expects a desired outcome (e.g., a raise in pay, an expression of gratitude for a favor done) and it fails to occur, emotional arousal may ensue, and, depending upon the context, it may be perceived as anger. If one appraises an event as a provocation, the occurrence of violence may still depend upon whether one expects violence to be instrumental in righting the perceived wrong or whether one can expect violence to be met with counterforce. One may, for example, regard having sand kicked in one's face as a deliberate affront and yet, upon learning that the agent of provocation is built like a football linebacker, have such low expectations for successful retaliation that violence is no longer under consideration. Alternatively, should the provocateur resemble Woody Allen, one's expectation that violence will prevail may rise accordingly.[2]

As inhibitors are reduced, and self-preservation is overshadowed by a desire to right a wrong or inflict revenge, violence might be considered even if there is risk of retribution — sometimes even if there is risk of death.

It is reasonable to be concerned that a problem employee might react adversely to an undesired change in status of position. When trying to predict his behavior you must assess the strength of his inhibitors versus the impact of the perceived provocation. So long as inhibitors are stronger than provocations, violence is unlikely. When the provocation is so great that it carries more weight than the inhibitors, a violent or harmful reaction is likely. This includes perceived provocations (or appraisals); to measure them, one must understand how the subject views himself. If he sees himself as a significant contributor to the company's success, he expects to be treated as such. An affront that might pass unnoticed by a "lesser" employee, is unacceptable to him.

Difficult terminations and situations involving threatening employees are similar to other volatile social situations, e.g., divorce, cutting off relationships, disputes with neighbors, disputes with financial institutions and creditors, lawsuits, dissolving partnerships, etc. A problem employee often has some of these problems away from work as well. The good things in his life, the inhibitors, are like dominos that have started to topple. Trust topples into Ability, which topples into Performance, which topples into Confidence, which knocks over Self-Esteem. The loss of his position or job is often perceived as a major provocation that threatens to knock over the few remaining dominos. The last one, and the one you mustn't unbalance, is the

2. Regarding appraisals and expectations, Dr. Monahan refers to the work of R. Novaco in *Cognitive Behavioral Interventions: Theory, Research, and Procedures*. San Diego, CA: Academic Press, 1979.

Dignity Domino. When that falls there are no inhibitors — and often only few options: threat, harm, and violence.

But months and sometimes years before the dominos started falling, there were things management could have done to change the course of events.

How You Got In — How To Get Out

To avoid this situation in the future, management should ask itself: What did we do, or fail to do, that brought us to this stage with this employee? Most often, the answer will include three principal reasons.

Reason 1: They hired him.

Are there indicators that an applicant might cause a T.I.M.E. problem and can they be detected in the pre-employment process? Yes and yes. Though a perfect predictive performance is impossible, you can increase the odds to your advantage. With each applicant, the hiring officer is making a prediction that the candidate either will or won't meet the needs of the employer by being a well-adjusted, capable, and productive employee. This prediction, like all predictions, will be better if based on the most complete and accurate information available. To meet this need, conduct background investigations before employment. Confirm facts in the application, check references, request credit reports, driving records, etc. Speak with former employers and co-workers. For most companies, the pre-employment process is the last chance to make generally unrestricted personnel decisions. Unfortunately, most employers do not take full advantage of that freedom.

During pre-employment interviews, (which can be videotaped[3]) ask the applicant the following questions:

"Describe the best boss you ever had" and *"Describe the worst boss you ever had."*

During which answer is the applicant more enthusiastic and animated? Which does he describe in greater detail? Is there a ten-minute speech about his worst boss, versus a brief statement about his best? Does he use expressions like "personality conflict" to explain why things didn't work out?

"Tell me about a failure in your life, and tell me why it occurred." Does the applicant describe a serious failure, or say he can't think of one? Does he take responsibility for the failure, or does he blame others?

"What are some of the things your last employer could have done to be more successful?" Does the applicant offer a long list of items and appear to feel he could have run things better than management did?

"Did you suggest these things to your last employer, and if so, how did they react?" The theme of a good answer would be: 1) I didn't really feel it was my place to make suggestions, or 2) Yes, an even though they didn't do everything I

3. We video tape pre-employment interviews asking for a restatement of much of the same information contained on the written application. When an applicant was dishonest on the application, he rarely recalls the exact details, so comparison of the video tape with the application produces valuable insights.

suggested, I think they gave my ideas fair consideration, or 3) Yes, and they acted on some of my suggestions. If the answer is "They told me to mind my own business," it can be an indicator that the tone or delivery of the suggestions was not good. Most managers and supervisors will accept suggestions with some grace if they are offered with some grace. Does the applicant tell of his coming up with great ideas that were either ignored or stolen? Does he tell "war stories" about his efforts to get his former employer to follow his suggestions? If so, ask if this was a one-man undertaking or suggested in concert with his co-workers. Sometimes an applicant will say his co-workers "didn't have the guts to confront management" or "couldn't see how good my ideas were." Statements like these are important indicators of a problem in this area. Information gleaned through these questions can be discussed with the former employer.

"What could your last employer have done to keep you?" Does the answer contain unreasonable conditions that the last employer would have to have met?

"How do you go about solving problems at work?" A good answer is that he consults with others, weighs all points of view, discusses them with involved parties, etc. A bad answer is "I go right to the source of the problem and tell him he'd better straighten up" or "I go right to the man in charge, and lay it on the line." Another bad answer is that he does nothing to resolve problems, saying, "You can't change anything."

"Describe a problem you had where someone else's help was very important to you." Is he able to recall such a situation. If so, does he appear to be appreciative and give credit to that person?

"Who is your best friend, and how would you describe your friendship?" Can he name a close friend, and describe a productive relationship? Some applicants cannot.

Reason 2: He wasn't supervised appropriately.
The concept of appropriate supervision calls for correction of errors and praise for performance. One must not ignore noncompliance. With the problem employee, supervisors have often given up. Considering the number of times that they had complaints or concerns, they really didn't seek to improve his work. He got little appropriate supervision. He was allowed to get away with so much that being fired for whatever reason now cited seems unfair and petty. Many of the problems could have been avoided by treating this employee appropriately at every step. If this type of person perceives that he is being "handled" or treated differently because of concern that he will react violently or with vengeance, the likelihood of such a reaction increases.

When an employee is treated in a manner that leads him to believe he has been the subject of worry, has been discussed as a "problem" to be dealt with, it can mold him to be just that. If he feels management thinks of him that way already, he has little to lose by fitting that image. In fact, this type of person usually defines his identity by how others view him. It is important to keep secret any concerns one might have about this employees likely violence.

Reason 3: They didn't fire him when it would have been easy.
Such a person is easier to terminate before he makes a substantial emotional investment, before the minor issues become causes, before disappointments become disgruntlements. The longer that emotional investment is made, the stronger it becomes, and the more likely it is that the termination will be difficult.

The Termination Interview
When trying to get out of such a situation, we can draw on some of the guidelines already discussed. One is to be careful not to knock over the Dignity Domino; prop it up whenever possible. Another is to keep secret from the employee any concerns you may have about various harms he might commit against the company or its personnel. This means think the worst if the indicators are there, but treat the terminated employee like he is what you would hope him to be. Treat him as though he is reasonable, as though you are not afraid of how he might react. Terminate his employment in a manner that demonstrates that you expect him to accept the news maturely and appropriately. This doesn't mean ignore the hazard. Prepare for the worst, but not in ways detectable to the terminated employee. Do not lead him to believe that you are anticipating threats or hazard. If you do, you may be writing the script for him to follow. Furthermore, you are letting him know you are vulnerable to threats and intimidation.

Make the termination complete.
Employers are often tempted to offer a gradual separation, thinking it will lessen the blow to the terminated employee. Though it may appear that this approach extends the term of employment for him, it really extends the firing, and the embarrassment and anxiety along with it.

Do not negotiate.
Once the termination decision has been made, your meeting with the employee is for the purpose of informing him of that decision in a straightforward manner. It is not to negotiate the matter, which he may well try to do. It is not a discussion of how to improve things. To rehash the issues and contentions of his history with the company will only raise sore points and emotion. It is not likely he will be convinced that terminating him is a good and reasonable idea. It isn't in his nature to recognize that, no matter what the evidence. Keep the presentation brief.

Cite general rather than specific issues.
Some employers want to justify to the terminated employee why they are taking this action. Many use the termination meeting for additional efforts to correct the employees attitude and impove him, turning the termination meeting into a lecture. Forget about that. A wiser course is to describe the decision in general terms, saying

it is "best for all parties." Say it is a two-way street. Say he is obviously a capable person but that this company isn't providing the best environment for him to excel in. You might say you are seeking another approach to the position he held and that a change is in order. Do not get dragged into a discussion about who will replace him. Answer that those decisions aren't made yet.

Keep the discussion focused on the future.

In concert with avoiding discussions of the past, establish some issues to be resolved during the meeting that are all about the future. Make him feel that his input has bearing. For example, "What would you like us to tell callers about where to reach you? Would you like us to tell them where to reach you? Would you like us to forward mail or advise the sender of your address? How can we best describe your time here to future employers who may contact us for a reference?" Basically, go along with every answer he gives. They are minor points but they direct focus to the future, to starting again rather than dwelling on the past. The whole theme of your presentation should be that you are confident he'll succeed in the future, find work he will enjoy, and do well. (You may actually feel he has emotional problems, is self-defeating, and will always fail, but there is nothing to be gained by letting those messages surface.) Wondering what a former employer will tell callers is one of several concerns that cause anxiety and embarrassment to the fired employee. By addressing them directly and showing that they are resolvable, they are not left simmering beneath the surface. The tone of the meeting should not be solemn and depressing, but rather matter-of-fact. "These changes are part of professional life that we all experience at one time or another. We know you'll do well and that this needn't be a setback for you."

Who should be present.

A higher level manager than the employee usually works with should make the termination presentation. It should be someone distant from the day-to-day controversies that surrounded the terminated employee. It should be someone who is calm and who can retain that demeanor even in the fact of threats and anger. When workable, a second participant can be someone in management with whom the terminated employee has had a good relationship or is known to admire.

Who should not be present.

Security guards, local police, or Big Ed, the tough loader from the warehouse, should not be part of the termination meeting. Their presence provides the wrong message. Though some employers believe that this presence puts them in a position of strength, it does exactly the opposite. It sets all your vulnerabilities on the table for the potentially dangerous employee to exploit. No equal co-worker or direct supervisor should be present either. They increase the likelihood of embarrassment, along with the likelihood of getting into a heated discussion. The manager running the termination meeting shows his strength by not appearing to need any "reinforcements."

How to respond to threats in the termination meeting.

To best apply a response strategy, an understanding of threats is needed. First, one must correctly define threat. A threat is a statement of an intention to do harm. Many people misuse the word to include intimidations, which are different. An intimidation is a statement of conditions that must be met in order to avert a harm. Intimidations contain the words if, or else, unless, or until: "If you fire me, you'll be sorry" or "There will be some damaged machinery unless I keep my job" or "Lots of people will be hurt if I am fired." These are all intimidations, not threats.

The essential difference is that intimidations are brought into play as high-stakes manipulations; what the speaker wants is for his conditions to be met. He does not want to inflict harm. With threats, no conditions are offered; in this limited context (that of terminated or disgruntled employees), threats represent more frustration and carry more likelihood of violence.[4]

An an instrument of communication, the threat is similar to the promise. With a promise, if we first judge that the speaker is sincere, we next assess the likelihood that he will retain his will over time. One may promise something today, but feel differently tomorrow. Threats and promises alike are easy to speak, harder to honor. Threats are most often spoken from emotion and thus, the speaker might lose the will to enact them over time.

Promises are made to convince us of an intention. Some threats are also made to convince us of an intention or to show us how strongly the speaker feels about the matter at hand. Remember threats and promises are not guarantees or even commitments.

There are three concepts to keep in mind when faced with threats:

1) Threats are most often the work of desperate people. The threat is a communication that betrays its creator by admitting failure, failure to succeed at communicating any other way; failure to influence events in any other way.

2) Serious threats are end-game moves. They are rarely an opening strategy for influencing others. Those used early or in a confrontation are usually designed to cause anxiety with a limited investment of time and emotion. In the context of this writing, threats late in the game are more serious.

3) Few threats are spoken from a position of power. Whatever power the threat may have is derived from the fear instilled in the victim; fear is the currency of the threatener. He gains advantage through intimidation, or by actually carrying out the threatened act. He must retreat or advance and, like all people, he hopes to retain his dignity with either course.

4. It is very important to recognize that violence and dangerousness are highly situational. The relevance of threats in the context of a terminated or disgruntled employee is much different than in other circumstances. These comments are not necessarily applicable to other social situations involving threats.

On this last point, the ways in which one responds to threats and intimidations determines how valuable an instrument they will be. If the target turns pale, starts shaking, and begs for forgiveness, he has made the threat or intimidation very valuable. A better reaction is to say, "I understand you are upset, but the things you are talking about are not your style. I know you are far too reasonable and have too good a future to even consider such things."

It is also important to let the threatener know that he has not embarked on a course he cannot retreat from. A good response is, "We all say things we don't mean when we react emotionally; I've done it myself. Let's just forget it. I know you'll feel differently tomorrow."

The worst possible reaction is counter-threat and intimidation. Think of violence as interactional. The way you respond to a threat might up the ante and turn the situation into a contest of threats, escalations, and counter-threats. It is a contest companies cannot win, for they have far more at risk than the terminated employee. Examples of this strategy include management saying, "Oh yeah? Well, I'll have the cops on you the minute you try it!"

This termination meeting will provide valuable insights into how the employee is going to cope with the change in status. It sets the stage for how he perceives management will respond to any of his future statements or actions. The information from this meeting should be assessed by a professional; his opinions can help to guide judgments about security and other relevant matters. (By professional, I am not referring exclusively to a psychiatrist or psychologist, but rather someone familiar with the assessment and management of threats).

Strictly from a security point of view, the employee should not be aware of the termination meeting ahead of time. It should take place without notice at the end of the day while other employees are departing. In this way, when it is over, he cannot immediately seek out those he might feel are responsible. Furthermore, he will then be going home at the same time as usual as opposed to finding himself home, for example, on a weekday morning.

The day of the week should also be considered. If fired on a Friday, he has the weekend off as usual and so doesn't feel the impact of having no place to go the next morning. Unlike on a weekday, he won't awake with the knowledge that his former co-workers are at the job and possibly discussing him. If fired on a weekday, possible targets of aggression are available to him at work while he is still at a point of high emotion. Some might advocate the termination not be on a Friday, reasoning that he might stew all weekend rather than go out and seek new employment as he could on a weekday. There is merit in both positions and, like many aspects of these difficult problems, it is a judgment call for management. All things considered, I have generally recommended Friday late in the day as the best time for firing.

Conclusion

The main theme of this chapter is that the fired employee should leave on that last day with more than his final paycheck. He should be able to retain his dignity. This is true for all employees, not just the difficult types discussed herein. The company should try not to provide him with anything he can perceive as a provocation or personal attack.

As I noted, these suggestions are not solutions. Some people will react in a harmful way regardless of the strategies applied. Being prepared for the most (from a security point of view) is important. Others might never have reacted violently in any case. Still others would have reacted violently in the absence of these strategies or in response to ill-founded and provocative strategies. The prediction of human behavior is tough enough with reasonable people; it is far more difficult with people like those discussed herein.

Not a week passes without someone seeking my advice on this type of problem. Regularly seeing the harmful impact of these situations upon companies and individuals, I have come to respect the value of avoidance and prevention. It is true that these people can't always be identified early in their employment. Still, one frequently hears, "We should never have hired him." That simple sentiment should guide the rest of us to approach the pre-employment process with added scrutiny.

14

Choosing the Right Professional Protection Agency

Philip Little

I have found that many people, even sophisticated business people, do not really understand what a detective agency does or how it can serve them. The stereotypical image perpetrated by television, that of the one-man agency whose private investigator spends much of his time in car chases, breaking through windows, and engaging in physical violence, does not apply to the reputable agencies in the United States.

A professional private detective and protective agency should be a one-stop service for all your investigative and security needs. The agency should provide a complete range of investigative services; this would include field investigations of all types of crimes relating to your company, with the primary focus on white-collar crimes, including embezzlement or the diversion of assets from the company for employee use.

In most companies it is quite easy for the dishonest employee to divert money and assets from the company. The employee of the federal agency of Housing and Urban Development (HUD) who diverted $5 million for her own use over a short period of time without being caught, is an example of just how easy it is within both companies and government. Even though the cases my company works on are not normally that big, the impact, percentage wise, is just as big or bigger to the companies that suffer the loss. With the larger losses, it is usually one person working alone. They either have the authority to call a bank to transfer money or can make transfers using computers. They develop accounts under phony names of companies or individuals and transfer thousands and hundreds of thousands of dollars into those accounts.

Another common method of large-scale theft is the use of company checks fraudulently made out to a dummy company or a third individual who launders the money then splits it with the employee. The most common white-collar crime against a smaller company is a diversion of material assets. In a recent case for an electronic firm, we documented over $1 million worth of material assets stolen by one employee over the period of one year. It was as simple as putting extra pallets of electronic goods on shipments and having the truck driver drop the merchandise off at a safe location where the goods were divided between the truck driver and the employee. In a recent investigation within a small chain of clothing stores we documented a more than $400,000 loss over a six-month period. Lax store management and overall company policies made it easy for employees to take large quantities of merchandise out of the stores.

The recent investigation inside a movie studio led us to uncover embezzlements and thefts on such a scale that enough equipment had been taken from the facility on a piece-by-piece basis to set up a full sound studio for the employees use and financial gain.

Many of the cases involving large sums of money that we have investigated in recent years have been related to computer crime because of the ease with which someone can move millions of dollars if they gain access to the equipment and have the proper passwords. If we are to see a decrease in white-collar crime, it is imperative that the proper security measures be taken around computer systems, particularly where it is possible to transfer money or give instructions to move company assets without duplicating authority or checking authorizations. Studies have shown that fifteen percent is added to the purchase price of many products because of this kind of theft. Companies have traditionally taken a very soft approach to white-collar crime, choosing to deal quietly with the person by firing them—sometimes getting restitution and sometimes not—rather then risk any publicity. This behavior has led many employees to feel that the risk involved in white-collar crime is minimal. This attitude must change. Companies must have strong preventive programs to make it difficult for even the most honest employee to steal; particularly the employee who would only do so if stealing is made relatively easy. We must take strong enforcement action, including prosecution, even if it does mean publicity. In this way, we will be sending a message to our employees and stockholders that we will not tolerate the diversion of assets that ultimately harms the profit margin of our companies.

Undercover Service

The professional detective agency should provide an undercover service for determining what kind of problems exist in the company. The undercover agent becomes the eyes and ears of the agency and, ultimately, management. The agent is hired as a normal employee, processed and paid as any other employee. In reality, he is working for the detective agency and being paid a second check from that agency. Normally, only two or three people at the highest levels within the client company, know of the existence of the agent. The line supervisors or lead people, no matter how trusted or how long they have been with the company, should not be told about the undercover operation. The undercover agent must, above all, be able to do the job he was hired to do and must keep this job on his own merit. This means he must appear to management—who doesn't know who he truly is—a model employee, prompt and efficient. He must be able to gain the confidence of fellow employees while listening, watching, and observing what is going on within the company. He would then report all illegal activities on a daily basis to the control agent within the detective agency who in turn reports to the contact within the company. At no time does anyone within the company have direct contact with the agent other than in a normal workday fashion. The undercover agent is effective because employees talk among themselves even when they are not involved, and wouldn't be involved, in illegal activities, they will not, for the most part, inform management of such activities. Perhaps they don't want to be drawn into the situation or perhaps they are afraid of repercussions. At any rate, undercover agents do not ever take any action or do anything that might draw attention to themselves. All actions taken to build cases, any surveillance that is needed, is performed by outside agents so the undercover agent can be withdrawn from the company without anyone ever knowing why he was there. Given today's environment, where the drug problem has eaten its way into every company, no matter the size, the undercover agent often has to be used for testimony in drug cases. In many instances it is possible to avoid using the undercover agent by introducing an outside agent to make buys and document illegal activities. Any drug related buys or purchases of stolen property are done strictly within the guidelines of the law and are documented and controlled in conjunction with whatever local enforcement agency the detective agency is working with. A chain of evidence is maintained and at the conclusion, the company has a case that can be won in court, secure against claims of entrapment or abuse of someone's individual rights.

Personnel

It is important that the detective agency use professional, competent personnel as undercover agents. Too many times substandard people without the proper training or supervision are placed as undercover agents. You are exposing yourself to great danger if you don't use a professional. If the agent is not reliable and does not possess the highest integrity, then very possibly he can become as big a problem as the dishonest employee. You should inquire as to the agency's screening, hiring, and training practices. How does the agency ensure that agents maintain their integrity? Any applicant for undercover agent at West Coast Detectives is subjected to a complete background check of their personal and business life: psychological and stress testing; and a polygraph test. If the applicant is favorably evaluated and hired, he is then trained as an undercover agent following the standards of West Coast Detectives. After training he is placed in an appropriate job and monitored on a daily basis by his control agent who directs all his activities, making certain the agent is collecting the information the client wants and the case requires, as well as operating within the guidelines of existing laws.

Support Facilities

The detective agency should have sufficient support facilities to complete any investigation, i.e. lab facilities capable of product examination and analysis of blood, fingerprints, urine, and substances on fabrics; document examiners to evaluate handwriting and the age of documents; typewriter analysis to compare and determine what typewriter might have typed a particular document, and polygraph examiners. These services should be provided on an in-house basis to maintain quality control. They can prove invaluable in solving cases. In recent investigation of major theft within an electronics company, we discovered product being shipped illegally on a contract carrier. The product was shipped in boxes bearing hand-printed labels. By analyzing the handwriting, we were able to determine who had written the labels; but the irrefutable final piece of evidence was our identification of the fingerprints on the back of the labels, which matched those of the employee who had written the labels. By having the proper techniques readily available, we were able to solve this case in an expeditious and economical way for the client.

Surveillance

Another area of service that the agency should provide is surveillance from the very simple to the very elaborate four or five car detail. The agency must have the proper equipment and trained manpower with the knowledge of how to run a multiple-car form of surveillance. The agency should be able to provide helicopter surveillance support, a valuable tool in many child custody cases, or for the dignitary protection unit or the safe transportation of persons who need to be moved discretely.

Operations Section

The agency should have a complete operations section that can provide plainclothes security. When we talk about security, we are not talking about guards or a guard company. For the most part, all guard companies have the same inherent problems: They start with substandard employees, pay them minimum wage or a bit more, and expect them to be professional, confident employees. The corporations encourage this behavior when they treat security as an after thought and are interested only in paying the lowest price possible. They do not consider security a serious professional need even though they have millions and millions of dollars at stake. We at West Coast Detectives have removed the word guard from our vocabulary.

As mentioned earlier, we screen our applicants as any police department would, with the same type of background checks and psychological and stress testing to make sure they are suitable agent material.

Labor-related Problems

The corporate world has now realized that it can operate during a labor work stoppage. A few years ago it was possible for a union to shut down a company and, for the most part, companies were powerless to stop them. With the changing economic situations and other pressures on the corporate structure, they had to find alternatives. The progressive companies realized that hiring "goons" and putting them in uniform was as counter-productive in many cases as the strike itself. These goons or guards were nothing more than substandard individuals looking for trouble and often caused more trouble than they prevented. They sometimes made a negative impact on the company by behaving in such a way that lawsuits were filed against the company because of their actions. In many cases, companies had to settle strikes to the unions benefit in order to end lawsuits that could have been very harmful to them. By providing a professional, police-type security force where plainclothes agents look like police officers, we can ensure that the company is able to operate while at the same time not violating the rights of the picketers. West Coast Detectives has developed a reputation in the area of handling strike-related problems. We first communicate with the picket captains and picketers, letting them know who we are, what we are there to do, and that we intend to ensure that no one is injured. We advise them of the law and of what they can and cannot legally do. We advise them that if they break the law, they will go to jail, that the company has a right to operate and we give them the guidelines under which the company is going to operate. We also let them know we will not allow someone to harm them or attempt to run over them or violate their rights. By treating the picketers as human beings and using some common sense, we are able to avoid many of the usual strike problems and keep our client company operating. Ultimately, we have assisted our client companies in getting favorable settlements. It is important that you have the proper agency for handling this type of problem.

Protection of Public Figures

Clients in the public eye, including entertainment, political, or business leaders, have special problems. It is very difficult to find individuals who can work with celebrities or other dignitary without being affected by their status. For example, West Coast Detectives agents that work in dignitary protection go through a special screening, special background check, and are monitored at the outset to ensure that they have the personality and psychological makeup for dealing with celebrities on a very close basis. The detective agency should not only provide the traditional bodyguards that might be required, but all of the related transportation services, trip planning, and other coordinated activities that the client might require. Agents start with the gathering of information on an ongoing basis to monitor any threats or activities that might affect the client. If they are planning a trip that might take them to another state or out of the country, complete up-to-date information should be collected to make a risk assessment and analyze what type of services or protection they may need (if any). The area to be visited, whether in the United States or out of the country, should be visited by the agent in advance of the clients arrival. It is important to make a local assessment of the area at that time and plan the airport arrivals, routing, hotels and other venues they might visit, as well as briefing local agents who might be handling the dignitary protection. It is important that the agency you select provide these services with their own people and not by contracting out to another agency in the area, whose employment standards are unknown to you.

Protection of Families

A major area of concern today for the corporate client and the top executive is that of the safety of their families, whether at home or traveling. The professional detective starts with analyzing the security needs of the home, including the placement of whatever security devices might be needed (such as cameras, alarms, perimeter security devices etc.), provision of a safe room within the home, and the training of family members in basic security awareness. Transportation for family members should be provided when and where required, 24-hour staffing of agents at the homes, when necessary, and a 24-hour operational center when the executive travels so that his family can reach him at anytime no matter where he might be in the world. This not only brings peace of mind to the family and to the executive, but also frees the mind of the executive for total concentration on achieving the corporate objective of his trip.

Conclusion

The first thing that the detective agency you retain should be able to do is to evaluate, assess and prevent major problems from occurring within your facilities. It can only be effective if you give the agency the proper support and tools to work within your own company. We are hearing much today about risk assessment. There are many who claim to be specialists in risk assessment; you must look carefully at the credentials and backgrounds of anyone professing to be a risk assessment specialist. The agency that you select should have professionals with bona fide backgrounds in investigative security, dignitary protection, systems development, and the knowledge and understanding to be able to provide a professional risk assessment for your company. The risk to all corporations is growing from the simple product liability case, to a negligence action case, to kidnapping and death of key corporate executives on a national or international basis. The agency that you select should be able to handle all these situations in a professional way and be able to gather the information needed to provide assessment of the particular risks for your company.

When selecting your detective and protective agency do not hesitate to ask questions. The first might be, how long has your agency been in business? Longevity usually does speak for quality, for those that last in our field usually do so because of providing consistent quality service. Find out the areas of the country and the world they service with their own people. Find out how they select, screen, train, and supervise their employees. Find out about their licensing and insurance coverages and how they have conducted themselves in the past, i.e., have there been law suits or complaints from clients. This can be checked through state agencies that monitor private investigators. Determine if they have verifiable references, either by letter from clients or from corporate law firms who refer their clients to the agency. Asking these questions will assist you in selecting a professional detective and protective agency to meet the needs of your company.

There are many advantages to having an outside professional agency provide your investigative and security services. If you have the right agency, it can become just as strong a part of your team as your own employees or internal staff. It is impossible for a company, itself, to duplicate all the services outlined previously. With the right agency, a company has at their disposal a professional when they need it. The right agency should be able to provide security consulting and design on a regular basis, along with having the operational abilities that bring continuity to fulfilling the corporate needs and plans when approval is given for go ahead.

15

Who is the Potential Victim?

"The purpose of terror is to terrorize. The use of terror, even killing the victim,
is deliberate and dispassionate, carefully engineered for theatrical effect and
involves extensive planning and rehearsal."
                                                    – Carlos Marighella
                                                    Mini-Manual for Urban Guerrillas

Given this description of the aims of terrorism, it is not hard to see where any person from any country, regardless of job, sex, or appearance, might find themselves thrust upon the stage to become an actor in terrorist theatrics.

Experience has shown that potential victims may vary from country to country. Americans have not always been the chosen victims of all transnational and national groups of terrorists. They have not usually been direct targets of Irish terrorist groups, nor have they been direct targets in France or Spain. American businessmen have not been primary targets of Arab terrorist groups either. The Red Brigade, a terrorist group recently wiped out by the Italian frontier police, went after Italian businessmen in Milan, such as executives of the Fiat Corporation. The Japanese Red Brigade has not targeted Americans at all; they go after Israelis — both military and civilian — and other Japanese.

However, in South American countries, favorite victims of kidnapping are Americans — those connected with a district branch of an American-based corporation, military personnel, and staff members of American government agencies or embassies. (Also popular are local people in business, government, or the military.) And though the Baader-Meinhoff gang in West Germany has not selected many Americans for targets — other than military personnel — things might be different with the newer group known as RAF. They may decide to go after American business persons as well as NATO officers and American military bases.

Wherever he is, the American businessman, military person, or government official may become an incidental or accidental victim because he is in the wrong place at the wrong time. The terrorist may not know what fish he has caught in his net. It is a certainty that once the American's identity is known to the terrorists, he will become a special prize in terms of ransom and negotiations.

A.P. Schmid[1] describes four objectives of terrorism, each of which may involve different or similar targets:

1. Inducing terror with large-scale acts of violence, such as the hijacking of airplanes bearing passengers.
2. Inducing terror in the primary target, i.e., killing children to make adults suffer, as did the Democratic Front for the Liberation of Palestine in May of 1974, when they murdered 22 children in the Israeli village of Ma'alot.
3. Satisfying a demand, such as a change in government, release of prisoners, or money.
4. Gaining attention from the media.

To obtain any or all of these objectives, national governments are favorite targets for terrorists. Symbols of this particular target include government leaders, police, soldiers, and military or public utility facilities. A second popular target is the corporation, particularly those of America and Italy. The third target is a wealthy citizen or a simple tourist. The fourth target is the political organization, commonly attacked by the Christian Image Movement organizations. A fifth favorite target is the labor group. A sixth is the minority group as defined by religion, ethnicity, or numbers in an area. The latter groups are generally targets of national terrorist groups in the United States, i.e., the American Nazi Party or the Ku Klux Klan. Not all potential victims are chosen by terrorists for the reasons I have mentioned. Some may be chosen by the mentally ill, simply because the target has some special meaning to the perpetrator.

One of the most significant factors in choosing a victim is his attitude toward personal security. People often object to restrictions on their movements even when the restrictions are in their own best interest. Examples might help to clarify this point.

- Some years ago, a top union official complained of receiving death threats. Private security personnel were hired and two agents followed him in a separate car to and from work. The union official apparently liked to challenge the abilities of his escort and would drive at high speeds, maneuvering his car so that it appeared he was trying to elude his own protection. After two weeks the security agents were withdrawn at their own request because it was apparent the union official was defying their security plan and his own request for protection. This union official was a natural target for a terrorist group.
- A well-known NATO staff officer and general had been receiving threats from the Red Brigade in Italy. Instead of moving back to a secure military base, he maintained his apartment in Milan. He was kidnapped and kept in custody for several days until the Frontier Guards located and liberated him.
- Another NATO general in West Germany ordered his driver to take the same road daily to and from work. One morning his wife wanted a ride and

1. Schmid, A.P., *Goals and Objectives of International Terrorism*. Defense Intelligence College Symposium Proceedings. Washington, D.C.: Defense Intelligence Agency.

as they stopped for a red light at a point some short distance from a hill, they were surprised to hear a rocket whoosh through their trunk. One more inch and they would have been a double homicide. The Russian-built rocket launcher was found but members of the RAF responsible for the attack were not.

Knowing why an executive is targeted may point to finding out who has done the targeting. All executives and security staff must appreciate that any member of a firm or government agency might become a victim of kidnapping, threats, or assassination.

Executives traveling in the United States must not feel unduly over-confident about their safety. This country is quite vulnerable because, as a free society all the usual terrorist targets are in the open. We are full of communications installations and equipment. Transportation centers are jam-packed with cars, trains, and planes. Dams, bridges, natural resource pipelines, and power networks abound in every community. Throughout this country are countless waterways, deltas, and large harbors. In all communities most government buildings and private business facilities are left unprotected and unguarded.

Terrorist actions against entire cities, using biological, or chemical weapons, are not impossibilities. According to Mullin,[2] the City of Orlando, Florida, was threatened with a nuclear bomb in 1970. The same thing happened in Boston, Des Moines, San Francisco, and Lincoln, Nebraska in 1974.

Obtaining the enriched uranium or plutonium for a nuclear bomb poses a problem for terrorists. The material has to be stolen from a shipment in transit, a reactor site, or purchased from a country sympathetic to a particular cause. Workers sympathetic to the cause could be used in any of these methods. On August 6, 1986, the *New York Times* reported that 6,000 pounds of weapon-grade plutonium could not be accounted for. Allowing for mistakes, that left 1,500 pounds of this material unaccounted for. Finally, a nuclear weapon itself could be stolen. One such effort was made in the past ten years in the United States when a group planned the theft of a nuclear submarine — and came close to achieving it.

Nuclear installations and facilities could be sabotaged releasing radioactive material into our atmosphere. The infusion of nerve gas does not require special technical skill. The formula for VX nerve gas is a matter of public knowledge. An ounce of anthrax or cryptococcosis bacteria released in a domed stadium would kill about 70,000 people. Brucellosis and Hemophyllis influenzae cause serious disease complications and could kill and/or immobilize great numbers of people. In 1975, the Nazi organization known as the Order of the Rising Sun planned on poisoning several large cities, including Chicago and St. Louis, with typhoid bacillus. In 1978 terrorists from the Arab Revolutionary Army injected Jaffa oranges with mercury; and in 1976 Arab terrorists were apprehended carrying an envelope that contained nerve gas. The Weathermen Underground made plans to steal bacteria from Fort

2. Mullin, W.C. *Terrorist Organizations in the United States*. Springfield, IL: Charles Thomas, 1988.

Derrick and the Symbionese Liberation Army had plans for the use of germ warfare. Federal agents found 200 pounds of sodium cyanide at the compound of the Covenant, the Sword and the Arm of the Lord.

Any of these methods of terrorism can be used in both discriminate and indiscriminate operations against citizens of the United States. Detailed knowledge about our external and internal enemies is essential to effective planning of terrorism prevention programs so that risks can be minimized for you, the potential victim. The American traveling at home or abroad must learn to maintain a constant state of vigil.

A non-victim today may be tomorrow's target.

16

The Terrorist Organization: How It Works

An internal terrorist organization is one that operates almost entirely within a particular country. This makes it quite different from a transnational organization because the terrorists are working in a hostage-like environment in which the local, and sometimes national, police are in hot pursuit. The goal is to topple the established government. Their operations are hit-and-run by nature and generally involve bank robbery or bombing of symbolic institutions. Hostage-taking is rare because negotiations are more difficult since they cannot count on outside resources or pressures from other countries. If a hostage is taken, he is usually killed because, if released, he can offer too much important information to the police concerning safe houses and places of confinement. This has been true of such organizations in Iran, Italy, Spain, Germany, and Ireland.

Because the internal terrorist organization is local in nature and uses local personnel, there is often more time for them to utilize surveillance because they can easily blend into the environment. This type of mission is designed to provide information about the victim, especially his security arrangements and time schedule. Surveillance might be carried out by motorcycle, car, bicycle, or on foot. Selection of an ambush site includes making certain the immediate area is free of police and has escape routes (such as side streets and reasonably wide alleys). Rush hour and locations with heavily trafficked streets would be eliminated as possible strike sites. With these factors in mind, a fixed surveillant will study an area for a long period of time. His mission is simple: to observe. He uses disguises to help blend into the background and conceal his identity.

Such surveillance procedures are used by transnational groups as well, except differences in language, appearance, and style of dress may make it more difficult for those surveilling to blend into the background.

The external type of terrorist organization usually operates in one of two ways. For example, a Balkan group, such as the Croatians, operates in a foreign country from within an area in which there are emigres. A few people operate within their new country and planning flows from those in the new settlement area. On the other hand, members of the PLO Abu Nidal organization who settle elsewhere, even in European countries, carry out plans that are always developed in the headquarters by staff. These plans are based upon intelligence supplied by members residing in the new and temporary communities. (Another difference between these two groups is that whereas, for the Croatians, terrorist operations are usually directed toward a particular enemy, innocent members of the community are frequently involved in PLO actions, such as when they shot into the crowd at a Jewish delicatessen in Paris or set off a car bomb in Beirut).

Despite the relative autonomy of such internal or external terrorist organizations, an ever-present, other external terrorist organization is always watching for signs of civil disorder, the Soviet-based KGB. This group is always willing to supply weapons, sometimes money and, most of the time, encouragement. The style and overall price tag is exploitation of whatever civil disorder or unrest occurs.[1] We must wait to see if current events in the Soviet Union and the Eastern European countries bring about a change in this situation.

Mullin[2] points out that many terrorist groups function like any other business organization, with goals, objectives and planning, a process for decision making, and leaders. They have chains of command and, like all businesses, have problems of staff recruitment and financing.

Many non-terrorist organizations have a pyramid structure where management sits at the top of the structure and is separated from the workers. In this hierarchical, bureaucratic structure, communication becomes difficult and changes in rules and policies as well as goals, objectives, and methods are slow and seem almost impossible to bring about. Unfortunately, most military and police agencies follow this structure and this one factor may account for much of the confusion in their response to a terrorist action.

The terrorist organization adopts a circular or solar system arrangement. The leader has immediate contact with and control of all members and groups within his organization. Leaders participate in actions and in so doing become/remain visible role models for their followers. There are no separate support services to run offices, etc., no secretaries or typing pools, so active members must perform these functions. Communication in this structure is almost immediate and thus allows tactical flexibility, i.e., quick response to targets of opportunity.

Because such a structure allows for intimate contact with the leader, his charisma and position of power is constantly reinforced.

This structure allows for efficiency, ease of eliciting support from other groups and helps make the achievement of anonymity possible. The leader can do his own screening and internal security is enhanced. In this structure the leader can detect rising stress levels and provide release by choosing a satisfying or exciting target. In this way he reinforces the self esteem of his members when reinforcement is most needed.

The basic unit of the terrorist organization is the cell.[3] Each unit cell is made up

---

1. Barrow, J. *KGB*. London, England: Transworld Publishers, Ltd., 1974.
2. Mullin, W.C. *Terrorist Organizations in the United States*. Springfield, IL: p. 3, Charles C. Thomas, 1988.
3. Sterling, C. *The Terror Network*. New York: Holt, 1981.

from three to ten members and functions autonomously, often without definite knowledge of the existence of other cells. A leader keeps the cell together and his function is to motivate the members. A cell may have a specialty like arson, assassination, kidnapping, or bombing. Some may be surveillance units, others communication specialists. One may be responsible for stealing cars and other vehicles needed for an operation. Some gather intelligence information and others may organize boycotts, demonstrations, propaganda, decoy operations, marches, riots, sit-ins, strikes, or slowdowns.

Group leaders may organize and supervise several cells. They may select targets, make recommendations to the leader for action, and keep track of recruitment and cell function.

At the top may be a central operations committee consisting of the leader and the group leaders. It establishes the short and long term goals and objectives of the organization and the ways in which those objectives and goals can be achieved. It functions like a board of trustees.

Some non-operational units, supportive in function, may be formed. These might include couriers to deliver messages or to use cut outs or drop points to relay communications. They may be used to buy weapons or supplies. In his later years, Carlos Marighella functioned in this job.[4]

All terrorist organizations rely on outside supporters for money and a supply of the safe houses that are used to store caches of weapons and members who need to hide out. All such groups also have umbrella businesses to either generate money or launder illegal money. Some of these businesses involve drug dealings. Others, like those used by the PLO, are legitimate businesses, e.g., farms, ranches, hotels, airlines, and real estate. Terrorist-backed businesses have traded stocks on Wall Street and the stock exchange in Tokyo. A seemingly respectable print shop is useful for publishing leaflets, flyers, newsletters, and other printed propaganda.

Finally, mercenaries are used by terrorist organizations to train members, serve as consultants, conduct operations, or perform specialized missions like bombing or intelligence gathering. Political ideology means little to them, as they work strictly for money. Most mercenaries have military backgrounds and are well experienced in guerrilla combat strategy and techniques.

Targets of Terrorists

Selection of targets is important to any terrorist group; potential targets must realize that their selection may be based on timing, circumstance, and opportunity, as well as the needs of the group.

To the political terrorist, the most popular targets have been symbolic in nature. These might be national leaders, strong political representatives of countries considered to be the enemy, or rival terrorist groups. (For example, efforts have been made to assassinate the current Pope because of his stand in support of freedom for his homeland, Poland.)

---

4. Smith, C. *Carlos: Portrait of a Terrorist.* New York: Holt, 1976.

The next type of target is a pragmatic choice, specific opponents such as military leaders who either led successful military actions against the terrorist group, or who encouraged such definitive actions to wipe them out. A corporate leader, bank president, or board member might be a pragmatic or practical target if one of greater symbolic significance is not easily available or necessary for the goals of a particular operation.

The third type of target is based on ease of opportunity, almost impulse, and may involve bombing an unprotected place where Americans gather in a foreign country. Or the target might be an unarmed military man in uniform, as in the case of the general who was shot through his open mouth as he struggled with his assassins while standing on a street corner in Paris. Becoming this type of target involves being in the wrong place at the wrong time. The terrorists may have been searching for no one in particular.

It should now be apparent that there is a high-risk group comprised of the political VIP, high-ranking government and military officers, the corporate VIP, key businessmen or supervisors of a foreign-based business with headquarters in the United States or some other country opposed to terrorism, and any highly visible person with a predictable routine.

Aside from newspaper photographs and other public media, there are many ways of identifying likely targets that are silent and not easily observed even by counterterrorist police and military personnel. Targets for the terrorist might come from identifying information contained in an airplane loading manifest, bills of lading, immigration records, customs records, military unit rosters, manning boards, housing assignment rosters (this was important in the Munich Olympic massacre), phone listings, national club memberships, license plates (especially diplomat plates), speeches that have been highly publicized or attended, luggage tags, and lost and found departments in transportation centers (airports, train and bus stations), and personal behavior.

By personal behavior I mean those who drive expensive cars, utilize chauffeurs, carry briefcases, employ bodyguards or otherwise display accessories associated with high-level or important personnel. Sometimes wearing a uniform is enough.

Political Philosophy and Propaganda

Regardless of whether the terrorist organization is internal or external, an international tradition ties them together. Experienced, well-equipped organizations offer basic terrorist training to smaller, internal groups from different countries: the PLO operated training bases in the Middle East for terrorists from Ireland, Spain, Japan, and the United States. Terrorist leaders meet periodically. They loan one another money, documents, maps, and weapons. This is particularly true of European operations.

Another characteristic of the terrorist network is the use of propaganda. Propaganda is more important than human life. Operations are designed with an eye focused on dramatic, sometimes gruesome, effect so as to attract maximum media attention. Millions of dollars worth of free publicity—something terrorists could not pay for or obtain through normal channels—contribute to achieving the goal of terrorism: to provoke over-response by the targeted government and topple that government through terror.

In Spain, Cuba, China, El Salvador, and countries in South America, an effective terrorist strike resulting in useful propaganda often involves taking land away from the landowner (and sometimes killing him). The peasants, wanting to end what they feel has been their subordination and exploitation by the reigning political system, will then often join the terrorists—better than letting the government regain control and install a new landowner.

What choices are open to government when making decisions with propaganda value to terrorists? Consider how the Bolivian government handled the captures of Guevara and his journalist friend, Regis Debray. When Debray was captured and brought to trial, the event was covered by hundreds of journalists. The government executed Guevara without a trial. Bolivian authorities felt that his trial would not only draw even greater propaganda victories for his terrorists, but would make him a martyr. Supporters of Guevara did seek out his hunters and were successful in killing some of them, but I believe they were deprived of considerable benefits from propaganda as a result of his execution.

Terrorist Membership and Supporters

Who are the members of terrorist organizations? Terrorists are drawn from rural areas, from universities, the military, and from the professional and working classes. They are even drawn from the priesthood. Students and teachers at the university level make up a large share of the membership. In keeping with Marxist-Leninist tradition and philosophy, blue-collar workers are actively sought. Because it is almost impossible for terrorists to receive hospital treatment, emergency first aid, or drugs through conventional channels, pharmacists and doctors have been heavily recruited. Female membership varies from group to group: in one study of German groups it was found that about 40 percent of the members were women. Women figure heavily in the Tupamaros group in Uruguay. In many groups four characteristics identify the members: youth, education, middle- or upper-class backgrounds, and a commitment to Marxist-Leninist philosophy. However, in a group such as the Irish Republican Army, the members tend to be older with less formal education.

The terrorist group may have only a small number of actual members. Sometimes several small groups fall under the umbrella of a large front organization, such as the Peoples Sacrifice Guerillas in Iran. The PLO main body has about 500 members: when additional support is needed, it draws from refugee camps. The Japanese Red Brigade has about 30 highly-trained members. The Baader-Meinhoff gang in Germany had about 50 activitsts and 300 sympathetic supporters. The New Peoples

Army (NFA), of the Philippines and the Revolutionary Armed Forces of Columbia (RAFC) each have about 1,000 members.

There are many people who offer support and sustenance to terrorists without actually joining the organizations or participating in the violence. They provide safe houses, medical supplies, food, information, and help with the spread of propaganda. In the urban setting, they are often students or faculty from the universities.

The other support group has been the Church. Protestant leaders supported terrorists in Brazil and Guatemala until Church leaders were ordered out of the country. The Franciscan Order supported Castro in Cuba, and the Dominican Order supported Francisco Caamamo in the Dominican Republic and Marighella in Brazil.

In Nicaragua the Church remains in the forefront of support for terrorist insurgency. In Spain, some priests of the Church publicly endorsed the idea of Christians supporting Marxist thinking.

The terrorists benefiting from their support refer to it as "Liberation Theology." It teaches that Jesus Christ was a revolutionary and that the state should control ownership and production of goods, energy, transportation, and education.

Although few members are criminals prior to their recuritment, once recruited, they are rapidly dispatched into criminal activities. This makes it difficult for them to rejoin society, either by choice or as a result of rehabilitative efforts following capture. Once they become criminals, it is hard, if not impossible, for the police to approach them for intelligence information. A terrorist who kills believes it is a moral act justified by his political/terrorist commitment: any police officer who approaches him will be killed.

The Self-Defined Image of the Terrorist

According to Carlos Marighella, author of the manual for the urban guerrilla, the terrorist is a revolutionary patriot and friend of the people.[5] He believes terrorists differ from bandits because they do not fight for personal monetary gain, but as devoted enemies of the government of a country and the men who run it. Their goal is to destroy and dismantle the economic, political, and social system of a country. Their strategy is simple. They act to: (1) demoralize and exhaust the police and military establishments of government; (2) destroy the economic base and wealth of the country; and (3) force foreign economic influence to leave the country and abandon holdings. Any means are justified to accomplish their goal. Moral superiority is defined as being able to kill and to survive. The qualities terrorists value in each other include: being an astute judge of character, a good shot, a strong sense of morality (which seems to mean a willingness to kill the "right people"), resourcefulness, decisiveness, and the ability to lead a clandestine lifestyle.

He must be able to live among people without appearing strange or being set apart

5. What he fails to recognize is that his urban guerrilla is a person who destroys property and takes the lives of innocent persons. Frightening a whole population is not an act of generosity or patriotism. There is no charity among the guerrillas or terrorists. Victims of kidnapping are "tried" for "crimes against the people" without recourse to legal counsel. Furthermore, not all terrorists live at the poverty level. Carlos Marighella always traveled first class and lived in plush settings. Yasser Arafat lives well, and so do many others. Many, however, do live rather primitively, especially in Asian and South American countries. It is certainly fair to say that the goal of the guerrilla or terrorist is far from political alone.

from them, yet must not reveal his identify to anyone. If identified and/or convicted he must be able to give up his apparently conventional work and lifestyle and survive in the underground.

He must be imaginative and creative, able to walk long distances, endure fatigue, hunger, rain, heat, and isolation. He must display initiative, flexibility, and be able to take command. He must not fear danger or be easily discouraged, must have unlimited patience, and a great ability to remain cool and unafraid. (These qualities are certainly true of the leadership and the professional terrorist. Many of them are the same qualities needed for successful members of counter-terrorist groups: They are the qualities of good soldiers and police officers everywhere.)

He must have a great capacity for observation, be knowledgeable about the area in which he lives, and well informed about the enemy's movements. He must be prepared to expropriate supplies, firearms, and money in order to survive as well as to function as a terrorist. Capitalists are seen as the funding sources for the revolution; expropriation includes robbing the banks of the wealthy and using kidnapping to extort money from them. This is why terrorism must be of concern to American businessmen and not simply the exclusive concern of the police or military.

Training and Technical Preparation of the Terrorist

Many terrorists come from the rural peasant group and learn by doing. In urban areas they have little opportunity to learn to handle their weapons as there are few places for target practice that would not draw attention. (Members of the Baader-Meinhoff gang practiced near airports to drown out the noise of gunfire.)

Because they do not learn the discipline taught in police training they are often not properly prepared to lead the life of a secure, secretive type of agent or terrorist. Like the victims they watch, they often fail to vary their routines. If a secret meeting in a certain place has come off without a hitch, they will have another meeting at the same place. Middle-class leaders of the Cuban 26th of July Movement posing as peasants were arrested by a suspicious policeman because they had mud on their shoes and he knew that no Cuban campesino would come to the city with muddy shoes.

Both the police and terrorist groups (especially those with an established base like the PLO) recruit and train informants who watch for and report on anything suspicious in an area, such as new arrivals.

Some terrorists receive professional training at camps in the Middle East, Cuba, Yemen, or China. In order to qualify for such a training school, the student-applicant must first demonstrate his ability to perform in revolutionary action against the enemy. He is trained to fight, attack, and defend himself. He hikes and camps and learns to survive in the woods. He rows, swims, climbs, fishes, harpoons, goes skin-diving, and learns to hunt and trap birds and game. He learns to drive, handle a motorboat, and in some cases even pilot a plane. He learns to understand and operate a radio and telephone and learns about electricity and electronic techniques. He learns to read and calculate distances, make timings, and use an angle protractor or compass. He may learn about chemistry, especially as it relates to making explosives, and how to make stamps and falsify documents. He learns about first aid and drugs he may need in order to recover from sickness and wounds.

In addition to all of the above, the essential training of a terrorist concerns the use of pistols, rifles, machine guns, shotguns, mortars, bazookas, and explosives. He must learn to make and repair arms, use incendiary bombs, smoke bombs and the like, as well as dynamite to blow up bridges, railroad ties, power stations, and large buildings.

Weapons of the Terrorists

Terrorists tend to use lightweight weapons such as handguns and automatic weapons with short barrels, and hand-held rockets like an RPG7. These weapons are easily concealed but difficult to control, use too much ammunition and waste many rounds. Not everyone can be trained to use them. Despite these problems, the light machine gun is the favored weapon of the terrorist. Long guns are not employed much because they are hard to conceal and not as portable. Long guns are for assassins. Sawed-off shotguns are popular as well, because practice is unnecessary so long as close range and pointing are all that is required.

Almost all shooting, especially for assassination, is short-range or close contact. As supplies of ammunition are limited, the terrorist must learn to shoot accurately and quickly, using as little ammunition as possible. This ability, coupled with the element of suprise, aids in his ability to escape.

A machine gunner is usually partnered with a firing group armed with revolvers or pistols, usually 38 caliber or 9-mm. They might carry hand grenades and smoke bombs (also considered light arms).

Molotov cocktails, homemade grenades and other explosives, including plastic bombs and ammunition, make up the balance of the assault and defense arsenal of the fire group.

These groups must be capable of acting on their own initiative, even when some governing body establishes the target. The firing group might make the decision whether to execute, kidnap, or simply rob the targeted person.

However, such fire units are not totally efficient because the weapons they use, especially machine guns, are not uniform, and ammunition and calibers are mixed. Obtaining ammunition is difficult and there is too little opportunity to train in their use.

Technique of the Terrorist Battle Plan

Terrorist operations may be either discriminant, that is, actions which are specific, usually against governments, or indiscriminant in nature. Discriminant attacks provoke confusion, fear, and turmoil, and attacked leadership is so busy dealing with the event they appear to let other duties go by the wayside. Terrorists hope to demoralize the citizenry and make government look vulnerable and incapable of protecting itself or its people. If the target is a corporation, the goal is essentially the same, i.e., throw workers out of employment, tie up corporate funds in dealing with the action, discredit and smear the corporation's name, decrease production.

Indiscriminant operations are attacks on the public. Shops, restaurants, night-clubs and malls might be chosen for this type of operation. Places or establishments where Americans or other targeted groups congregate might fall into this category, as was the case in Paris when a Jewish delicatessen was machine gunned.

Terrorist operations, even the indiscriminant ones, are carefully planned, beginning with target analysis. The final choice may involve consideration of the following factors: Will destruction of the target interrupt production, operations, movements of personnel, or layoffs of personnel? Transportation sites are chosen if transportation can be interrupted (a switching site in a railroad yard, airport tower, or a bridge).

How easy will it be to reach and damage the target? This involves evaluating the size and construction of the target, and its security/protective devices.

How easy is it to enter the target, perform the operation, and escape successfully? Security fences, building design, security measures, and geographical location all are of significance here.

How well can the target recover from the operation?

What impact will the operation have with the target population? Desirable effects of fear, panic, unrest, disruption and demoralization of government and population rate highly when targets are chosen. Turning the public against government is the most highly desirable impact a terrorist group could hope for.

Once the target is chosen, the next step is intelligence gathering. Drawings or pictures of the target are taken. Information about security, shifts, passive security devices, materials required to enter a facility (such as entry passes) is collected.

After intelligence information is obtained and analyzed the next step is planning the operation: personnel needed, equipment, entrance and departure from the site, use of and type of explosives to be used, weapons to be drawn and routes of travel to be employed. Dry runs are made to time the operation. If diversions are to be used they must be planned.

An outline of the main steps in a terrorist operation are as follows:
1. Investigation and information
2. Observation
3. Exploration of the terrain for the scene of action
4. Study and timing of routes
5. Mapping
6. Mechanization and transportation
7. Selection of personnel and relief

7. Selection of personnel and relief
8. Selection of firing capacity
9. Rehearsal
10. Completion
11. Cover
12. Retreat
13. Dispersal
14. Liberation or transfer of prisoners
15. Elimination of clues
16. Rescue of wounded terrorists

These factors were clearly taken into account in a number of terrorist kidnappings throughout Europe and South America. The kidnapping of Aldo Moro is an excellent example. He was the leader of the Christian Democratic Party, tipped as the next president of Italy.

• Early one morning he left church and headed to Parliament. Enroute he sat in the back of his blue Fiat reading a newspaper: his driver and security guard sat in front. This car was followed by another containing three security guards. Suddenly, a white Fiat with diplomatic license plates cut in front of his car, forcing the driver to brake hard. The escort car ran into the back of the Moro car. Occupants of the white Fiat jumped out, apparently to see if their car was damaged. However, they pulled pistols and immediately killed Moro's driver and guard. Four men dressed as Italian soldiers standing on a nearby corner drew automatic weapons from flight bags, and fired and killed the three policemen in the escort car. Moro, unharmed, was dragged from his car and thrust into another blue Fiat. A woman and man watching the proceedings jumped into a car and thus completed a three vehicle escape motorcade.

• The entire episode took 30 seconds. Police were tied up investigating bomb reports (later discovered to be false) and phone service at the kidnap site was mysteriously out of commission for 15 minutes after the kidnapping. The diplomatic license plates had been stolen from the Venezuelan embassy more than a year earlier.

• With the telephone system knocked out, the members of the Red Brigade were on their way and long gone before the police were even notified of what had happened. The terrorists had gained at least 30 minutes. When the police arrived at the scene, there were no witnesses or clues.

Terrorists operate from a mobile group, not a fixed base, as would be the case in conventional warfare. Retreat always follows a lightning attack. A terrorist group's function is to wear out, distract, and demoralize the armed forces or government. To accomplish this, the terrorist must take the enemy by surprise, know the terrain better than the enemy, have greater mobility and speed than the police, better intelligence information than the enemy has about him, and be in decisive command of the situation.

Through surprise, the terrorist gains an advantage over government forces and compensates for his lack of firearms. The size of the force to be attacked is known to the terrorists, but the target group has no knowledge of the size of the terrorist group. The terrorists fix the time of attack, its duration, and its objective. The government or civilian target remains ignorant, as does the police or military organization charged with their defense.

The terrorists know the terrain, how to attack the group, how to escape, and where to hide. They know the backstreets, alleys, and sewer system. They know the foot routes, where to drive, and what kind of vehicles to use for each of these escape routes. They know where to assemble afterward and how to evade and deceive the enemy. Those terrorists native to the city have all these advantages, whereas the foreigner has less knowledge than the police, unless he works with a local group.

Mobility and speed of operation are enhanced by the use of light weapons, disrupting the enemy communication system, and using small, lightweight transportation to aid in escape. The terrorist knocks out the telephone system to prevent early warning to the police or military.

At times, escape is assisted by obstructing routes with illegal vehicles. The obstructions, inconveniences, and damage delay police action and mobility. Even police on horseback can be thwarted by ropes tied across the street.

The combat strategy of the terrorists is to tie up government forces to such an extent that pursuing forces will be withdrawn to guard foreign businesses and power and utility facilities. By using lightning-quick attacks, the terrorists hope to keep government forces pinned down to the urban setting. As government troops and the police tighten a reign of control over those who live in the city, the terrorists hope to pick up support from those who develop resentment toward the military, police, and government.

The more enemies against the government that are formed after the terrorist movement begins, the better the information and cooperation that is made available against the government; as a consequence, there is less and less information available to identify and trace those in the terrorist movement.

Thus, urban terrorist action models involve the following: assaults, raids and penetrations, occupations, ambush, street tactics, strikes and work interruptions, encouragement of desertions, expropriation of arms, liberation of prisoners, execution, kidnapping, sabotage, armed propaganda, and a general war of nerves. The most likely targets for assault are banks, commissaries, government jails, government property, and commercial and industrial businesses, including those which produce arms. Executives of businesses and government agencies are favorite targets for kidnapping. Credit establishments, armored cars used by money carriers, trains, ships, and planes are all popular robbery targets. Street tactics involve groups which construct barricades, lock arms while marching down the street in parade fashion, hurl stones and marbles at the police, and hide in buildings under construction. "Net within a net" is a terrorist operation involving surrounding a police officer, disarming, beating, and robbing him, then permitting him to escape.

Street tactics also involve mining escape routes used by terrorists so that pursuing police cars will be blown up. Encouraging desertion by police and soldiers makes it possible to reduce the numbers of persons hunting them and also makes possible the flow of modern weapons and explosives to the terrorists.

Sabotage results in a destroyed or impaired economy, interferes with agricultural production, disrupts important communication and transportation, as well as otherwise timely police and military action or counter response, weakens a repressive military or police system and, most important, destroys the properties and investments of North American or Western businesses. United States embassies and trade centers have become likely targets today. Railway transportation is another likely target because it carries fuel, industrial machinery, and food. Bombs can destroy all forms of transportation, but simple derailment is effective against trains.

As all of these forms of terrorism mount, the government responds by imposing censorship; often there is a news blackout. Terrorists exploit the lack of information by feeding misinformation to the police in the form of false leads about terrorist locations, locations of bombs, kidnapping and assassination plans and targets. They stimulate the distribution of rumors and ensure that all misuse of judicial process and violence by the government are protested through the United Nations, the papal nunciature, and any available international organization or judicial commission. Amnesty International is an agency interested in publishing such information, but it also reports stories of terrorist abuse of citizens.

Long experience has shown that the wounded terrorist cannot be left behind. If taken into custody, security is impaired. In one Central American country, the police do not believe in keeping prisoners. Terrorists are tortured, killed, and the remains fed to caimans. Terrorists are no gentler with their captives. They like to have their dead victims found as a form of intimidation and as a warning to the government.

Police infiltration is the largest security danger to the terrorist group. In some groups, great pains are taken to destroy personal phone books and any papers or documents of the organization. Laxity about security can never be permitted.

The mini-manual of the Urban Guerrilla lists seven basic sins that can increase the margin of error of an individual terrorist. Inexperience might allow him to see the police, government, or military as being stupid, and he can overestimate the strength of opposing forces. Second, he may boast about his actions. Vanity is the third sin. It allows him to feel pride about his success at the expense of ensuring that security and organization are running well. His fourth sin is exaggerating his own strength and taking on missions for which he is unprepared. Precipitous action, based upon fear or impulse, is his fifth sin. Anger felt intensively preceding an attack of the enemy is the sixth sin. Failure to plan action and relying on too much improvisation is the seventh sin.

Once the civilian population takes their action seriously, terrorists feel their success is almost guaranteed. They count on the refusal of civilians to cooperate with the police. This has not happened in Italy and Bolivia, or in the United States with groups like the Weathermen, the Symbionese Liberation Army, or the Black Muslims. Terrorists hope that the local population will see the folly of elections because the ever-present threat of terrorism maintains the repressive military regime. They seek to prevent a political election solution to the country's problems and they do not want various parties reorganized. They wish to preserve the military base of their work and the response of the government. They hope to encourage the development of struggle between the masses and the military dictatorship or section of the government.

17

Executive Security and the Female Terrorist

Dr. Deborah M. Galvin

Everybody in New York City is looking for something. Men are looking for women and women are looking for men."
Donald E. Westlake [1]

Act one, scene one: the bar of the Plaza. Man meets woman. Man asks woman out to dinner. Man invites woman to his room. Man found dead. It is an old tale, one of the oldest. Yet, so often successful. So many men, men known to be cautious, men who are reckless, men who are faithful to their wives, men who are philanderers, men who are religious, men who are atheists. All are capable of falling into the trap. Sometimes the *femme fatale* is a woman they have just met, a chance meeting, perhaps. On others, the encounter only appears accidental. On occasion, the woman has been known to the man for sometime, a mole, perhaps within the organization, a planted set-up. Victimization is facilitated by knowledge; the target becomes easier prey. The whereabouts of the intended male victim are known to those who wish to do him harm, his weaknesses can be more carefully analyzed and exposed. Nor are these possibilities of victimization confined to such deliberate designs or those having terroristic overtones. It is also possible to fall prey to a disturbed female employee who feels some injustice, real or imaginary, has been done to her within the workplace. These scenarios are talked about, joked about, and in the minds of many are improbable: "not something which will happen to me." They make an interesting cocktail conversation or party talk, yet, it is always something that happens to the "other guy." So do traffic accidents. The truly security conscious executive should always "expect the unexpected."[2] Those in business must, prudently, allow for unaccustomed violence to enter their lives at some point or another. Those whose business takes them into the terrorist gambit must take special precautions. And, these days, where there is widespread terrorism, there will be

1. Evans, M. *Dancing Aztecs,* New York: (1976), p. 3.
2. See, "Expecting the Unexpected", H.H.A. Cooper, XLIX *Police Chief,* April, 1982, p. 54.

118

female terrorists. Potential targets need to know how some of these women might look and behave. They are not always what they seem and they are rarely what they seem to others.

The media has played up terrorist women as psychopathic, overly aggressive, unreasonable, and more violent than their male counterparts. There have indeed been females who fit this picture but others all but portray the opposite. When looking to construct a female terrorist profile, the authorities may have a difficult time in presenting a representative one. In truth, a valid, reliable profile simply does not exist. Female terrorists have been from all age groups, young adolescents to grandmothers in their eighties. They are of all nationalities, as likely to come from those countries in which women are not allowed to uncover their faces in public with separate education from men to those liberated societies in which women are nationally as free as men to pursue their dreams and goals. They come from societies and cultural backgrounds where there is little if any mass media influence in individual domiciles to societies in which every home has at least one television set. Some are extremely beautiful, and would be able to compete in and win beauty contests, while others are unattractive on the scale of those who count to ten. Indeed, there appears to be no useful correlation between level of education, appearance, race, socio-economic status, class, political affiliation, age on entry, marital status, number of children, or religiosity. Some are extremely intelligent, others are dull, some are born leaders with charismatic qualities, while others are content to serve in a subordinate capacity. Quite frequently involvement in terrorism by males and females is a reaction to a feeling of "powerlessness" and of being in a situation in which the "terrorist" solution appears to be the only choice left. Yet, like the Little Drummer Girl, a number of females (as well as males) become involved quite accidentally, by being at the wrong place at the wrong time, by making one bad decision, by taking one miscaluclated step. There are more Ann Murphys than the public might care to believe.[3] Some are enthusiastic, some are not.

It is an interesting process how a "good" girl becomes involved in terrorism, and in someone else's battle for a goal not originally one's own. The case of Patricia Hearst is an extremely instructive one in this regard.[4] Was she actually kidnapped? Did she play a role in her own abduction as some have theorized? Was she brainwashed when she joined the SLA? What battle was she fighting? Independence

---

3. Ann Murphy was 32 when she met Nezar Hindawi at a house near Heathrow Airport, and within a year became pregnant by him. She miscarried the first time, but became pregnant again. Although he did not want to marry her initially, he unexpectedly proposed marriage and a holiday in Israel. Murphy was a single, simple Irish girl, who had no knowledge of the 3 pounds of plastic explosives given to her to carry on board the El Al jet bound for Israel by her supposed husband-to-be, Jordanian terrorist Hindawi. Not only was she surprised that he proposed marriage, but she was also surprised at his background and her suicide mission which was aborted fortunately by El Al security officers at the airport. Ms. Murphy had been a chambermaid at the Hilton in London, she came from a large family, and left school at the age of 14 and had worked as a machinist in Dublin. The bomb her lover had hidden in a package he had given her to carry was set to explode 5 hours into the flight, 39,000 feet over Austria. What can we trust? Our very basics are challenged when pregnant, mothers-to-be from working class families are utilized in the manner in which Ann Murphy was recruited and set-up.

from her parents? A reaction to being in a bad relationship which didn't work? Or was she convinced that the SLA's ideology was correct? That the poor would be helped through the free food program? Was she victim or victimizer? Although the Patricia Hearst case appears to be unique, there are a number of other cases which involve women who may have been coerced into acting a terrorist role. Some who appear aggressive, independent and effective in the role of terrorist, and who espouse the propaganda of the group as their own have actually been manipulated by others to act in this traditionally non-feminine role. Many are even willing to die for the cause.

Other terrorist women like Susan Stern[5] or Marilyn Bucks[6] are acting in their own right and have purposely chosen to become involved in the politics and power plays involved in the use of terrorism. Although these women have independently chosen their destiny as "terrorist," they are not necessarily more dangerous than those who have been manipulated into the role. Indeed, the orchestration and outcome of the action may have little relationship to the process by which a woman becomes involved in terrorism. The terrorist's success in accomplishing their goal may have more to do with the preparedness of the target. In hostage-taking situations, when the need for negotiation is present, the psychological reasoning for the initial involvement might be useful in promoting a successful outcome of the negotiation.

Protection Against the Female Terrorist
> "Full security comes from leaving nothing undone."
>
> Richard W. Kobetz & H.H.A. Cooper
> *Target Terrorism* [7]

It is difficult to imagine protecting oneself against all the known and unknown dangers which might challenge the executive's private, personal, familial and property interests. There is just too much territory to cover completely. Terrorism is designed to attack the individual's sense of security, to prey upon his/her mind in an attempt to wear it down and gain advantage in the play for power. Terrorism is an idea that knows no bounds. The coercive fear created by terrorism furnishes the terrorist with the means to go on winning in an unfavorable arena. The terrorist enjoys the tactical advantages of surprise and initiative. The female terrorist provides an additional element of surprise. No matter how well trained security

---

4. Patricia Campbell Hearst was kidnapped on February 4, 1974 by the Symbionese Liberation Army. Her abduction, the SLA's demands for millions of dollars to feed the poor people in California, her later involvement in terroristic activities, all shocked the general public in America. In her book, *Every Secret Thing,* (Hearst, 1982, Doubleday & Company: NY), many of the questions the public demanded answered were addressed. Still there are many issues left unanswered.
5. S. Stern, *With the Weathermen,* New York: Doubleday & Co., 1975.
6. Marilyn Bucks, Kathy Houdin and Judith Clark were all part of the Old Left, the radical underground, and the Days of Rage. With the Brinks robbery they resurfaced in October, 1981. For information on these women see: *Diana: The Making of A Terrorist,* by T. Powers (Houghton Mifflin Company, Boston, 1971), *Growing Up Underground,* by Jane Albert (William Morrow, NY, 1971), and *The Big Dance* by J. Castellucci (Dodd, Mead & Co., NY, 1986).
7. *Target Terrorism,* Gaithersbury, MD IACF, p. 5.

professionals may be, how cautious in taking any form of risk, the danger of the female terrorist remains a challenge even to those who have done their homework and attended all their lectures. One small error can lead to the fatal consequences against which all are warned.

In the book, Vengeance[8], for example, "cautious" Carl, a man with many years experience with the Mossad, was caught in the "honey trap." He was found murdered in his hotel room after having had dinner with a "blond woman." Was she an old friend? Did she kill him or have him set-up? These were the questions his companions asked after it was too late.

For the executive, his family and his co-workers, this type of set-up seems too remote, especially for the executive who is skeptical of being victimized in the first place. But is it really? Only the executive can know the answer. How many are prepared to ask themselves the hard question?

How does one protect against the female terrorist? In the United States, we live in a society in which females are equal to men. They share the business place, meet men outside of traditional arrangements, are free to travel, check into hotels and motels by themselves, telephone and converse with anyone they might wish, to drive cars, pilot aircraft, and even act in the role of bodyguard. Even with these freedoms, men and women have both continued to view the female as the "weaker" sex, more passive, less likely statistically and perceptually to become involved in violent crime, especially in terroristic activites.[9]

In the 1960s, it was projected that with women's rights, the woman would become as involved in crime as men. Those who projected into the future saw women as men's equals in every sense. Although women have joined the work force in greater numbers, becoming one-parent child supporters and two member mortgage holders, they still have not joined the ranks of men in terms of numbers involved in crime or terrorism.[10] Moreover, even increased participation has failed to give them status. Few, indeed, have risen very high in the ranks.

Perhaps the best protection against the female terrorist is the attitude that anything is possible in terrorism. Hard intelligence concerning specific terrorists in any given situation before it occurs is difficult to come by. However, if security precautions designed to prevent attacks are followed equally for women as they are for men, this, in and of itself, would reduce the possibilities of infiltration by females. Understanding the terrorist, the interactions between hostage/terrorist, for example, given a difference in sex, and the variations in reactions by security and police personnel to these differences can all aid in the protection of the executive. Knowledge has to be developed through research and analysis. Case histories must be carefully studied. Crisis management and contingency planning need to incorporate policy making for more effective functioning to prevent terrorist events as well as coping with them during their occurrence. Knowledge and the training at skills necessary to employ

8. George Jonas: *Vengeance*. NY: Bantam Books, 1984.
9. F. Adler: *Sister in Crime*. New York: McGraw Hill Book Co., 1975.
10. D. Galvin, ed: "The Victimology of Terrorism." *Crime Victims*, R. Mawby, Plymouth England: Plymouth Polytechnic 1986.

that knowledge wisely are the executive's best protection against the female terrorist.

Dangerous Situations and the Female Terrorist
One of the basic elements comprising a successful terrorist attack is location: day, night, summer, winter, raining, clear, public, private, congested, secluded, home turf, or foreign land. Much has been written in this area of "crime prevention through environmental design."[11] Yet, terrorism is no ordinary crime and the fact of the perpetrator being female can alter the basic underlying findings of the research in this area. Crime prevention through environmental design of what Oscar Newman[12] has labelled, "defensible space" theories. Assume that there is less crime in public situations where there are a number of "public eyes" on the street. In terrorism and for the female terrorist, the public setting can be more appealing, more protective of her purposes, than a private one. The best hiding place is often beneath the lamppost. The public place with the large number of strangers mingling and passing through can be an excellent place to make initial contact with the target. Public areas have a sense of security, with so many eyes looking on, as defensible space theories suggest, crime is less likely in these places. Target figures feel safe at Disneyland. The executive, his family, co-workers and other possible related targets, assume that "probably nothing will happen." There are distinctive feelings associated with "safe" places. The female terrorist is quite likely to meet her prey in a relatively safe location,[13] one in which the target feels falsely comfortable, one in which the target is less likely to entertain a suspicion of being set up. Finally, in public, terrorism can be more successful in reaching its goal, for here with so many people at hand, the greatest amount of fear and impact on the public mind may be made. Terrorism is at its most effective when it "endangers or destroys the fundamental freedoms of the innocent."[14]

Depending upon the type of terroristic activity, the exact design for the event will be established including time and place of initial contact, specific details about how the action will be carried out and contingency plans for alternative strategies. If the target has a repetitive or consistent schedule, the planning of the operation becomes easier. For example, if the target has a regularly scheduled barber or hairdresser appointment, the female terrorist can develop a plan of attack encompassing a range of possibilities: a job at the place of business so as to be easily in place at the set time; a position at a nearby shop adjacent to the location; a role as customer with an appointment of the same time; or any other convenient and plausible role which

11. Oscar Newman: *Architectural Design for Crime Prevention,* United States Department of Justice, LEAA, GFO, 1973.
12. Op. cit.
13. On April 13, 1982, Yaacov Barsimantois, an Israeli diplomat was slain by a young woman in the lobby of his apartment building in Paris. She was acting for the Lebanese Armed Revolutionary Faction.
14. H. Arendt: *On Violence.* New York: Harcourt. Brace and World, Inc., 1969. Also, H.H.A. Cooper, "What is a Terrorist: A Psychological Perspective." *Legal Medical Quarterly,* 1(1), 1977: pp. 16-32.

would coincide with the target's known whereabouts at that specific time. For this reason, ransom patterns of behavior are recommended by security professionals. High risk targets will have closely held schedules.

The office or place of business is one location that the employee and executive, generally, tends to trust as "safe." One does not expect terroristic activity there, much less extreme domestic violence such as the burst of gunfire as an ex-IBM employee burst through the glass doors of the IBM facility in Bethesda, Maryland[15] in an effort to finalize a dispute with an estranged spouse. But these things can and do happen underlining the potential hazards of even the best regulated work places. The female terrorist can easily obtain a trusted position as secretary, assistant, security guard or office cleaner. These are positions favored by terrorists as well as spies. In these positions, the female is in a strategic position unobtrusively to enter into the work environment during normal working hours and gain access to personal or property targets. The worker's presence, and frequently a friend's presence (boyfriend, husband, girlfriend, etc.) is rarely questioned. In certain cases, they might even be able to have large equipment moved into the building, plant bugs or bombs, or sabotage on-going work. When a bomb went off in the Staten Island[16] women's restroom, which was conveniently located next door to the FBI offices, it was most likely a female perpetrator who had gained access.

Truby, in his IACP article on Female Terrorists, [17] recounted the story of a female terrorist who purposely transmitted a sexual disease to a top executive in a corporation. The female, aware that she was infected, transmitted it over a period of three days to be sure she had accomplished her goal. The executive was embarrassed both at home and at the office. The terrorist organization was able to make good use of the cleverly acquired propaganda tool in making further demands and breaching security. With the introduction of the AIDS virus, the dangers this disease might cause seem endless. Photographs and home videos are always good for blackmail. Locations such as hotel rooms, private homes or apartments, office buildings, or the client's own residence, have been used in many of these sexual encounters turned terrorist events in the past.

If a terrorist cannot easily assassinate her target in the proper sense of the term, she may be able to assassinate him politically through the use of sex as a moral and ethical question. The Gary Hart case has some interesting and suggestive parallels. Likewise, the deliberate passing of a virus such as AIDS would also accomplish the same end, and in an even more damaging manner. The possibilities for doing harm are endless. Women in positions of trust are able to poison their targets quite easily

15. Crazies and the mentally ill have been discussed in the literature as a major typology of hostage-takers and kidnappers. These individuals are difficult to plan for and even more difficult to negotiate with. See, *The Hostage Takers* by H.H.A. Cooper (Boulder: Paladin Press, 1981) and *Crusaders, Criminals, Crazies* by F.J. Hacker (New York: W.W. Norton & Co., 1976).

16. Bernadine Dohrn of the Weathermen was involved in the 1974 bombing of the California State Attorney General, Evelle Younger. Judith Wand bombed the London National Defense College also in 1974. More recently, there has been a large number of car bombings, where young female teenagers have been used as the suicide bombers.

17. J. David Truby: *Women as Terrorists*. Gaithersburg: Md: IACXP, 1976.

by placing chemicals within their food or drink. Who makes the boss's coffee? More sophisticated possibilities still suggest themselves. By placing sedatives, depressants, or stimulants in the executive's intake, the female terrorist would be able to control his psychological being, ruin an important business conference and his/her reputation. And how easy it is to remove a drugged executive from the office.

These "honey traps" leave a bitter taste. By nature and the social environment, the female terrorist is well placed to gain the inside track.

A well known example of the use of sex to lure a target was accomplished by the League of Women, an IRA off-shoot, known as the Cunann namBann.[18] Three young Irish women invited three British soldiers to an apartment in Belfast, the latter assuming they would receive more than tea. Sadly, they were right. Instead of tea, they were shot down with submachine guns.

This is not an isolated case. This old technique has been used more than many would like to admit, and not only in Northern Ireland. Men like to think that they are in a powerful position in terms of the male/female relationship. Although this may be true in a great number, or even the majority of cases, they are at their weakest point in the boudoir of the wrong woman. Just as women have been known to be more easily manipulated, psychologically, after they have entered into a sexual liaison, men, too, can become easier prey, physically. Being caught, literally, with one's pants down is not merely embarrassing, it may be down right dangerous. The bedroom can lead to blackmail, espionage, hostage-taking, kidnapping, and death. This recital will not, of course, deter the amorous executive. But is should give him pause.

Bars, nightclubs, discotheques, and hotel lobbies have all been and will continue to be places in which the female terrorist can meet and dazzle her prey. The female does not always work alone here. A young couple, male and female, often appears safer to outsiders.

Charles Sobhraj, [19] for example, frequently used female companions to take his targets off guard, drug their drinks, and later have the female accomplices assist him in robbing and at times murdering his victims.

These are also locations where alcohol is served, leaving the potential target in less control of the situation than if he/she had been in a more sober environment. People who would not be likely to associate with strangers and converse in any other situation are given social license to introduce themselves, carry on intensely personal conversations, and reveal themselves in unlikely and unaccustomed ways.

Air travel has a similar effect on many. Airport lounges in far away places rival the bedroom as danger spots for the eager and unwary. Under these conditions, the female terrorist is again at an advantage. Being of the opposite sex, and thus seen as non-threatening and an object of pursuit, she is in a position to gather intelligence, ingratiate herself so as to establish a future prospect or even, in some cases, an immediate invitation to some other more private location, thereby opening possi-

18. Trudy, op. cit.
19. T. Thompson: *Serpentine*. New York: Dell Books, 1979.

bilities of access to the corporate world by means of a job offer, luncheon engagement, consulting arrangement, or the like.

The female's appearance undoubtedly plays a part in some of these encounters, but all types of women have been successful in this role. Crossing the social barriers not previously easy to break, opens the target to a number of possible threats, aggressions and attacks, and critically exposes weaknesses. The woman is the pry-bar. Anything can follow once the door is open.

Executives sometimes employ security personnel to act as bodyguards.[20] While such protection is no longer reserved for the very rich, it is still an expensive business. It is the body guard's job to be with the executive to fend off any potential threat. He/she must be close, physically, to do the job effectively. This is, some-times, literally a hands on performance. However, in many cases, the executive feels "overprotected," smothered almost, or feels that he/she would like to conduct private affairs away from the watchful eyes of the protectors. In some, executive protection induces near claustrophobia. By seeking much desired privacy in this way, the executive is inviting the mischief against which the protection is estab-lished. If the escape is to rendezvous with a female outside the executive marriage, the executive is particularly vulnerable. The woman, herself, may not be a knowing terrorist agent, but the knowledge that the victim frequents the location without personal security leaves a dangerous opening for an attack. Countless cases attest to this folly. The location may be as varied as the number of scenarios which can be dreamed up: restaurant, hospital, church, home, a lonely country road or even a graveyard. Those who have bodyguards dodge them at their peril. In all situations, it is highly dangerous not to include the body guard as a part of any social activity. If you rate one, you probably need one. If you must have "extra-curricular" activities, take your body guard into your confidence. If you feel you cannot, he (or she) ought not to be your body guard.

Male as Victim of Female

The literature contains much about the female being victimized by the male. Little has been written about the male being victimized by the female. The literature has traditionally labelled the female as a "victim." Von Hentig, Mandelsohm, and other victimologists have all placed the "female victim" in their typologies. Psycholo-gists, sociologists and feminists have all noted that women have been socialized as the "weaker sex," to be dependent upon men, afraid of success, physically less capable, not taught the rules of the game, and "wounded" by their socialization. Although there are many studies indicating that the female tends to be victimized by her male counterpart in the business place, at home, and even in terrorism, less attention has been paid to the male's attachment to female relationships and possible victimizations arising from such attachments.

We must ask how did Agrippina so easily administer poisonous mushrooms to

20. "The Hardest Question", Richard W. Kobertz and H.H.A. Cooper in *Terrorism and Personal Protection*, ed. Brian Jenkins. Brookings Inst.: Butterworth. 1985, pp. 388-394.

Claudius and when he expelled this poisonous potion, how was she again able to repeat her performance, only this time successfully to poison him with the juice of the fungus (orally and anally).[21]

Another example of seemingly facile victimization was Jean Paul Marat, comfortably relaxing in his bathtub listening to a lovely young informant, Charlotte Corday, whom he had never met before. She assassinated him with a knife which she had concealed in her blouse.[22]

There is an almost Shakespearian quality about these cases. What causes this lack of discretion in males? What is this interesting attachment to the female? Why, we might ask, are such powerful figures apparently so careless?

The male can be vulnerable to the female as he assumes her to be the weaker sex, more volatile, less powerful and easily manipulated. He assumes, even in the bedroom, that he is in charge. He rarely questions this assumption. He feels he is able to control the situation, any situation, despite training he may have received to the contrary. There are variations on this theme that try to explain evidence of male weaknesses. Many feel it is only the older man being taken in by the young, "innocent" woman. Although this scenario has successfully been accomplished in the past and will no doubt continue to be used, women of all ages seem capable of victimizing men of all ages in the same way.

There are still some who believe that terrorism is the province of men. It is falsely assumed that men are expected to do these terrible things, not women. There is still a shock factor involved when a female is involved in an act of terrorism, as though it were somehow unnatural. The female terrorist is seen as an incongruity, an aberration and this is almost universally accepted. These assumptions have important tactical significance. Beyond the initial act of surprise, the male's ego is easily exploited by his need to believe that he is in control of his destiny, especially when it comes to his relationship with a woman. We might almost say he is socially programmed to think in this way. "Johnny" knows that "Debbi" grew up with dolls, that "Debbi" is easily manipulated given the right circumstances. This is, indeed, the product of everyday experience and none can be blamed for thinking these thoughts or extending the consequences to include all women in all activities.

There are still many in the business place who believe that although you must accept a few women into the boardroom, they can be easily controlled by men through the proper use of power. The analysis is shallow, but experience seems to bear out the thesis. Likewise, females are easily controlled through sex in many cases. Once in a sexual relationship with a woman, the male assumes that he is able to gain, and more importantly keep, control. Frequently this is the case, often enough, indeed to reinforce common beliefs. This is associated with the underlying sexual theme of subjugation: "The girl being forcefully taken," "the male in the conquering position," "the woman submitting to the man and changing her point of view to fit his." It may well be that there is a man behind these things, but it is beside

---

21. D. Galvin, "Women as Assassins," *TVI Journal*, Vol. IV, Numbers 7-9, 1984.
22. op. cit.

the point from the victimization angle. The victim is blindsided because regardless of who is behind it all, women are just not supposed to do these things, particularly when the victim seems to have the poor little woman in his power.

In detection, "cherchez la femme" is often used as a rule of thumb. In terrorism, it is "cherchez l'homme" for it is usually assumed there must be a man behind all this. Hence "women who do awful things for awful men."[23] All run counter to the female acting in the role of terrorist, victimizing the male executive. Indeed, these images also run counter to the female victimizing the female executive. We must free ourselves from impressions that erode the strength of our natural defenses.

Perhaps the usual senses which warn one of danger are simply subdued when it comes to the female terrorist. Although one might normally suspect something is wrong, the executive shrugs it off when it comes to the female terrorist. The greater his (or her) ego involvement in the on-going situation, whether it be business or personal, the greater the disbelief. We are continually reminded of the "after the fact" lines such as "she was always so normal," "she was just like everyone else," "she was a cheerleader in high school," "she attended church and came from a good family," or "she was so pretty, I just didn't think." All reactions to the inevitable: why didn't we read the writing on the wall? Yet, to change the gender, were not such things said of Nazi war criminals thirty or forty years after their awful crimes? Female terrorists do not carry the obvious mark of Cain on their foreheads. But, worse, there are those who would not believe it if they did.

That males are victims of female terrorists more frequently than females, is for the same reason males are more frequently victims of terrorism in all cases: they tend to be societal symbols of power. Like Everest, they are there. The female terrorist marks her victim not *because* he is a male, but rather for the reason that the victim might provide her and her organization the recognition, media attention, and level of fear for which the terrorist event was planned.

With extensions of women's liberation and particularly, more women in higher level executive positions, which has yet to reach its potential, the female executive will become more of a target. We hazard the guess that female terrorists will continue to blindside these women exactly as they did their male counterparts. Aside from the obvious sexual implications, we hear echoes in this of Rex Harrison: why can't a woman think more like a man. Female executives can, and do, and often treat their female subordinates in much the same way. Many, from their new-found arrogance would, incongruously, echo the masculine cry: Why she couldn't possibly do that: she is a woman!

The social psychology of terrorist groups has, for obvious reasons, not been the subject of reliable scientific study. Most of what is known or conjectured is based on the most impressionistic of evidence. Those concerned with these matters must be careful how far they can stretch the evidence. In each terrorist event, the individual's peculiar psychological make-up will interact with those factors affect-

---

23. "Women Terrorists: Victims or Victimizers", Fifth International Symposium on Victimology, Zagreb, Yugoslavia, 1985.

ing the social cohesion of the terrorist group and thus produce an impact on the outcome.

Where negotiation is involved, or interaction with outside groups, the social group as a participating terrorist will also have an impact on the events as they occur and on the outcome of the event itself. The mere fact of being female, in and of itself changes the course and dynamics of the terrorist action. Within the terrorist group, there is typically a lack of confidence that the female will "come through" in the same fashion as a man. Even though she may have passed many tests of endurance, skill and fortitude, she is never accepted by the males, and, nor, frequently by the other females in the group as an "equal" in the true sense. Any show of weakness, such as tears after a long, highly tense situation (a normal reaction for a female which often is only a form of tension relief and/or defense mechanism), will be used as a reason to doubt her strength and ability: "just like a woman!" Despite the anatomy is destiny argument, there is no reason to doubt the female terrorist's performance as a terrorist. Given the right situation, she can act as methodically and swiftly as any male counterpart. Men who witness the female act in any fashion which could appear as "weak" should not assume that she will not or can not carry out her duties as a terrorist in any given situation. To a kidnap victim or hostage, the female may appear to be more "motherly," and giving in nature, yet, let the victim beware as the female can be as deadly as the black widow, the pretense only a part of the role playing before the attack. All these factors must be taken into account by those orienting negotiation strategies. Will they make it easier or harder to reach an agreed, non-violent way out of the impasse? How should the "female factor" be approached? Who should deal with the woman terrorist, if dealing seems desirable?

Women in Surveillance and Support Roles

Women have served in all areas of terrorist surveillance: choosing the target; selecting the technique (clandestine or overt); keeping observation; collecting the information; maintaining the information in some orderly fashion (database, etc.); and determining how to use what has been learned. The effectiveness of women in these roles has been proven time and again. To accomplish these tasks, the female has functioned in a number of arenas: mistress, functionary, secretary, office cleaner, database analyst, and security official. You name it, they do it. Obviously each of these and other job positions would lend themselves to various opportunities to access data, gain useful levels of trust, and set-up the target. Such women can be quite useful in obtaining schedules, telephone numbers (published and unpublished), family members names and relationships, blackmail information, and a wealth of other data useful in planning assassinations, kidnappings, hostage-takings and other forms of logistical support activites such as funding teroristic organizations through extortion, blackmail, fraud, robberies and white collar crime. Their placement within organizations is not only useful in targeting specific executives of that entity, but also in obtaining access to information leading to the ability to target related institutions and personnel. Depending upon the organization and the woman's position within it, she may be able to obtain entrance to a number or social settings not previously accessible: private parties; media events; international and national travel; friendships with family members; personal ties with close friends, etc. Women seem so *natural* in these positions. Their good faith is taken for granted.

Women have been used both voluntarily and involuntarily, knowingly and otherwise, in these positions. To find out things of operational value, and to facilitate the introduction of others who could not, on their own account, gain entry.

Sylvia Ageloff[24] is a good example of a female insider who unknowingly facilitated the introduction and entry of a professional male assassin. Ageloff, a 27 year old psychologist, met and was lured into a love relationship by "Jacques Mornard." Mornard, a Soviet agent, was aware that Ageloff's sister happened to be Trotsky's secretary in Mexico. Prior to this well-thought out plan no one had been able to breach Trotsky's physical or personal security. Mornard was able to gain a trusting familarity with Trotsky based on his relationship with Sylvia. The assassination, its initial plan, and execution was then all made possible by Mornard's use of Ageloff. Unwittingly, she supplied the information and, more importantly, the much needed accreditation.

Perhaps one of the best placed voluntary spies was the woman known as "Tania," if CIA sources are correct in their assumption and assertions concerning her role.[25] According to CIA sources, "Tania" was one of the best known infiltrators. She was an Argentine born German, working for the Russians when she became Che Guevara's lover. The CIA contends that as a plant, she was able successfully to set up the defeat and death of Guevara. Many claim that she received her money and orders from some source higher than Che. Yet, Cuba and others still contend that this was disinformation and that Tania was a great revolutionary heroine who died bravely in the Bolivian jungles fighting for the revolution. Perhaps we will never know the true story.

It is never easy acknowledging a mole within the organization, especially one who infiltrates as soldier, companion and lover. The higher the position and the more trusted the individual, the greater the embarrassment, especially if sex is involved. What is interesting, if the CIA story is true, is that the Soviets should have chosen a woman for this job. With unerring sensitivity they recongized the great "Che's" weakness, and exploited it accordingly. But whatever the case, it is evident they felt no qualms about sending a woman to fight, to kill, and to die in the jungle. As with all intelligence-based operations, what is fact and what is fiction may never be known. But it does contain many of the lessons we have adumbrated here.

Women have been placed in certain positions to gain access to monetary sources for funding "the revolution" or terrorist activities. By simply occupying traditional female slots in the workplace, they arouse no suspicion when they pervert them for

---

24. op. cit.
25. This note is from J. Truby, "Women as Terrorists", op. cit. Yet, it is also relevant to cite, *Women Spies,* J. Bernard Hutton (New York: W.H. Allen, 1971), H.H. Cooper and L.J. Redlinger, *Making Spies* (Boulder: Paladin Press, 1986).

more sinister purposes. The Black Hebrews used a number of women in travel agencies to ticket false names in a scam which resulted in the extortion of thousands of dollars. [26] Men can and do commit such crimes, but the consequences are usually more serious if they are discovered.

The numbers and types of other white collar crimes and illegal rackets are innumerable. Among other forms of illegal activities is stealing information from a wide range of databases, data which can help these organizations to plan and execute more successful operations. The advent of the computer has aided terrorists enormously and changed the way they procure information. Women employed as database consultants have easy access to such files. Is it inconceivable that they may be Fawn Halls working for subversive organizations whose loyalties are to these rather than their normal bosses when they carry out documents in their clothing? Office cleaners can clean gargabe cans of output which has been discarded or simply heist information off desk tops or shelves. After all, this is their job. And are they not too stupid to know about anything that might be harmful? Why, many of them do not even speak English, let alone read it. Or do they?

As information gatherers and in planning positions, women quite often work with a man as a team. The West German profile labels the typical spy couple as: professional, childless, and married late in life. As professionals, these individuals are privy to huge amounts of information from the highest places. Unfortunately for the West Germans, a review of their database came too late to capture Herbert Willner and his wife, Herta Astrid Wilner.[27] Both were unmasked as spies after their successful escape on vacation to Spain. Herbert Willner was a defense expert with access to high-tech information. His wife, Herta Astrid, was even in a more promising spot, she was a secretary in the office of Chancellor Kohl. The resulting scandal was most embarrassing.

Another successful, recently apprehended spy couple were Russian emigres: Nikolay and Svetlana Ogorodnikov, apprehended in Los Angeles. Svetlana lured FBI agent Richard W. Miller into the operation with sexual favors in the guise of a love relationship.[28] As part of a couple, each operant is able to gain access to many individuals who assume falsely that a married couple is more trustworthy than a single person. Being married is a socially acceptable role, one which shows stability, willingness to take on responsibility, to act maturely, and hence, to be trusted. These assumptions are simply turned, adroitly, against those who make them. Likewise, there are many positive aspects from the point of view of terrorist organizations for members to operate in couples. It is always dangerous to trust outsiders, women or men, who are not part of the organization. Intimacy is

26. Other religious groups which have been suspected of terroristic activities include the Aryan Nations, founded by the Rev. Richard G. Butler, in Idaho. Many of these groups have their female followers in terroristic activities.

27. Truby, op. cit.

28. Another interesting case, in the traditional fashion, is that of Lonetree and Bracy, U.S. Embassy guards in Moscow, led into a spy scandal by Soviet women agents at the embassy. Violetta Seina, a former receptionist at the Ambassador's residence seduced Lonetree into allowing KGB agents to enter the Embassy. Corporal Bracy was seduced by a Soviet cook, Galina.

antithetical to the clandestine lifestyle. It is difficult once operational to have love or sexual relationships. To establish them outside the organization is asking for trouble. Being a couple allows for easier contact. The spying business, like terrorism, is lonely, and stable relationships among "comrades" makes for a more successful long-term use of personnel within the organization. Jane Albert obtained much needed information for her male companion, Sam Melville. [29] Had it not been for Albert, Melville could never have been as successful as he was, for Albert was clearly, the "brains" of the two. In terrorist couples, often enough the woman supplies the brain and the companion the brawn.

One member of a "spy or terrorist couple" may not be aware of the involvement of the other. Some may be aware of the involvement, but are easily manipulated into active participation themselves. The "church-going" CIA clerk from Virginia[29] was manipulated by her boyfriend, Michael Agbouti Soussoudis to provide information concerning CIA operations in Ghana. Many believe that this lack of discretion led to the death of a CIA informant in Ghana. Involvement is slight to begin with, but then deepens as the partner becomes accustomed or resigned to the role. There are probably more "unknown" cases of this type than we would care to imagine.

Females are frequently drawn into "doing awful things for awful men" through the use of sex by a master manipulator. Others participate for fear of losing their partners. Whatever the motivation or inducement, there are mutual benefits. There is a binding from which the organization is the real beneficiary.

Women and Weapons
Women should never be underestimated on their ability to know their weapons and use them professionally. There are women, just as there are men, who wouldn't know the difference between an Uzi or a b-b gun. There are a number of women terrorists who know nothing of guns, weapons of any sort, but whose job it is to be involved in another aspect: writer of propaganda, safe house operator, information gatherer. For those in operational positions, if the women don't have the knowledge of how to handle a weapon before they enter the organization, they have the intelligence to know that they had better learn their weapons, and they do. In facing the barrel of a gun held by a woman versus facing one held by a man, it is just as dangerous. The well trained woman may be more feeling, sentimental, easier or harder to coax into negotiation or putting down the gun, or have less combat experience. These are not the factors one should be analyzing when facing the gun. When the decision to fire comes to play, the amount and type of training is of greater importance, and the victim rarely knows the history and training of his opponent.

When Lynette "Squeaky" Fromme went to shake the hand of the President with her Colt .45 pistol, she may have been intent on killing President Ford or she may have only wanted to act theatrical to gain access to the media for her causes, however, it is most likely that she did not have the means to shoot him. There was no chambered bullet, and she was surprised to find that the gun failed to fire. For a

29. Sharon Scranage, "Spies." *The Economist*, July 20, 1985, p. 20.

woman with small hands, the Colt .45 is difficult to handle. A female terrorist who meant to succeed in her deed having small hands or other physical weakness would know that in action, the bullet should have been chambered, the safety latch released. Although some weapons are more difficult to use than others (even for males), a well-trained terrorist, as the Little Drummer Girl[30], Squeaky, Hearst and all others have been taught, will know the gun in every way. Both females and males need to practice with the weapon and be comfortable with it. The Colt .45 weighs over two and a half pounds unloaded, and it is difficult to carry, even more difficult to conceal. Fromme's case is worth a careful look on these facts alone. Other firearms in the terrorist arsenal, including the carbine and assault rifle, submachine gun, shotgun and machine gun are all heavy and hard to conceal. They are standard military equipment and many regular armies now have combat ready female units. These weapons are frequently as difficult for men as they are for women to handle. Yet, it has been reported that women guerillas carry these weapons and others successfully through jungle terrain, over mountain roads, and in adverse weather conditions. A determined woman, and there are many, will make light of the load. It is little comfort to those providing executive protection to know that these Annie Oakleys are numerous and increasing all the time.

The recent sentencing of Marion Monica Sprag[31] for bombing police stations and political party offices on behalf of the African National Congress in South Africa, might be the first for a white woman in that country, but women have been involved (black and white) in similar terroristic activities in a number of countries for quite some time. Not all women, like Ann Murphy, were unknowing victims of some male terrorist, able to plant a bomb in property in their possession. Women like those of Peru's Sendero Lumineso are now the rule rather than the exception. Many women quite voluntarily carry bombs under their clothing, pretending to be pregnant, or in baby carriages, grocery carts and book bags. Country and culture have little bearing upon the use of women in bombing incidents. It is more a question of operational utility. In April of 1983, Thye Sieu Heong[32] was executed with her husband for carrying nine hand grenades in Malaysia. It was the first time a woman had been executed for such a deed in this small country. In Beirut, teenaged women have been dying delivering car bombs. Whether they do it of their own free will has been an interesting question. That, in the nature of things, is not susceptible to any easy answer. Not only do women carry bombs, but they are quite adept at making them. We all have heard of the deaths of Cathy Wilkerson in the New York townhouse and Diane Oughton while they were making bombs. There have been advances since those days and many women are gainfully employed in this profession. Where women excel is as deliverers of deadly ordinance. Hence the need for security personnel to be especially alert on this account.

Women are involved with both gun running and gun dealing. Obviously, the drug

30. D. Galvin, "The unmasking of the President, 1975: The Girl who Almost Killed Ford Revisited," Denver, Colorado: ASA, 1983.
31. "South African Gets 25 Years in Bombings", *New York Times*, Nov. 7, 1986.
32. D. Galvin, op. cit. "Women Terrorists: Victims or Victimizers", 1985.

milieu has encouraged this development. In January of 1984, police had a gunfight with two males and a female in Bronx, New York, when they were attempting to apprehend them for selling weapons to terrorists. Some of the best weapon dealers in Europe have been reported to be women. Thus, not only are women capable of handling their weapons, they are also capable of dealing in them, a profession demanding knowledge of the wide range of available sources and types. Yet, there is still a continuing male arrogance about all this: women do not really understand weapons or how to use them. To the unbiased security professional, we simply say, you be the judge.

Negotiating with a Female Terrorist

Bargaining in any terroristic event, which by its nature permits it, is always difficult. Not every act of terrorism gives rise to a bargaining situation. Bargaining with a female terrorist changes the rules of the game by definition. The injection of the woman into the equation alters its dimension. Tactics will always vary from incident to incident. The negotiation process, in any on-going kidnapping or hostage-taking, is complicated. There are a number of variables which vary from case to case: among others, location, time, psychological background of victim and perpetrator, power positions of each party, individual weaknesses, fears, prejudices and flaws. All of these factors are important in the negotiation. Having a female with whom to negotiate introduces the added variables of the problems of female psychology into play: do women know "the rules of the game;" are women inherently weaker than men and even if it is only culturally assumed, do they have to react more aggressively to overcompensate; are they as cool as men; are they able to give in; are they dependant upon their male counterparts? The male negotiator frequently has not been trained specifically to deal with female kidnappers and hostage-takers, and if there are female negotiators, they too, may not have had proper training in this regard. Negotiation is a process for bringing about a meeting of the minds. How can minds meet if they have no common ground or no real understanding of how each mind in this interactive process works? Understanding requires deep and extended study of the female mind in general and that of the female terrorist in particular. Those to whom negotiating responsibilities are likely to be assigned should be carefully selected and adequately trained.

In any negotiation, hostage-takers or kidnappers need to be in a powerful position if they are going to succeed in their demands. There is an abiding impression that the female terrorist walks into any negotiation lacking power, by the mere fact of her sex. One speculation is that the female must then take on or assume an added toughness to overcome this initial lack of power. The Marian Coyle case has provided a classic material for study. Recently released from Irish prison for the joint hostage-taking of Dutch businessman, Tiede Herrema, she chose not to communicate in any way with her hostage throughout the ordeal. Her male counterpart, Eddie Gallagher, and Herrema on the other hand, quickly developed an ongoing, daily, almost comradely communication. Had she not become ill, the negotiations might not have been able to break through her hardened stance so as to prosper. Herrma might not be alive today to plead on behalf of the release of Gallagher. Gallagher was a hard man, his female accomplice stands out as a much harder woman.

There are evidently important psycho-sexual dimensions to the relationship between the male victim and the female terrorist. The woman is perceived by the male as "out of her milieu" in all of this. It is self-evident that this is the product of social preconceptions. That it is, necessarily, a kind of defensive mode for most men, especially those used to exercising authority is no less important if less easily recognized. Some men encountering the macho woman for the first time in these terrifying circumstances, uncritically conclude such female terrorists must be a bunch of lesbians. A scientific study of the sexual preferences of female terrorists has yet to be undertaken. But the observation itself says much for the preconceptions that pervade the thinking on these matters. The male victim's reaction to the female terrorist is all but fixed, sociologically and psychologically. The male has a blinkered approach to the dangers. The female terrorist, still seen as an anomaly, is cause for distrust and apprehension. She is seen as highly unpredictable and hence more dangerous, because she is a woman. The male is not used to being victimized by a female, whether in a terroristic event or otherwise. Or, at least, he's not used to admitting it until long after the event. His masculine role is doubly threatened, both by being victimized by the event and being held by a woman. To date, there have been no reported cases of male victim female hostage-taker/kidnapper generating anything analogous to the Stockholm Syndrome. Yet, logically, the possibilities are ever present, if the dynamics of the Stockholm Syndrome have been correctly understood. The male, in his need to survive, might very well turn to the female for some potential relationship other than that of hostage/victim in order to reduce cognitive dissonance and relieve the pending fear of death. Although the Stockholm Syndrome, as currently defined, is essentially male generated and a product of physical, male domination in a palpably life-threatening situation, bringing about unexpected changes of allegiances, it is clearly possible for the male to be subjugated in the hands of his female captor, so as to perceive in this relationship something essential for the purposes of survival. This is not something the male mind can readily accept. The male ego can be easily wounded if taken advantage of by the female terrorist. How readily a man can adjust to his misfortune is dependant to some degree upon the amount of involvement he had prior to the event with his victimizer. Adaptation to role reversal is never easy. If he has been taken in over a long period of time by a female (with or without an accomplice), he may never recover his former strength or authority: the trauma is devastating. This, along with his victimization, can readily alter his self-perception. He can easily become overwhelmed by self disgust. As with the female, the male ego is complex, and many factors are involved with each action and reaction. Simple formulae do not exist. However, with enough time, pressure and insecurity, the male does succumb to victimization. It is an old adage that only the strong survive, but in this case, it is a well worn adage. Some people are simply worn down more quickly than others.

What type of negotiator should be assigned to dealing with the female terrorist? Males might symbolize male chauvinism, an authority figure, one who might have to be overcome with greater force. Confrontation is to be avoided if negotiation is to produce a favorable outcome. On the other hand, he may just as likely represent a father figure, a person to be trusted, listened to with respect. The female negotiator might be seen as a threat or as a comrade. There are not hard and fast rules in this matter. Each case stands on its own and assignments based on an informed judgment of what is likely to prove most effective. The need to develop a rapport with the terrorist is important if the negotiation is to be successful. There are practical difficulties that must be considered. Depending upon the location of the hostage-taking, a female negotiator, trained to negotiate with a female hostage-taker might be hard to find. Further, in most larger cities where females have been included in negotiation training, the female is generally not given the real, on-the-job, practical experience needed in the event. Female negotiators are generally regarded as supplementary rather than as principals. Thus, more frequently than not, the male negotiator is chosen to end the stand-off, however the matter might proceed. More training in this area is needed, we need to understand better the dynamics of negotiation with the female terrorist and to train women negotiators generally, in the fine art of negotiation.

Discussion

The female terrorist is hardly a new phenomenon, nor is she one to ignore. She can be at least as dangerous as her male counterpart, she has been involved in all phases of terrorism, and her prominence in our times should come as no surprise, although it often does, to those who are in counter-terrorism positions. There is a frightening potential for improvement. There is little consolation for us in this, as we reflect that the next female assassin may be a lot more competent than "Squeaky" Fromme or indeed, John W. Hinckley. Product contamination proceeding out of the Tylenol scare that has been with us since the fall of 1982 and continues to plague us from time to time in a number of cities, lends itself especially well to the purposes of the female terrorist. The current and continuing spread of AIDS, threatening us like the plague, is an especially dangerous malady which can be deliberately spread through the female terrorist. Much of the information available on female terrorists has been distorted, hastily developed and out of focus. Many curious and unhelpful statements have been made about female terrorists due to the embarrassment they have caused law enforcement, private security officials and others. Many of these assumptions still remain clearly embedded in the literature. Along with these assumptions are the many analyses and projections which have not materialized, or at least not to date. Women were supposed to become involved in terrorism more intensively and extensively, their numbers were to increase exponentially, their degree of proficiency was to give rise to special problems of control and containment. In short, this was to be an epidemic. Although these predictions have yet to be fulfilled, although the Terror Decade did not bring forth more or as many women terrorists as men, the female terrorist is still a reality, one which should not be overlooked in any training program or operational procedures. Woman as terrorist is a formidable adversary who is here to stay. Understanding the female terrorist and being prepared for her is not academic. Before the end of this decade, there may be dramatic changes which will alter our entire perspective on terrorism in general and female involvement in it. While the new generation of female terrorists has yet to emerge, their progenitors are still very much involved in the game.

18

Terrorism in the United States

The reader might be tempted to question why a chapter on national terrorism should appear in a book dealing with executive protection. The answer is simple. Many businesses unknowingly hire persons who are members of various terrorist organizations. Inside information about targets becomes available to those terrorists and they can be on the lookout for suitable executives to kidnap or terrorize. In addition, they can become familiar with facilities and plant bombs without suspicion since they are employees.

International terrorists also pose a threat but there are many safeguards available. Accents and appearance are hard to hide. Documents can be checked and the mark of a stranger is easier to recognize. However, the national terrorist looks like the rest of us and with any charm can even be disarming. Thus, our own citizens can present an increased security risk with the potential for business loss and personal harm.

In the United States there are basically three types of terrorist organizations. The first is the nationalistic or separatist movement. For example, there are left wing and other groups which advocate the overthrow of the government with a preference for a Communist form of government.

A second type of group engages in terrorist actions designed to bring about government reform. They adopt the Communist Manifesto as a significant document to declare their hope for change. To this group, like so many others, change is brought about by revolution.

The third group operating in the United States is the far right extremist type which also seeks massive government reform. This type focuses on particular groups like Blacks, Jews, abortion clinics, Asiatics and other foreign groups.

Because we read so much in the newspapers about different national groups and because of the threat they pose, it is pertinent here to describe some of these organizations.

The FALN (Armed Forces of National Liberation), a group formed in 1974, specializing in bomb and other forms of sabotage. They operate in Puerto Rico, New York and Chicago. Membership numbers about 40 persons who have engaged in about 150 bombing operations. In 1980, 13 members were arrested and the group has declined since then.

The EPB (Machete Swingers) is based primarily in Puerto Rico and operates against military establishments and engages in bombings. It attacked a group of American sailors with gunfire a few years ago. As a result of several arrests in 1985, its power has dwindled.

Omega Seven, a group of exiled Cubans, are anti-Castro and chose as targets businessess favorable to the Castro government. Bombing is its favored method of action and the group operates in Florida. Because of several arrests in 1985, it has now become almost extinct.

The American Communist Party is one of the oldest terrorist organizations. It is structured into three groups. One, the Maoists, see Communists as an elite, imperialist group which trades with capitalists. They believe in violence and revolution and see all opposition as justifying assassination of the opposition. The Trotskyites is the second faction; see Communism as being international in scope. To them revolution must be immediate and at all costs. The Stalinites are the third faction and see Moscow as being the true center of Communism. Control of the movement rests in Moscow and they see terrorism and revolution as being the paths for change. For all factions in this political group, revolution is the agreed upon vehicle for change.

The United Freedom Front is a leftist organization. It has been involved in a dozen bombings plus some fund raising types of bank robberies from Connecticut to Virginia. They carry weapons, attack law enforcement personnel, killed a police officer in New Jersey and maintain a cache of automatic weapons and bombs as well.

Other left wing groups include the May 19 Communist Organization also known as the Armed Resistance, United Revolutionary Fighting Group and Red Guerrilla Resistance. It is a Marxist group with ties to the FALN. Some of their members come from the Weathermen and Black Liberation Army.

The New Afrikan Freedom Fighters, a New York group, has the goal of establishing a socialist republic in South Africa. In 1958, 8 members were arrested for bombing attempts against police officers. It was a ruse and diversion to liberate a "political prisoner", Nathaniel Burns. The New Afrikan People's Organization believes in the extablishment of a new socialist republic in New Afrika, but is non-violent.

According to the Republic For New Africa, in Alabama there should be a new and separate Black state. Other southern states would be acceptable to this group. Further, this highly political group feels and demands that every Black citizen of this country should be paid $10,000 as damages for slavery. This group is intellectually political at this time.

The Irish Republican Army operates in the United States under the title of the Provisional Irish Republican Army. It functions to collect funds and weapons for the IRA in Ireland. Many of its dual citizenship members have been arrested. Its activities of violence have been limited to collecting and exporting weapons to the battle zones in Ireland. Government police agencies keep a watchful eye on this group.

An anti-IRA group called the Ulster Volunteer Force sees the IRA and Catholicism as a danger to Protestantism in Ireland. None of its members have been arrested, but efforts have been made by them to purchase weapons.

The Jewish Defense League has existed since 1968, founded by a highly controversial Rabbi, Meir Kahane. He is met with disapproval in the United States and in Israel where he currently lives. His group is a militant one, whose purpose is to defend Jews against anti-Semitic acts by Arabs, Russians and other extremist groups. It has engaged in bombings of Russian business establishments and trains its members in California in a desert area with sophisticated automatic weapons. It is primarily pro-Israel, and acknowledged bombing the Metropolitan Opera House and Lincoln Center in New York in protest of the Russian National Ballet appearances. It has been suspected as being responsible for the bombing of a prominent Arab leader in Orange County, California, a few years ago.

[I have had contact with this group and have found its members to be clumsy, self-styled James Bond type characters. Their moves are obvious and in phone conversations they refer to themselves by their initials and refuse to identify their group. Many of their members, who have appeared at Jewish rallies of some kind, are boisterous, overly aggressive, use a soap box at any turn and are offensive. They train in violence, not security as it should be practiced. Their aims of protection of Jews is compromised by the lack of professionalism in their work and their acceptance of violence and headline making as the method for dealing with safety issues of Jews.]

Although Neo-Nazi groups will be discussed later, at this point they should be identified.

The New Order/National Socialist White People's Party was founded in 1958 by George Lincoln Rockwell, himself later assassinated. It embraces the teachings of Adolf Hitler and the German Nazi Party. It is racist against Blacks, Jews, other minorities and Catholics. It has pursued violent terrorist missions, has chapters all over the United States, especially through the southeast, middlewest and west. It has engaged in assassinations, smears and assaults against other similar right-wing extremist groups.

The National Socialist Liberation Front resides in Louisiana, and is one of the most violent of all Neo-Nazi groups. Karl Hand formed it in 1969. It advocates the violent overthrow of the United States government. It recruits members from prisons as prisoners have the skills and termperament to carry out acts of violence and terrorism. It has attacked other white supremacist groups.

A similar group is the National Socialist Movement led by Robert Brann in Cincinnati, Ohio. It advocates political terror and armed violence.

The National Socialist Party of America/American Nazi Party will be discussed as a key group.

The National State's Rights Party was founded in 1956 by Eugene Wilson in Georgia. It represents a mixture of the KKK and American Nazi Party. It has engaged in terrorist attacks against Blacks. It bombed the Bethel Baptist Church in Birmingham, Alabama in 1958 and again later in 1967 killed four black children when its bomb exploded.

In Westlake, Michigan, in 1979, the Security Services Action Group was formed. Leaders adopted Nazi names and play the role of special Gestapo members. They wear black uniforms similar to SS ones. Their demonstrations are heralded with much publicity and they operate in southern Michigan and Cleveland, Ohio.

In 1974, the National Socialist League was formed in San Diego, California. It is a homosexual, Neo-Nazi group. It blames Jews and Communists for the AIDS virus.

The Christian Identity Movement throughout the United States has been active and frequently successful. It is right-wing politically and rests on three major concepts: white supremacy, patriotism and survival, and Christian conservatism. They believe that Jesus cannot return to earth until God's law is established and this can be done only after the white race becomes predominant and powerful and a new government to replace the old is established by this movement. They view Jews as a race established as a consequence of Eve's seduction by Satan. To them all Blacks are derived from animals. They discount the Old Testament as being an Israeli book and vehemently deny that Jews are the Chosen People of God. They argue that minorities and Jews must be separated from the human race, that these targeted groups are decendants from space and are agents of Satan.

Members of this movement met in Hayden Lake, Idaho in 1982 and formulated a new constitution. It was filed with the county clerk and was entitled the Nehemiah Township Charter and Common Law Contract. It proclaims Jesus Christ as the Executive Officer of the new government and its avowed purpose is to protect the Christian faith.

It believes that Apocalypse is near at hand, will come from changing economics, societies and technologies. Associated with it is a total collapse of the world's agricultural system. Those who survive will grow their own food. They feel that Armageddon will result from nuclear war which will cause the government to fall. This appeals to survivalist groups. It could occur as a result of natural disasters as God's rage over Christians allowing Jews and minorities to flourish. Racial conflict is another route by which Armageddon may occur, they feel, and they actively support this direction. Finally, they feel that it could occur as a result of the spread of world Communism.

In a book significantly associated with this movement, The Turner Diaries, the movement accepts the book's format of survival by killing off police, non-Aryans and race criminals and advocates a nationwide campaign in which Jews are hanged along with Catholics, Blacks and other minority groups. They perceive police officers as being Jewish agents of Zionists. They try to provoke police officers by being deliberately disobediant and have killed several police officers.

The Aryan Nations, founded in the late 1970s at Hayden Lake, Idaho, by Richard Butler, is the largest right-wing Christian Movement group in the United States. It is white supremicist and anti-minority group in its philosophy. Membership can be acquired by killing any type of police officer. It stockpiles all kinds of dangerous weapons and explosives and recruits ex-felons. It assigns various points toward membership for assassinating valuable leaders, including the President of the United States. It advocates an establishment of a White homeland in Washington and other northwestern states, denounces the current government, protests currency and taxation and trains its members in urban guerilla warfare. It has bombed several facilities and passed counterfeit money. Utilities and sewage systems have been bombed along with bridges.

In the 1980s a faction broke off, the Order, later called the Silent Brotherhood. It has been known also as the White American Bastion, the Aryan Resistance Movements, the White American Army of National Liberation for the Aryan Nations and believe themselves to be "God's Army." It believes police officers are agents of Satan and need to be eliminated. It assembles lists of assassination targets in terms of political leaders, law enforcement, judicial and prosecutors and human rights leaders.

A faction of this group lives and survives in San Quentin Prison. It is called the Aryan Brotherhood. It has engaged in murder of minority prisoners and dedicates itself to violence against such groups as well as police officers.

The Christian Defense League founded in Louisana in 1977 is intensely anti-semitic and anti-Zionist and publishes articles about Jewish ritual murder, sex practices of Jews and other topics of distortion and hate.

In the same year in Illinois, the Christian Patriots Defense League was founded and cultivates survivalist activities and training programs. It has formed a private militia called the Citizens Emergency Defense System and a fund raising program called the Paul Revere Club. It publishes a self defense booklet called the Christian Patriots Defense League and passes them out to those who attend Freedom Festivals.

The Covenant, the Sword and the Arm of the Lord as a group was founded in 1970 in Arkansas. It has a 224 acre compound where they engage in training and weapons supplies. They are white supremacists who believe the chosen race of God is white. Hatred of Communists is intense. They deny Jews as being the chosen people but are anti-Christ and train Blacks to kill Whites. Its training programs run the full gamut of personal protection, martial arts and use and types of weapons. It provides protection at the Christian Patriots Defense League Freedom Festivals.

Police raids have uncovered caches of weapons, explosives and hoards of gold. The organization has engaged in a number of bombings, including a natural pipe line, a Jewish community center, a church for homosexuals and arson of a Jewish community center. They killed a state trooper.

In 1973 the Sheriff's Posse Comitatus began in Portland, Oregon. Its purpose was to protest taxation, elimination of the Federal Reserve System and the Federal Judicial System and to limit the power of law enforcement. It also professes and establishes hate programs against Jews, Blacks and federal officials.

Members of this group have assaulted and killed police officers, conduct armed training, establish weapons caches and many of their members declare they are ministers of the Life Science Church.

The Arizona Patriots hold the same views and purposes as the Posse Comitatus and urge the overthrow of the government in Arizona. They train and have made plans, some of which have been discovered, to bomb various government installations. Like the rest of these groups, they stockpile weapons and explosives.

The National Alliance is made up of ultra-conservatives who share the same old anti-Jewish and white supremacist views and publish pamphlets which espouse their beliefs and arguments.

Other groups are the White American Resistance from San Francisco, California, have planned assassinations and the Armed Resistance Movement which is a replay of other groups and is very opposed to Communists.

The Black Hebrews or Yahweh Church, is right-wing, believes that Whites are devils and that any one opposed to the church should be killed. They promote racial war and members of this group have been involved in murder, arson and various physical assaults.

These groups have some television programs, publish hate literature and have large memberships, like the Aryan Nations which boasts of having 2,000 - 3,000 members. Some, like the Christian Identity Movement, are using computers for networking and electronic message boards to get their messages out. The groups making up this movement share information, propaganda techniques, training, materials and finances.

Among outside groups functioning in the United States, Armenians have targeted and actually assassinated the Turkish Counsel General in Los Angeles and the Honorary Turkish Counsel General in Boston in 1982. Further incidents stopped with the arrest of the assassins. The Indian Sikhs planned two assassinations but were stopped by the FBI. i.e., Indira Ghandi while a visitor to the country and the Chief Minister of Indian State of Harya during a similar visit.

The pro-Kaddafi terrorists assassinated members of the anti-Kaddafi group and similar activites have been conducted against Iranians in this country. However, various PLO groups have not been involved in more than fund raising and some active recruitment of supporters at this time.

Since the 1960s, world attention has become increasingly focused on the explosive and dramatic happenings of transnational terrorism. Citizens and authorities in the United States feel a mounting concern about targets here: when will such groups direct their efforts against our country on its own soil? Certainly the American hostages taken in Iran brought the problem home and generated great fear and resentment about the take-over of an American Embassy by a foreign mob with approval by the host government. Most intelligence gathering in the United States concerns such groups and most security measures seem to accept the premise that such a group might strike.

Although possible menace might come from the transnational groups, the

American situation is a little like watching the back door as the criminals enter through the front door. That is to say, we expect a terrorist assault from persons of countries and groups from another shore. What we seem to ignore or fail to appreciate is the menace posed by the National terrorist groups described in the United States. As discussed earlier, among such groups are the Ku Klux Klan, the American Nazis as well as their ballooning variant groups. Let's take a look at the history of the two oldest groups. In my opinion, these groups have been picking up members and now pose a greater threat to the United States. No one aside from law enforcement and targeted groups, seems to take them seriously.

The Klu Klux Klan
The first Klan was formed as if it were a non-violent fraternity in a Tennessee town called Polaski, south of Nashville. A judge's son, Calvin Jones, Richard Reed, Captain John Lester, Frank McCord, Captain James Crowe, and Captain John Kennedy met. They had fought for the Confederacy, were unemployed, and bored. The Civil War had ended a short time earlier.

One night while sitting around an open fire they decided to form a mystic society. They developed ritual based on absurd rules and chose a name from a Greek word, *Kyklos*, meaning circle. They played with the word and stretched it to *Kuklux*. From this group name, it changed to Kuklux Klan. The leader was known as the Grand Cyclos and the vice president as the Grand Magi. The secretary was the Grand Scribe and the greeter of new candidates was called the Grand Turk. The two messengers were known as the Night Hawks and the two guards were called Lictors. The rank and file members were Ghouls and the meeting place was the Den. The den was located in the ruins of a storm-wrecked house on a hilltop. The Ghouls and others met in its basement.

The town buzzed with excitement as the lights were seen flickering on the hill. The setting lent itself to stories of ghosts inhabiting the ruins. As the members of the Kuklux Klan were delighted with the effect, they rode through the town one night wearing bedsheets. Everyone was excited except town Blacks, who were steeped in superstition and perceived the galloping ghosts as the Confederate dead. Because of this effect, frightening blacks in this manner with bedsheets became popular sport. In addition, some blacks would be met by a Ghoul at a well, where the Ghoul would drink water apparently unendingly. The water slipped into a rubber bag through a tube unseen by the Black. The drink would be followed with a statement, "I haven't had such a drink of water since the Battle of Shiloh!"

It should be apparent that through this hoaxing, "Klan Fun," there were only implied threats of violence. New chapters developed in other communities. Despite the presence of the Klan, peace prevailed through 1866 and into the spring of 1867. However, the development of this group did not go unnoticed by some old Confederate generals. They sensed the Kuklux Klan could form the base of a guerilla organization to fight the Carpetbaggers and others from the conquering North. This support of the Klan emerged during a time of great stress in the backlash of the Reconstruction of the South. Resentment mounted toward those in power: the Radical Republicans and Blacks. Hatred of those Southerners who cooperated with the North, the Scalawags, mounted. These enemies of the pre-war South enlisted Blacks into a society known as the Loyal League. Arms were issued to members and drills were held in public. Elaborate ceremonies were held by torchlight. This upsurge of Black power added more fuel to the flames of resentment toward all who sided with the conquerer.

In April 1867, George W. Gordon drafted a prescript or constitution for the Klan at a meeting in the Maxwell House in Nashville. The prescript read:

> "This is an institution of Chivalry, Humanity, Mercy, and Patriotism embodying in its genius and its principles all that is chivalric in conduct, noble in sentiment, generous in manhood, and patriotic in purpose..."

The men who attended this meeting were all respected, well-educated, and esteemed members of the community. There were no rednecks or roughnecks. In this way control of the Klan shifted from youthful pranksters to experienced men with ideas. The name changed from the Kuklux Klan to the Ku Klux Klan. The new group challenged the Loyal League with blazing guns and flogging of Blacks. Hooded riders rode through the night and the robes they wore disappeared into the night. All who opposed them were punished. Others in the South reacted to the Klan as if it battled for Justice, protected Southern womanhood, and was the last hope of the South. Thousands flocked to join the Klan. Other organizations existed separately, but worked in league with the Klan, which was more popular. Such groups were the Knights of the White Camelia, the Invisible Circle, the Pale Faces, and the White League.

The Klan became the Death Brigade, a group which killed by lynchings, murders, beatings, burnings and mutilations. By 1869 the original leaders of the Klan were sickened by its operations and General Forrest, one of the original leaders, ordered it disbanded, but the Klan persisted and grew.

In 1871 the Congress passed a law directed to limit the Klan. Penalties were provided for the types of crimes used to prevent citizens from voting. President Grant used Federal troops to bring Klan members to justice and many were imprisoned. The Klan began to fade in 1872 when Congress restored full rights to all ex-Confederates. A period of 40 years then passed without the Klan being more than a memory.

In Atlanta, in 1915 William J. Simmons, a self-styled "Colonel," decided it was time to revive the Klan. He rationalized its need on the basis of not only preserving Protestant supremacy in the South but also to fight the menace of foreigners, anarchists, Catholics, Jews and labor unions. The hooded white robes returned on December 4, 1915 when the Knights of the Ku Klux Klan, Inc. was chartered in the State of Georgia. A cross was burned on Stone Mountain and Simmons declared himself imperial Wizard of the Invisible Empire. He defined its direction as being a benevolent and charitable society.

By 1920 Blacks who had fought in France returned to their homes in the South and North and no longer wanted to tolerate being treated as inferiors. In this country then, there was political, social and economic upheaval. Youth was rejecting old moralities and crime surged and flourished because of Prohibition. Simmons' Klan offered an opportunity to defend against the changes occurring and threatened by the times. Within 15 months 90,000 members joined at $10 per person. Its size and violent activities brought the Klan once again to the attention of the Congress. This time, the Department of Justice developed prosecutorial interest in the organization as well. By 1922 President Harding received a call for help from the then Louisiana Governor, John M. Parker. The governor wanted help to break the stranglehold of the Klan on his state. He felt powerless otherwise to move against this "terrorist" organization because so many of his police officers were also members. J. Edger Hoover dispatched agents to Louisiana and murderers were arrested while others became undercover workers for the FBI. Despite this governmental action, however, the Knights of the Ku Klux Klan reached maximum strength by the mid-twenties: five million members. Millions of dollars poured into its treasury.

By the time the Depression hit this country, corruption and the need to turn to ways of basic survival brought the Klan to a state of collapse. Thereafter from time to time local Klan organizations and ones on a state level periodically appeared. Inner fights for control, power and money encouraged division within the organizational ranks. Klans disappeared and re-emerged under new names.

In 1961 the largest Klan organization was the United Klans of America. It was chartered in Georgia. Robert Shelton, former Grand Dragon for Alabama, became its Imperial Wizard. Since 1954 when the Civil Rights movement really began, the Klan grew because of renewed interest and angry resistance to the Supreme Court's landmark integration of schools decision. The Klan's battle cry became "Never."

Another movement at that time - McCarthyism - lent some support to the Klan from the standpoint of McCarthy's insistence that communists abounded in our government. With the help of the Rosenbergs, atomic secrets found their way to the Soviet Union. Thus the Klan organization built an appeal on the basis of patriotism and a fear of communism. Similarly, the Klan charged that giving rights and power to Blacks would only return the South to the terrible Reconstruction period.

By 1963 when Blacks were recruited to be registered to vote, the Klan came to life in Mississippi, a voting registration target state. The Klan moved against that organization which sought to register Blacks, the Council of Federated Organization (COFO). The Klan announced its return to political and terrorist action by burning crosses on the lawns of Blacks near Natchez. Members of the Klan felt the Civil Rights Movement was a "Jewish Communist Conspiracy," one operating from Washington, D.C. The Klan leader, Sam Bowers, had achieved some college education while serving in the Navy and this gave him rare credentials for this organization at this time in its history. In his circle within the Klan, Bowers was viewed as being an intellectual. He had money, easily quoted passages from the Bible, and had disconnected himself from an interest in women. As a loner with all these qualities, he was ideal as a leader. One story has it that he sewed a Nazi swastika on his arm and issued a "Heil, Hitler!" salute. He spread a story that Blacks were training in Cuba and Secretary of State McNamara would mobilize the state's National Guard and federalize them. Blacks would land on the shores of Mississippi and McNamara would use troops to evacuate white loyalists to the United States. Then Blacks would occupy the state. Despite its unbelievability, Klan members bit the story and accepted it on faith. The Mississippi Klan pulled out of the Louisiana Klan and formed its own White Knights of the Ku Klux Klan. Sam Bowers had become its leader when it was formed in 1973 and was elected Imperial Wizard. He recruited members from a beer joint across the street from the Masonite Plant near his home. He won recruits as he talked about the danger of Black men taking the jobs of white men. He talked of Blacks raping white women. A collision course began when COFO gathered together 30,000 students to register Black voters in their civil rights campaign that summer.

On April 4, 1963 a dozen crosses burned at various places in the country. On April 24, thousands of posters appeared.

Here are Twenty Reasons WHY you should, if qualified, join, aid and support the White Knights of the KU KLUX KLAN of Mississippi.

Because it is a Christian, fraternal and benevolent organization.

Because it is a very secret organization and no one will know that you are a member.

Because the goals of the KKK are the total segregation of the races and the total destruction of communism in all its forms.

Because the KKK has twice saved this nation from destruction as history clearly records.

Because there are today many alien forces entering the United States of America bent upon its destruction.

The list went on. And below the twenty reasons was a text that said in part:

The White Knights of the KU KLUX KLAN of Mississippi is, of necessity, a SECRET organization. The administration of our National government is now under the actual control of atheists who are Bolsheviks by nature. As dedicated agents of Satan, they are absolutely determined to destroy Christian Civilization and all Christians. We have nothing dishonorable to hide, but we must remain SECRET, for the protection of our lives and families.

... Our members are Christians who are anxious to preserve not only their souls for all Eternity, but who are MILITANTLY DETERMINED, God willing, to save their lives, and the life of this Nation, in order that their descendants shall enjoy the same, full, God-given blessings of True Liberty that we have been permitted to enjoy up to now.

We do not accept Jews, because they reject Christ, and through the machinations of their International Banking Cartel, are at the root-center of what we call "communism" today.

We do not accept Papists, because they bow to a Roman dictator, in direct violation of the First Commandment, and the True American Spirit of Responsible, Individual Liberty.

We do not accept Turks, Mongols, Tartars, Orientals, Negroes, nor any other person whose native background of culture is foreign to the Anglo-Saxon system of Government by responsible, FREE, Individual Citizens.

... The issue is clearly one of personal, physical, SELF-DEFENSE or DEATH for the American Anglo-Saxons. The Anglo-Saxons have no choice but to defend our Constitutional Republic by every means at their command because it is, LITERALLY, their Life. They will die without it.

If you are a Christian, American Anglo-Saxon who can understand the simple Truth of this Philosophy, you belong in the White Knights of the KU KLUX KLAN of Mississippi. We need your help right away. Get your Bible out and PRAY! You will hear from us."

On June 15, 1964 the Klan made the decision to get one of the leaders of the COFO who was coming to Mississippi to register black voters. They named him Goatee because of the beard he wore. His name was Mickey Schwerner. Tension in Mississippi mounted.

On a fateful evening in 1964, June 19th, Mickey found himself together with Andrew Goodman and James Chaney, a Black. They were traveling in the COFO station wagon on Highway 19 outside Meridian, Mississippi. Police stopped the car on some pretext, brought the occupants to the Madison County Jail where Klan sympathizer officers had arranged for their arrival. Deputy Cecil Price gleefully brought them into jail. After a short detention and small fine, the three were released and never seen alive again. Sheriff Lawrence Rainey, Prices's boss and colleague of hatred, was not available when COFO officials tried to locate their three members who had failed to appear at their appointed destination. On August 4th the bodies were found on property known as the "Old Jolly Place." On property which was a part of it, a dam construction site, the bodies were excavated at three different levels.

Eventually the killers of the Civil Rights' workers were found and tried. Their conviction brought success to the efforts of the FBI and other government agencies to challenge the Ku Klux Klan. Local and state police agencies had been weakened prior to this event because the Klan had infiltrated police positions and hamstrung investigative interest and efforts to contain the Klan. This case had become the stabilizing force in an otherwise explosive situation. It broke the Klan organization for some years.

Despite this long past landmark investigation and prosecution of the Ku Klux Klan, its message continues without interruption. It sees itself as fighting the last defense against communism. Its role, as the Klan defines it, is like a lone sentinel, a patriot engaged in an almost religious mission to destroy an enemy which had induced a conspiracy against the United States by the FBI, civil rights' leaders, Blacks, and Jews.

Over the past 10 years much of the power of the Klan has dissipated. Its aims are fed by anger toward its objects of political and terrorist action. Klan violence has taken a softer and more secretive quality. Hit-and-run sniping has been its style.

Another measure of continued Klan activity and its quest for membership expansion and power is the fact that it has continued in recruitment efforts. According to a report from the National Education Association, its members had undertaken action to combat a recruiting drive by the KKK to recruit school children into the Klan's hooded ranks. It claims that the Klan has approached children as young as 10 years of age for the KKK Youth Corps. It further claims that the Klan exploits racial tensions and targets such schools with recruitment fliers. One such flier read, "Are you fed up with the special privileges afforded blacks by school administration, simply on account of their race?" They stated that the Klan preaches hatred for immigrants, Jews, homosexuals, and non-whites.

The NEA pointed out that a group of Whites attacked a gay bar while wielding baseball bats in Oklahoma City, that a group of youths wearing Klan T-shirts set fire to a school bus during an anti-bus rally in Decatur, Alabama, and children have been taught hand-to-hand combat with racist ideology outside Houston, Texas.

In August, 1979 in Greensboro, North Carolina, some marching anti-Klan communists were fired upon by members of the Klan. Five were killed and others were wounded. Mutual gunfire was exchanged between both groups. Two of the Klan killers were Jerry Paul Smith and Coleman Pridmore and like others, were acquitted on the basis of self-defense, and received awards for their "steadfast defense of our constitutional rights" at an "Americanism Awards" banquet in Marietta, Georgia. *Klanwatch* noted and quoted, "Smith and Pridmore seemed to have interpreted the verdict as a 'green light' to continue their racist organizing." Both men have gone on to organize other hate efforts, one in a North Carolina town and the other in Albany, Oregon.

Since early 1981 Klan members have been riding on shrimp boats of militant American fishermen off the coast of Texas. They have combined to form a campaign of violence and intimidation against immigrant Vietnamese fishermen. With the aid of the Southern Poverty Law Center, a federal lawsuit was filed and an injunction against the Klan was obtained.

Klan activites have not been limited to the United States. Rightist white mercenaries from the Klan were recruited from the United States and Canada to join in an operation with black terrorists to take over the small, poor Caribbean island of Dominica. The ultimate plan was to establish a drug, banking, and gambling empire under a cooperative, left-of-center prime minister.

This plot was given away by a jailed Dominican army officer who wrote a note ultimately picked up by a disabled American Vietnam veteran who helped federal agents trap the invaders before they left Louisiana. Ten persons were involved, three face trial, and the money man behind the operation will be indicted soon. The invaders had automatic weapons, 10 pounds of dynamite, handguns, 5,246 rounds of ammunition, a Nazi flag, and a rubber raft. One of the operation's leaders, Michael Perdue, age 23, had been a Klan member since high school. He was the one who approached the disabled veteran who operated a 52-foot charter boat. Perdue told him he was with the CIA. The veteran was suspicious, called the State Department, and was referred to ATF which sent an undercover agent to work out an arrest plan.

In addition to the Klan members there were others with some Neo-Nazi connections and affiliations. Formal terrorist group sponsorship was not behind the invasion plot.

Despite periods of disinterest since its inception, the Ku Klux Klan currently has an estimated 11,000 members, a figure which has doubled since 1976. Within the Klan are splinter groups but the largest section is the Invisible Empire, Knights of the Ku Klux Klan. Under the leadership of its Imperial Wizard, Bill Wilkinson of Denham Springs, Louisiana, there is a network of training centers. One such center is a 47-acre spread in Jefferson County, Alabama. It is for training in ordnance and all kinds of weapons and tactics. Such efforts are designed to meet the anticipated racial war which Wilkinson felt would result when President Reagan removed all Blacks from the welfare rolls.

Other military training centers are located in Texas and Northern Alabama. The Klan is well-armed and well-funded and membership seems to be climbing. Aside from police agencies, which have been effectively monitoring this organization and assisting in its prosecution when crimes have been detected, one of the most effective methods of fighting it has come from the Southern Poverty Law Center which frequently takes the Klan to court for civil suits. It has long fought racism in the South and in the past 10 years has brought suits to integrate the all-white Alabama State Troopers, has defended Joann Little, integrated the Montgomery YMCA, represented many black prison inmates on death row who otherwise would have been electrocuted, and has produced Klanwatch which documents all Klan groups in the United States.

Klan violence shows in four ways: violence from non-members who are stimulated by Klan propaganda; Klan members acting independently; groups of members acting without express permission of their leaders, and those acting with permission or on orders of their Klan leaders.

Recent expressions of Klan-inspired violence can easily be seen. On February 11, 1979, 200 armed Klansmen mobbed a Decatur, Georgia supermarket as two Blacks were picketing it. A Confederate flag was wrapped around the head of one of them and the hat of the other was set on fire. Another Black citizen was knocked back inside his car and another was fired upon as he drove by. The only ones arrested were the two black pickets.

In Forsyth County, Georgia, Robert Neal Davis was convicted of aggravated assault and sentenced to 10 years in prison for attacking and shooting a young Black couple who were picnicking. This occurred in a county which had billboards reading, "Nigger - Don't Let the Sun Set on You in Forsyth County." The Klan in its publication, *Thunderbolt*, commented that if the county had not removed the sign, no Black would have been foolish to violate the time-honored tradition in that county.

The same *Klanwatch Intelligence Report* carrying the report about Forsyth County, Georgia, described Klan activities in Toronto, Canada. In April, 1981, the Klan members tore up signs for Liberal Party members, attacked Nigerian exchange students, and distributed hate literature in schools in Vancouver where there had been racial violence.

These types of incidents occur almost daily in some community across the United States and now in some sections of Canada. This is not 1865. It is the 1990s and the beat of the Klan goes on and can be heard with more frequent and louder thumps. Missing are the lynching and burnings. Present are the physical assaults and shootings. Present also is the domestic terrorism which this organization creates for the nation and community in which anti-social and anti-democratic demonstrations occur. It should be apparent that the Ku Klux Klan is not a local or purely Southern phenomenon. Proof of the expanded structure of the Klan is the fact that there are four major Klan factions. The largest is the Invisible Empire, Knights of Ku Klux Klan led by Bill Wilkinson which is based in Denham Springs, Loiusiana. Robert Shelton leads the United Klans of America in Tuscaloosa, Alabama. Don Black from Tuscumbia, Alabama leads the Knights of the Ku Klux Klan. James Venable in Decatur, Georgia leads the National Knights of the Ku Klux Klan. All have chapters in various communities throughout the United States and Canada.

The Klan is not limited to the North American continent. A recent Department of Defense consultant revealed that Klan activities have increased in virtually all Army, Air Force and Navy commands in Europe. Klan membership cards and on-post literature is appearing and 'cross burnings' are appearing on the walls of military buildings. With such a wide distribution of Klan efforts it should not be surprising that such efforts will spill or have spilled out from the military establishment to the European civilian setting.

It should be apparent that the Klan is still invasive and clandestine in its structure and aims. It is real terrorism of the 90s and beyond until it can be contained through education, litigation, and appropriate police monitoring and legislative action. With the armament purchased by Klan organizations, a real menace and danger confronts each police department as it strives to protect the various targets from this national and historically powerful terrorist organization.

The American Nazi Party

When the pounding boots of Nazis goose-stepping through Europe, and the noisy guns of Hitler's Army ceased at the end of the World War II, all persons who fought in that war or lost relatives breathed a sigh of relief that Hitler and his exterminators were dead. VE day in the United States and other countries was a carnival of affection, relief, and celebration that soldiers would return home. And the killing and genocide of Jews would stop. Additional hope seemed to materialize following the Nuremburg Trials with the full exposure of Hitler's atrocities at Auschwitz, Treblinka, Buchenwald, Dachau and the countless other concentration and extremination camps. Once the surviving Jews and other members of those camps began to fatten up and lose their ghost-like appearance, the pain of the war and what Hitler had wrought upon our civilization began to fade. For most of us, Hitler would be remembered only in history and those of us in the United States would never again have to face his menace.

In the 1950s, however, the ghost of Hitler appeared in the form of George Lincoln Rockwell who founded the American Nazi Movement. Among his early efforts he picketed the White House in 1958. He predicted his movement would place him in the White House in 1972. In 1967 he was shot to death by a disgruntled follower in an Arlington, Virginia parking lot. With his death, however, his declarations and shouts of "Send the Blacks back to Africa" and "Send Jews to the gas ovens" did not die. Although he never had more than 400 to 500 followers, he did have some financial support from wealthy anti-semitic contributors and followers. Despite this support, he and his band of drifters and ex-convicts were forced to subsist for periods of time on canned dog food.

Rockwell was not the average hate monger. He had been educated at Brown University, was a skilled cartoonist and propagandist, served as a pilot in two wars, and was a Lieutenant Commander in the Navy. He had failed in several businesses and marriage but was determined to be known and achieve some special meaning in his lifetime.

Following his death, a struggle for leadership of the movement occurred. A major in Rockwell's movement, Matt Koehl, became the "Fuhrer." He was from Milwaukee, Wisconsin, and had been a member of the National Renaissance Party, a Neo-Nazi splinter group. He was a friend of several Klansmen and joined Rockwell in 1962. In 1958 he had been co-founder of the National States' Rights Party.

Prior to assuming command he changed the name of the Nazi movement to the National Socialist White People's Party. By 1970 the party structure and organization fell apart because he was not the leader Rockwell was.

In 1973 he tried to blame Jews for the oil embargo by Arabs. Then these neo-Nazis began picketing the White House, foreign embassies, and synagogues. Organizational hate literature was distributed. His group invaded board of education meetings, defaced public buildings and school walls with hate slogans, and announced the opening of four party offices. These moves were good for a significant amount of media coverage and talk show invitations. However, as world sentiment favored Israel, by 1974 the Nazis once again faded from the limelight.

By June 1978, in addition to the Arlington main party, there were about another dozen Nazi groups. One splinter group called the National Socialist Party of America is led by Frank Collin of Chicago. It boasts having 15 to 20 uniformed troopers and has achieved considerable recognition. Collin has attempted to organize and unify the warring factions.

A university drop-out, he combs his hair like Hitler and wears a small moustache. His father was a Jewish survivor of Dachau, a fact he bitterly denies. His organization is now at odds with the National Socialist Congress.

His power was challenged by another college drop-out from Lincoln, Nebraska, Gerhard Lauck. The West Germans laid blame for some trouble with resurging Nazism to his effort and forbade him to enter Germany in 1974. He defied their ruling in 1976 and 1977 and has been arrested for his activities in Great Britain and Belgium.

Allen Lee Vincent from San Francisco, California, became another leader in the National Socialist White Workers' Party. He has banded together a group of six helmeted men wearing swastikas. This man has served 10 years for various crimes and has also been confined to a California state mental hospital for 11 months as a criminally insane patient.

In Reedy, West Virginia, German-born George Dietz is the leader of another group, the White Power Movement. He also operates Liberty Bell Publications, specializing in anti-semitic publications including a resurrection of the infamous "The Protocols of the Learned Elders of Zion." The latter instrument was produced by the secret police in Russia in the early 1800s, and had been published by Henry Ford in his Dearborn Independent newspaper in the 1920s and 30s. It has been used as the "factual" base for many well known anti-semitic hate mongers such as Gerald L. K. Smith and Father Coughlin. Dietz promotes literature which denies that 6,000,000 Jews perished under the reign of terror brought about by Hitler.

Bill Russell, a former American Nazi captain in Michigan, has formed a new Nazi splinter group, ROW (Rights of Whites). He has a ninth-grade education, is disabled because of a rat bite while employed at Chrysler Corporation in 1974, and has been diagnosed as suffering from a schizophrenic reaction, paranoid type. Before becoming a Nazi he joined the Communist Party. His membership is limited to a few members. He feels the American Nazi Party has lost the spirit of true National Socialism as propounded by Hitler but his hatred of Jews and Blacks is just as deep as it was when he was a captain in the American Nazi Party. He achieved some prominence in the Detroit area when the community protested his operation of a Nazi book store and the lease for his store was cancelled. More will be heard of this group as time passes. The leaders are keeping a tight lid on their activities at this time.

Running throughout all these groups are certain common threads. They have no substantial leaders, no programs, no philosophy except hate, and no factual base to their arguments. They do not address themselves to the real problems of blue collar workers and middle America, namely inflation, crime, unemployment, or taxes. They stage provocative situations and demonstrations such as parades, hate phone calls, racist and anti-semitic slogans and stickers, and paint messages on the walls of various public buildings and synagogues. Their themes are invariably the same, e.g., "Hitler was right!" and "Death to all Zionist Jews!"

Fortunately they have had little success since their inception in the middle 1950s. They still continue to gain recognition, however, through the media. Pictures of their demonstrations and parades appear in all newspapers and occasional national network interviews of these various leaders are seen. At times, their appearance is connected with violence.

I for one do not see this movement as benign. According to *U.S. News and World Report,* Nazi candidates have run for office in five states, received 16% of the vote in a Chicago City alderman race, received 55,000 votes in a Westland, Michigan council race, and have been actively recruiting in high schools, prisons, and among blue collar whites. They have held white supremacy meetings and rallies in New York, Los Angeles and Portland, Oregon. Violent confrontations with police at such rallies occurred in 1977 in St. Louis, San Jose, and Oakland, California. A major march in Skokie, Illinois, a heavy Jewish population area, was almost successful and was called off only as a result of a massive public protest and a court order. Swastikas have been painted on homes and businesses of Jews in Detroit, Memphis, and Chicago, and Stars of David, a symbol of Judaism, have been burned near synagogues. Both Jews and Blacks have received threatening phone calls from persons identifying themselves as Nazis and their hate literature can be found everywhere.

A prominent case involving a Nazi supporter, Fred Cowan, made headlines in New York in February, 1976. He had killed five persons and then himself. His home was searched and two Nazi flags, Nazi uniforms, and an arsenal of weapons were found. In his notebook was written, "Nothing is lower than Blacks and Jews, except the police who protect them.

Another supporter, a 17-year old boy wearing a swastika, committed suicide after firing 12 shots into a crowd of 200 Blacks at a Labor Day picnic in Charlotte, North Carolina. One person was killed and three others were wounded.

It is suspected that Nazi groups have a mailing list of 200,000 and an annual income of about $100,000. The activity of their movement seems to have arisen from several factors. Initially, there has been an upsurge of community interest in Hitler's life and the origin of his Nazi movement. The American Nazi movement exploits this basic historical interest. This was complemented by a former best seller, *Adolph Hitler*, by John Toland. This book was exploited by a New York publisher who also distributed the diary of Goebbels. Revisionist histories of what happened in World War II written by authors such as the British writer, David Irving, dispute the horrors of Hitler's war. Another, Arthur Butz of Northwestern University, questions whether Hitler was even aware of the extermination camps. A sellout movie was made and shown in Europe and the United States called, *Hitler: a Career*. An English language musical, "Rock Opera: Der Fuhrer," was created and paints a protrait of him as being an evil genius who offered his despairing people a faith and type of religion. Finally, Nazi era memorabilia have appeared in shops and gun shows and have been picked up by American Nazi groups and Klan members.

Thus far, a fairly clear picture of two hate groups should emerge. The Klan, a much older movement, has functioned by developing scapegoats such as Blacks, Jews, and now Vietnamese immigrants. Organized violence and hate literature have been directed against them. Rationalizations about the prospects of a war have been made and military training camps in order to prepare for that war, have been developed. Recruiting has been successful and the arms have been plentiful. Four groups have emerged and efforts to coordinate them have been undertaken.

The American Nazi movement has been more recent to the scene. The same basic terrorism structure and direction has been fashioned as the Klan and the organizing figurehead is the ghostly charisma of Adolph Hitler. In his death he has landed on the shores of his American enemy.

Naziism and the Ku Klux Klan
Either organization by itself is a matter of grave public and police concern in the United States. Although there has not been a successful merger because many American Nazis feel the Klan is too ultra-conservative, they have touched base in jointly-shared projects, marches, and printing of hate literature. The efforts of both groups release poison in the bloodstream of a patriotic and democratic society such as the United States. These groups encourage expressions of hatred toward other citizens and deeds of violence toward these same citizens. One does not have to wait for a large group massacre to sense the danger of these groups in terms of any single citizen having his rights compromised by either of these groups.

Apropos of the point concerning the possibility that national terrorist groups may cooperate in terms of publications, propaganda, and sharing weapons and destructive technology, this terrorist format has existed in Europe since 1968. Large numbers of weapons were stolen from Swiss military depots are stored in various "safe houses" in many other countries such as France, the Netherlands, Ireland, Turkey and Spain. This illustrates another reason why terrorism either national or transnational, must be viewed and dealt with seriously as various terrorist groups may use one another to accomplish their primary goal, mainly, destabilization of our democratic system.

In the March, 1981 issue of *Klanwatch: Intelligence Report* it was reported that in Toms River, New Jersey, Klansmen and a Neo-Nazi leader were indicted for shooting into the home of a Black family. It also reported an incident in Buffalo, New York where a Nazi-Klan celebration occurred to honor "a great White warrior" who was killing Black citizens. This celebration was designed to detract from a celebration of Martin Luther King's birthday.

In Michigan the Nazis and Klan joined with other similar groups such as the Minutemen to mobilize an effort to support the state's tax revolt. Robert Miles, former Klan Dragon, formed His People's Mountain Valley Congregation, a church in Cohatah Center, in Livingston County, Michigan, and his hate printing shop can be found in Howell, Michigan, in Livingston County, where a personnel carrier is parked in front of the shop building. This location is well known to both Klan and Nazi members. Their literature asks for public lynchings in the street and an enemies list of all federal officials and IRS agents who have talked or worked against these types of groups.

Control of National Terrorism Groups
It should be apparent from the examples cited throughout this chapter that vigorous law enforcement under existing legislation at the local level should do much to contain the range of activities and victimization which these groups produce. The work of the FBI in Mississippi to bring to justice those who killed the three young civil rights workers who had attempted to register black voters was a landmark piece of law enforcement. The convictions of those responsible for those crimes brought the Klan to its knees and afforded greater safety to those minority group citizens who

lived in Mississippi. Whenever law enforcement takes that important step to stop a criminal activity, safety follows.

It is also true that once terrorist groups are deprived of publicity, their efforts fail as their actions fall on deaf ears. In this connection, the press, media and entertainment fields have a contribution to make by depicting such terrorist efforts as unfair against people, as dangerous to the vested interests of a true democracy, and as the acts of disordered and frequently ridiculous leaders and followers. The criminal and psychiatric backgrounds of such persons should be placed in the forefront of stories about them.

In regard to the Klan, religious groups should question and attack its premises as being a Christian movement on moral grounds as well, and peaceful church groups have not spoken out with enough fervor about such groups. Unfortunately, the Jews themselves through the Anti-Defamation League, is one of the few such organizations. Yet here too is the voice of a minority group. Its efforts extend far beyond the interests of its own religious and ethnic minority group. It sponsors educational programs against such groups, gathers basic intelligence about them and supports litigation and stimulates legislation against them.

Most states and communities have enough local laws to control and prosecute violations by these groups. There is a need, however, for some federal and newer state laws to control some of the more awesome and potentially violent activites of these groups.

George Fleming, the only Black in the Washington state senate, introduced Senate Bill 3342, which provides that for malicious harrassment by violence or threat of violence, a felony would be committed when such harrassment is based upon color, race or religion. The bill establishes actual civil and punitive damages. It passed the Senate 47-0 and was sent on to the House Law and Justice Committee at the time of this writing.

The Anti-Defamation League has constructed a model bill. It aims to control efforts at paramilitary training for such hate groups. It calls for imprisonment and/or fines for persons convicted of operating paramilitary training camps or receiving training at such camps. According to Michigan Police Chief Newsletter, Connecticut became the first state to outlaw paramilitary camps. The law, which took effect October, 1982, follows the model of the Anti-Defamation League proposed control measure. It provides for penalties up to 10 years in prison and fines of $5,000. It is also a crime in Connecticut to teach, train, or take instruction in the use or manufacture of firearms, explosives, or fire-producing devices for the purposes of carrying out violent public disturbances.

In Georgia, State Senator Julian Bond introduced a bill which would make it illegal to teach the use of firearms, explosives or other devices, and techniques which could cause injury or death to another person from assembling for such training. Violation of this law would be a felony with a fine up to $5,000 or imprisonment up to a year. It passed the Senate 54-1 and was sent to the House Subcommittee.

State Senator Diane E. Watson introduced California Senate Bill 266 which outlaws meetings for the purpose of committing or advocating violence. Civil procedure to provide civil injunctions for such meetings are also provided in the bill. The bill also prohibits cross burning or defacing facilities by using terrorist signs and symbols. Violators would be punished with fines up to $5,000 or imprisonment up to a year for first offenders. Fines up to $15,000 could be rendered against subsequent offenders. The bill awaited a hearing in the Senate Judiciary Committee.

Steps seem to be needed at the federal level as well. Although I am not an attorney and am certainly not an expert in any sense on constitutional law, it seems to me that the Bill of Rights did not have terrorist organizations in mind when it provided for freedom to assemble. Furthermore when such groups as those discussed in detail in this chapter meet to formulate and plan for violence against citizens of various minority groups, they are violating their rights, especially when such plans are carried out and innocent persons are kidnapped, killed, harrassed, beaten and forced to move or give up their rights to vote or earn a livelihood. It seems to me that federal legislation to control such organizations in all states would not invade the important sanctuary of states rights.

The United States and Terrorism
The arrival of different peoples from different countries and cultures has served as an influence in this country to support the notion of separateness and difference among our citizens. In a position way this has helped foster a sense of separation and uniqueness and has laid a firmer foundation for the very essence of freedom in a truly great democracy. Having visited five Eastern European and Soviet-dominated countries, I feel more convinced that such uniqueness and separateness is sweeter and helps us as a nation savor our humanism and political democracy.

Along with our freedom we have our problems. Some feel that freedom is license to practice any faith or philosophy and others feel it is freedom to maintain whatever control is necessary over the lives and interests of those who blend into the background of the front sights of a rifle or who occupy a building which has been wired with explosives. Agreement on just what freedom and civil rights mean and entitle all Americans to has been debated since it was placed into our Constitution in 1776.

Along with the freedom debates and laws, terrorism and organized violent protest groups have always existed in this country. Certainly the Boston Tea Party and the Minutemen and Paul Revere and all of those who supported the American Revolution helped that type of image. They were considered freedom fighters and heroes rather than terrorists. Those who have developed violent protest groups and causes since then have been considered either outlaws or terrorists. The Klan and Nazis are examples but have not been the only such movements. In more contemporary history the SLA, Weathermen and Black Muslims represent other examples. There were groups of terrorists throughout the Country's history.

In 1767 the Regulators, a vigilante type of organization, rode through the hills of

South Carolina to maintain its own law and order. Other similar vigilante groups formed all over the United States and the Bald Knobbers in the Missouri Ozarks were violent in purging from their Christian country all of the gamblers, thieves, and prostitutes. In 1887, the governor called out the state militia to quell them.

Following the Civil War, such groups flourished and employed the rifle as an instrument of random terror and justice. The term "dry gulching" comes from this period and refers to ambush, a technique of military strategy which was employed.

The most long-lived and prominent of such groups was the Ku Klux Klan. It liked to employ hanging like the German Fehme group but changed tactics in the 1960s when the group confederated on a national scale, as noted.

Like the modern Klan, Robert Bolivar DePuch, who formed the Minutemen in 1960, advocated use of the high-powered rifle and scope to deal with traitors. The rifle as a still ever-present instrument of settling a score with traitors or the "enemy" of such groups was endorsed by an American Nazi group called the Nationalist Socialist White People's Party. It offered the FN Model 1949 semi-automatic rifle as a preferred weapon for that purpose.

Truly revolutionary groups in this country adopted the philosophy of Carlos Marighella, the famous Brazilian, who went beyond the revolutionary rhetoric and battle plans of Regis Debray, Che Guevara, Mao, Trotsky and Lenin. Marighella felt that terrorism was the key for starting a revolution.

Modern day groups employed bombing, kidnapping, and sniping. Many groups, especially the Black Panther Party led by Eldridge Cleaver, and the Black Liberation Army, were responsible for 138 terrorist incidents in 1972; 77 in 1973, and 86 in 1974. In 1972, under such a philosophy, 14 police officers were killed and 44 were wounded. From 1969 to 1973 there were more than 50 such ambushes against police, a figure which was quadrupled for the period from 1962 to 1966. These assaults were unprovoked.

In 1968 the Black Panthers published a credo for rioters and looters:

> America, you will be cleansed by fire, by blood, by death. We who perform your ablution must step up our burning — bigger and better fires, one flame for all America, an all-American flame; we must step up our looting — loot until we storm your last hoarding place, till we tramp your last stolen jewel into your ashes beneath our naked black feet; we must step up our sniping — until the last pig is dead, shot to death with his own gun and the bullet in his guts that he had meaant for the people. . . .

Of no lesser importance in the United States has been the most destroyed minority group, the American Indian. Unquestionably as a target of genocide, official and subtle, the American Indian stands out as a truly sad and tragic blemish in American history. In keeping with the spirit of the times in the mid 1960s and 70s, the dissident Indian groups also took up the rifle and terrorist banners. Six armed Indians seized the Bureau of Indian Affairs Law Enforcement Center on the Red Lake Indian Reservation in northern Minnesota. Forty-five vehicles and six buildings were destroyed and a media news helicopter was shot at and forced to land. Such militant protests, exploding after centuries of resentment toward Washington and government in general, brought home their bitter feelings and created fear in all government officials who tried to mediate a peaceful solution.

Some Current National Terrorist Activity
As has been discussed, paramilitary groups seem to be forming throughout the United States. The ones mentioned base their rationale for being upon hatred for others, for the good of either racial or religious Christian purity.

Other groups have been forming and are arming and becoming involved in paramilitary training. For example, the Christian Patriots Defense League trains for battle in rural Illinois. The Brown Berets, a Chicago group, charges the enemy, utters a battle cry, and achieves firearms proficency in the Southwest. The Posse Comitatus, a virtually unknown group, trains in Wisconsin and the Hare Krishna trains in California. Most of these groups unite through striving for religious purity against a threatening enemy, one fantasied to be out to destroy true Christian Evangelical identity and unity. For other such groups the second issue seems to unite members against communism. For example, the Christian-Patriots Defense League gathered in Flora, Illinois in 1981 to offer instruction to Whites about racial problems and solutions, combat medicine, demolition and camouflage, street action, knife fighting, guard dog training, aircraft usage, and anti-tank and anti-aircraft techniques. This league is mobilized against Communists. Underneath it all, however, they are really talking about immigrants whom they actually categorize as non-whites along with Blacks.

This latter organization makes it pitch for members in the following way:

> WANTED: Patriotic men and women, especially veterans, who see the decline and possible collapse of our social, political, economic and military structure to help staff, operate and train others for survival at scores of emergency gathering points made available by Patriots throughout the United States for this specific purpose. For details contact the CHRISTIAN-PATRIOTS DEFENSE LEAGUE or CITIZENS EMERGENCY DEFENSE SYSTEM, Box 565E, Flora, Il 62839, or call (618) 665-3937, day or night. (46)

I believe it would be a serious mistake to limit any judgment about the seriousness of such groups to whether they have armed themselves or sought military training of location. Some organizations appear to be heading in that direction even if they are not actually there yet, according to what group watches have been able to observe.

For example, Chick Publications of Chino, California, has been publishing a blatantly anti-Catholic 32-page comic book which passes off as truth the unsupported claims of an alleged agent of the Jesuits that the Vatican has incarcerated Protestants in concentration camps. At a meeting of the 1981 Christian Booksellers Association in Anaheim, California, Jack Chick, when introducing the speaker of such distortions, Alberto Rivera, said, "There's very few with the courage to stand up, because if Rome pulls this off, we'll all be in concentration camps." In that dimly lit room, Rivera offered an amazing dialogue and set of charges that nuns and monks carry machine guns, and that such persons as officers of the Church were responsible for the assassination of President Abraham Lincoln. When questioned about his charges, he would defensively shout, "You are not a Christian! You are not a Christian!"

In a parallel manner, other Christian groups seem to be spreading the same type of distortion and hate material. For example, Daniel Fore, Moral Majority leader from New York, claimed that Jews have a God-given "ability to make money" and "control the media." Furthermore, he said later that the Inquisition was run "by Catholics, not Christians." Jack Chick, through his anti-Catholic comic book, claimed that the Vatican has a computer with all the names of Protestants so that they can be rounded up for a future Inquisition. Dr. McEvoy was quoted in the same article as stating that the religous right, with other extremist groups, has given a green light to anti-Semitic vandalism and violence, a form of discriminatory behavior which has increased tenfold in the last 18 months (1980-81).

In El Cajon, California, there is a radio station, KMJC (King, Master, Jesus Christ). A listener called the program in response to a request from Michigan Evangelist, Rosalind Mussleman, to pray that the Pope would not heal from his assassin's bullets. The caller, Cliff Kirby, a worshipper at St. John of the Cross Church in Lemon Grove, California, claimed that Rosalind Mussleman said that the shooting of the Pope was the work of the devil to bring about sympathy and support for a religious leader who is really anti-Christ.

Another caller to that program spoke of the Catholic Church as being "a harlot, a fallen women, a prostitute, the whore of Babylon." Embellishing his charges, he stated that the Roman Catholic Church was plotting to deprive evangelical Christians of their religious freedom and that the Jesuits were trying to take over a coming one-world government.

Mussleman has been dropped from that radio station but another rightist religious hater, R. Kenton Beshore, persists in his anti-Catholic preachings.

People such as those two use a strange interpretation of the Apocalypse, Chapters 12, 13, and 17. In Chapter 12 the symbol of a dragon (Satan) is used. It turned over its authority to the beast with seven heads (seven hills of Rome) and 10 horns (individual governmental). Following their connection of these passages with the Roman Catholic Church is the passage which refers to a fatal wound to one of the heads of the seven-headed beast. These rightists use this as a reference symbol to infer symbolic meaning to the wounded Pope.

As stated earlier, such "Christian" type groups appear innocuous at this point. There are no known arms caches among them. In my opinion, however, they bear watching, close watching. They all follow a typical paranoid type of thinking. Those who oppose the concepts of the movement are viewed as sources of special evil—the enemy, sources of inquisitions and demonic possession by the devil who directs their breathing and activities. In these groups the Master Race concept of the Nazis World War II has been replaced by the Moral Majority or spiritually "clean" type of evangelical Christian.

If we can assume that this is their style of thinking, it cannot either be far away that some substantial effort will be made to install a paramilitary super-structure to the set types of right wing religious groups. When or if that happens, the people and courts will have their hands full because churches have been exempt from taxation and close public scrutiny. The only close-up view has come by police infiltration and former members exposing actions of the movement or group.

Within such paramilitary and religiously right wing groups are the seeds of national terrorism. Let no one mistake the reality that any moral crusade can be as bloody as the historical crusades which killed in the name of God.

So long as we hold to the right to bear arms, assemble, and engage in free speech, we will have a thriving democracy. We will also have such groups who use the protection of the law to recruit others to share in their campaigns of hatred and harrassment of other citizens in this country.

Ultimately such problems must be anticipated in a true democracy. All have a right to be heard. That is part and parcel of the American way. However, when such groups abuse our Bill of Rights and Constitution and turn to terrorism as a means of achieving power, ridding themselves of enemies and compromising the rights of others, local and national law enforcement agencies and legislators must recognize the problem and establish law and order through constitutionally approved means. Police agencies and legislators alike must take a realistic view of the history and potential of such groups. Intelligence information must be gathered and shared. Such responsible persons must also prepare for the possibility of armed confrontation. The one fact which supports that truth is that since this country began, and especially in the period of modern-day revolutionary activity in this country since 1960, the list of dead innocent citizens has grown longer.

I take them seriously, devote much of my time in an effort to study their activities and warn others of them. I feel that continued survival in this country requires appropriate vigil to safeguard the freedom which such groups so consistently attack.

19

Hostage-Takers

The frightening and bizarre practice of hostage-taking has become a major, menacing way to achieve a goal. All police departments, political offices and state departments recognize the danger and importance of this problem which generates fear and news coverage. The crisis is charged with emotion for all participants and management of the situation by police becomes a matter for public view.

Although a special police unit does not have to be formed, each department must take the time to understand the problem, develop a policy, and assign personnel to develop contingency plans for such an event.

Psychological insight into the hostage-holder is essential. All police personnel must be aware of the nature of the problem and some personnel must know the theory and practice of tactics for dealing with it.

Basically, there are four types of hostage-takers: the robber, the emotionally disturbed person; the unorganized group and the terrorist. [1,2,3]

This chapter will focus primarily on terrorist hostage-taking, as well as some aspects of non-terrorist hostage-taking.

The robber is usually armed and, as his primary mission, sets out to rob some type of business, wealthy person, or home. During the course of his robbery either a silent alarm is activated or an unseen witness notifies the police, who arrive at the crime scene before the robber can safely exit. He panics, grabs one or more of the people present, and makes demands for safe passage and escape or the hostages will be killed.

Usually, the robber hostage-taker is the easiest person with whom to negotiate. Its a safe bet that he has been in contact with police before and knows something about how the criminal justice system operates. Basically he does not want more trouble than he has. He wants out, not more trouble. He does not want to be beaten or shot. Initially, he will make demands for safe escape but in the back of his mind, he knows it's futile. Rather, he wants a promise of non-violence for himself.

He knows that if he surrenders rather than being stormed by a police assault, it will be better for him in court because he will have the image of being cooperative; this

---

1. Mullin, W.C.: *Terrorist Organizations in the United States*. Springfield, Illinois: Charles Thomas, Publisher, 1988.
2. Bolz, F.A.: *How to be a Hostage and Live*. Secaucus, New Jersey: Lyle Stuart, Inc., 1987.
3. Maher, G.F.: *Hostage: A Police Approach to a Contemporary Crisis*. Springfield, Illinois: Charles Thomas, Publisher, 1977.

can be pointed out to him during the negotiations period. By the same token, he needs to know that surrender is his only choice, and that he stands to gain clemency by not adding more crimes to his growing list of offenses.

Some police departments negotiate to drop some of the charges which might otherwise be pressed, such as kidnapping, but keep the rest of the charges, such as armed robbery, felonious assault, etc.

The mentally disturbed hostage-taker is another matter. If he uses hostages to force a wife or girlfriend into a decision not to leave him, the problem may be less complicated. Sometimes that woman can help in calming him down so that he will release the hostages. At times, the hostages are his own children or family members. This can go good or bad. Usually it is safe to assume the hostage-taker has feelings of love for the hostages, but, unfortunately, this is not always true. Imagine as a hostage a mother-in-law whom the hostage-taker has felt played a role in breaking up his marriage. At this time of stress, it may be hard to count on him feeling love for her.

These hostage-takers might have multiple personalities, each with different behavior from the others, even including dialogue and handwriting, and each with no memory of the actions of the others. They complain of physical symptoms such as headaches, numbness, and weakness, and also exhibit behavior which may involve drug abuse, suicidal behavior, (especially wrist cutting), stormy interpersonal relationships and even hallucinations and delusions. One of the personalities is both conscious of what is going on and remembers the events despite a general anmesia most of the other personalities may have.

Surprisingly, although usually there are no more than 3 to 4 distinct personalities, as many as 17 to 22 have been reported. I have treated one woman with 16! Sometimes they express themselves as men and women in terms of personality. Each may dress with distinctively different clothes, hair colors and styles, and walks. Most multiple personalities are women but men can be easily found among such psychological oddities. They may even appear to be of different ages from one another. Among men many will be diagnosed as sociopathic personality and wind up in prison when other personalities go undetected. Homicidal behavior is not at all uncommon.

More commonly, according to Mullin, the mentally disturbed hostage-taker is seriously disturbed and may be a paranoid schizophrenic, manic-depressive, (now known as Bipolar Disorder, mixed type.) The latter type suffers from either a Passive Aggressive Personality, Dependent Personality Disorder or a Histrionic Personality Disorder. Finally, the anti-social personality is very common in the criminal and terrorist groups. He enjoys the power over a hostage. The dependent personality hostage-taker suffers from lowered self esteem, feels inadequate and chooses hostage-taking to achieve a sense of power. He may savor the opportunity to try and possess someone who to him may be a fantasied or real love object who wishes to break ties with him.

In the light of these problems it should not be difficult to imagine how hard it could be in negotiating with such persons for the release of hostages. Use of a psychiatric consultant is essential.

Emotionally disturbed hostage-takers present a difficult problem to the police because they may be irrational and delusional about a plot being hatched against them by some foreign power or mystical agent. Internal voices might be giving them orders to take hostages and kill them, like Abraham was ordered by the Lord to kill his son, Isaac, to prove his loyalty to God. When this type of situation occurs, a consultant psychiatrist is essential.

Let's take an example of psychotic behavioral problems. This one does not involve a hostage-taker, but rather a barricaded woman armed with a 410 ga. shotgun. Police had been called to serve commitment papers filed by her family through probate court. She had been hallucinating, hearing voices which told her to do simple things such as bathing, eating, shopping and dressing. She developed the delusion that people were out to harm her. In November, 1979, she purchased a shotgun. In December, her pet bird died. In mid-May, 1980, she lost her job and began to deteriorate under the pressure. When the officers attempted to pick her up, serve the commitment papers and bring her to the local hospital, she fired her shotgun at them. A three-day siege occurred before the Detroit police used Iron Mikes to fish her out and get her to the hospital.

Before that happened, I was called to help. I arrived at the scene with my body armor and obtained some psychiatric information from the family. I read the commitment papers. From the intelligence information I obtained, I knew that trying to talk with her as a psychiatrist would be futile and inflammatory as she had reacted this way because she felt threatened about going to a psychiatric unit from the beginning.

I decided to adopt the role of a veterinarian because I knew her bird had meant much to her. She also had a cat, Tigie, in the apartment with her. I talked through the night, left and returned and established myself once again in the stairwell talking to her about the things which meant the most to her. This did not work because she was in a mute state. Eventually, forced entry was necessary.

Under the heading of emotionally disturbed hostage-taker, there may be angry ones who want to redress some wrong from an employer, a boss, or company which had turned down a loan application or committed some offense against the hostage-taker. Their motivation is to publicize their grievance, not harm the hostages. Usually, they can be dealt with swiftly by a promise from the boss or company to offer special attention and help correct the problem.

The third type of hostage-taker is the unorganized group which might be involved in a riot and takes some hostages. This situation is different from a terrorist group, as there is no formal leader. This may be seen in prison or a protest rally where some people explode and take a correctional officer, staff or innocent bystander. If this occurs in jail or prison, action must be prompt and some concessions might be granted, but not escape. Usually officials of the institution handle the negotiations, not the police. This type of hostage-holding is easier to deal with than that of the terrorist group.

[Kobetz[4] classifies a fifth category of offender. This is the skyjacker. He fits into a separate category because it is an action involving a particular setting and group of hostages. Such hostage-takers could involve criminals planning an escape or extortion, more commonly terrorists, and, of course, the mentally disturbed type.]

The primary or high priority type of hostage-taker is the terrorist. [5,6,7] He carries such importance because his self-denied image is that of a solider in a war against society or the established power structure. He is prepared to die or kill because he sees this as a patriotic action. His plan has been well worked out, his leader is dedicated and determined not to compromise very much, and his mission is the bring about an over-response from the power structure of government. He or she is prepared to accept the risk of being killed, hurt, or imprisoned. He hopes that citizen sympathizers will be stimulated to join the movement or support it in some way. This form of hostage-taking differs from the first two because it is not impulsive, has been well thought out and rehearsed and the use of hostages was planned right from the start.

As of this writing, there are more than 2,500 transnational terrorist organizations in the world with a membership of thousands of persons. They are known as Bureaucratic Terrorist Organizations, or BTO. They employ experts, weapons, utilize recruitment, have special documents, and maintain an active training program. They may start as a form of rebellion and end with some type of legal-like negotiation and settlement. They have excellent sources of funding and keep going by kidnapping for ransom and committing armed robberies. They develop special secret ties with respected government leaders. They exact loyalty to the point of death for those who leave the membership or wish to do so. They use the life of a hostage as a wedge to wring out some form of political concession from the government and to accomplish this, they dehumanize the victim so that he is expendable property, not a person.

Why does the terrorist movement succeed? The BTOs employ fear, force, intimidation, and an assertion of power which makes terrorism in itself its own authority. [5,6,7] It is always extra-legal and is not bothered with such important social concerns as civil or constitutional rights. The action of such groups is always purposeful, fear being a part of the broader purpose. Terrorism is used to resolve a political power conflict. It employs assassination, kidnapping, and hostage-taking.

From 1975 to 1977, hostage-taking was popular; from 1977 to 1978, kidnapping was used, and in 1979, it was assassination. Now all three are popular, but bombing is the favored method of assassination.

The hostage is used to bargain in the confrontation between hostage-taker and those in authority or political power. He may be used as a shield in aiding an escape

4. Kobetz, R.W.: *Hostage Incidents: The New Police Priority.* Gaithersburg, MD: Internal Association of Chiefs of Police, May, 1975, pp. 32-35.

5. Sterling, C.: *The Terror Network.* New York: Holt. Rinenart & Winston/Readers Digest Press, 1981.

6. Kobetz, R.W. & Cooper, H.H.A.: *Target Terrorism.* Gaithersburg, MD, 1978.

7. Elliott, J.D. & Gibson, L.K. (Eds): *Contemporary Terrorism: Selected Readings.* Gaithersburg, MD: International Association of Chiefs of Police, 1978.

effort. By way of contrast, a kidnapper does not take a victim as a shield. The kidnapper knows the victim has value to others but he usually does not want to kill that shield because his only aim was money. The terrorist has little concern about the victim, wants money, and also wants power in terms of obtaining political benefits or concessions.

In dealing with terrorists, you must determine who they are, what they want, what they will take, and what is the government prepared to give them. Their structure, political base or ideology, membership size, kind of support, use of men and women, and weapons are also important facets of field information to obtain.

The Terrorists

Most are men, but as time passes, women seem to be playing a more prominent role. In some groups, women hide weapons and documents, serve as couriers, spot targets, and provide cover for men. However, women organized and supervised the Baader-Neinhof group and Symbionese Liberation Army. They played front line roles in the PLO and other Arab groups, in the Bolivian group, and in the Weathermen in this country.

Those in their early twenties were seen in the Uruguayan Tupamaros and are now in the Spanish Basques, among the former Iranian groups, Turkish, and Northern Ireland groups. Persons in their late twenties were found in the Japanese Red Brigade, the PLO, Black September, and German Baader-Meinhof groups. However, teens were found in great numbers among the Spanish Basques. Younger members are found in the Italian terrorist groups also; their leaders are between 30 to 35 years old.

Most terrorists are unmarried, making them difficult to track down. For example, although he was not a terrorist, Adolph Eichmann was trailed by Israeli agents through his wife. Being single allows a terrorist greater flexibility, security, and opportunity for total dedication to the terrorist cause. The only notable exception among terrorist groups is the Tupamaros, where 30 percent are married.

Most terrorists come from and reside in urban centers. Cities offer better hiding places and fewer people who get to know their neighbors. Most universities are located in urban centers and that is where so many terrorists and terrorist leaders are recruited. Many from rural areas attend urban universities and are then recruited, or live in urban centers away from their country and return to the urban setting for revolutionary activites. More targets are available in urban centers, i.e., government buildings, public utilities, and opposition political leaders. The notable exceptions to the urban dweller are the PLO and Spanish Basques.

Generally terrorists come from middle to upper class families. Their parents are often professionals in law, medicine, government service, engineering, and even the military. Such parents are often liberals and frequently advocate significant social change to promote a new social structure. A special exception here are members of the IRA.

Among American terrorist groups, some members seem to have backgrounds with criminal records. This was seen among members of the SLA and BLA who were easy to trace because there were fingerprint material and probation reports with much intelligence information about them. Such groups combined anarchist theory with revolutionary activism, and members feel impotent in terms of social power until defiance can be expressed through the terrorist group. More political and better organized groups would not permit persons with a criminal record or ones with a need to steal to become active members because such persons are too easily traced by police. In American groups the terrorists may profess racial supremacy and try to make the government sound like it's controlled by Blacks, Jews or minorities.

In general, about two-thirds of such group members have some university training. Among the Basques, it is about 40 percent and among South American groups it is 75 percent. Few intellectuals are found among the IRA.

Groups may commit acts of terrorism as a justification of their religious beliefs, as do the Shites.

Their political philosophy is usually a mixture of anarchism, Marxism, Leninism, and some form of nationalism. Most reject what they consider to be the passive outlook of Communism and favor the violent form of revolution promoted by Carlos Marighella.

Guess when this profile of a terrorist was written:

> The revolutionary is a doomed man who has no feelings, no interests, no property, no name, no relationships only revolution. He has broken ties with civil order. He rejects all science except destructive technology to further revolution. He despises all public opinion and romanticism. He has a hardened attitude toward himself and others. He can only accept another tested revolutionary. He has no sentimentality. He is dedicated.

It was written by Sergey Niechaev in 1869.

From a psychological point of view, the terrorist as a person is action-oriented, politically motivated, cannot channel his emotions, and tends to stick to one reality — he puts all his eggs in one basket. He is introspective, keeps searching within for answers, is moody, egocentric, or is only self-directed. He tends to be exhibition-istic about his forms of protest, and seems to have a need to be a martyr. He is capable of forming a blind and fierce faith in and loyalty to his terrorist leader.

Rand Corporation has observed that terrorists seem to be satisfied by a life style involving both a 'cause' and a dangerous, adventuresome type of life. They enjoy freedom from all of the usual routines. Their life is nomadic and they have contact with all kinds of groups in all different kinds of places. Jail does not matter much to them. As members of a group they stick by one another. They enjoy not being a member of the establishment with the usual goals of education, marriage, family and a job. Instant action is what they want as they feel that the usual channels for bringing about social change are not effective or available. They enjoy lots of money which comes from bank robberies or similar sources of financing. They view others as being foreign to their ways and this may be the result of having been raised in a narrow social situation, one which did not provide for contact with others from a different life or culture.

Rand has also found that terrorists are an insensitive group. On the one hand they perceive the proverty, sufferings and injustice to others but are insensitive to the suffering they have produced, e.g., homicide of hostages like Moro, destruction of property, frightening hostages and their families. Their emotions may range from elation or a real high of happiness to the depths of despair. Planting bombs and planning on taking hostages may be exhilerating but once away from adventure as a terrorist, they may feel empty, miserable and very much alone. They may commit acts of terrorism to acquire weapons or money.

The leader is usually older and charismatic—he is a magnetic leader and is almost hypnotic in terms of drawing followers. He trains them to speak in a commanding voice and crush anyone who offers resistance or opposition.

Terrorists, in my judgment, suffer from a "Baby Snooks" snydrome. They play the role of the mean little kid who is manipulative, confrontive, and provocative, who attempts to cause the forces of authority to react with an over-response or over-kill. In this way, even though death is a decided risk, they live as martyrs and cause an erosion of popular support for the government which over-reacts. Such persons settle for living through history and in the media, rather than searching for a more ordinary way of achieving recognition.

Despite any emotional instability they may show, and regardless of their demands and threats, their use of fear and force, they rarely ever double cross the authorities or kill when their demands are met.

Psychological Profile of the Terrorist
Mullin points out that the terrorist, generally, is well-educated, has received state of the art training, is goal oriented, capable of great fanaticism, and is dedicated to success. Some have a history of being an outsider and all too many have been shunned or humiliated by peers. This leads to lowered self esteem and social isolation. Some have a negative self-image and I feel that, especially in the case of the typical member of the Christian Identity Movement groups, there is a projection of that inner sense of worthlessness to minority, ethnic and religious groups which these terrorists consider unimportant.

Thus, the terrorist group offers a social connection, an opportunity for self esteem, a chance to take revenge on a rejecting society and peer acceptance among others with similar backgrounds and emotional needs.

Successful missions and operations offer confidence, approval and improved self esteem. These terrorists feel they are a part of some important movement and have basic social worth. They feel they are contributing to the group and are heroes of a sort, even prepared to lay down their lives. Their misperception of reality is reinforced by the group to which they belong and there is no one present except law enforcement to question their view of and action toward the society in which they live.

Many, especially members of the right-wing groups, define themselves as the elite. They see their morality as superior and their mission divine. Compromise is a gray area they are unable to see. Their thinking is simplistic, goal directed and morally right.

The leadership and group itself exploits idealism. Such idealists carry out dangerous missions like collecting intelligence, criminal acts and even dying for the cause.

Through dehumanization the terrorist removes the human factor from those he kills or hurts and depersonalizes them to assuage guilt for his action. To him and the group the enemy are undesirables who contaminate society and the government against which they protest. Thus, through these psychological defenses, they can distance themselves from the reality of their unfair and destructive behavior.

Dangerous rationalizations occur. Victims are not assassinated, they are executed after trial. This was clearly seen as the rationale for executing Colonel Higgins by the Hezbollah group. To them and in their propaganda, Higgins was an American spy using the United Nations observer assignment as a cover. Kidnapping is not kidnapping, according to terrorists, the enemy is being held in a people's prison for crimes against the people.

The Terrorist Leader

This person is key to the group as he has confidence, excellent self esteem, often is battle experienced for the cause, and, as was stated earlier, is a charismatic leader. This leadership tries to recruit those who psychologically are looking for leadership from another. Through such followings he gets them to do his bidding. He konws how to manage and manipulate others.

Personality qualities this leader possesses often involve a paranoid suspicion, finding it both easy and convenient to blame others and feeling that those who oppose him are his enemies. He may exploit a religious or political doctrine to support his cause as seen especially in the right-wing groups in the United States as well as in the Middle East Shiite groups. When followers accept this view of the world and enough form a group, the terrorist body becomes a dangerous collection of irrational people.

The leader views past ideologies as flawed and sees that his mission, according to Mullin, is to improve and correct these errors. His followers maintain loyalty to him as he promises significant and sweeping changes, to overthrow the government, and thus adding more recruits. Ideas rather than concrete change are considered the only important reality and morale is preserved by only promising change. This was a technique employed effectively by Jim Jones in developing loyal followers. He avoids being pinned down by lamenting, "This is not the time for change." He promises to extricate all from the old ways and the past through overthrow of the government. He sells his followers a personal type of salvation, a form of greatness and harmony unknown to them in their lifetime.

Complementing his charismatic profile is his need to make himself into a messianic figure. Being and feeling worshipped is important and this is accomplished when planned actions come off successfully. These actions enhance his image and the confidence of his followers.

Being and acting in an amoral, "mother is the necessity of invention," the "end justifies the means," manner makes anything possible, even mistreating and killing innocent victims. It feeds his megalomanical need to feel omnipotent and in control of life and death.

Basic dependency of the group members makes it possible for the leader to exploit them and keep them close at hand as they need to be nurtured. They obtain such emotional support through their leaders and fellow terrorists.

Seizing this opportunity to achieve power and purpose, the leader rules with an iron hand, makes decisions, and his judgment is not to be challenged for he will not tolerate departures from his wisdom or decisions. Functionally, he becomes a god-like figure. This power base gives rise to fanaticism on his part and brings about self-confidence and a megalomanical sense of his own importance and greatness. He feels infallible and invincible. This quality can be seen in examples from all areas of world history, e.g., Castro, Lenin, Jim Jones, George Lincoln Rockwell, Hitler, Stalin, Mao, Ayatollah Khomeini, Charles Manson, and a host of others.

Psychological Aspects of Hostage Negotiation

In my experience as a hostage negotiator with the Wayne County Sheriffs Department, in Detroit, Michigan, and other police agencies in that area, I have found hostage negotiation to involve certain process phases.

Basically, there are three psychological phases associated with hostage negotiation.

In the first phase, there is *confusion*. The hostage-takers make demands and the negotiators make counter-demands. At times, tempers flare on both sides. The hostage-takers are flushed with victory. If they are terrorists, they have trained, rehearsed, and executed a successful plan. Their morale is good and opposite to the morale of the police, who are still struggling to organized themselves, especially if the terrorist act occurs in a community unprepared for such an event.

The next phase is *negotiation:* the terms of a deal are hammered out after patient listening by police. If the act has transnational involvement, the State Department may have to make the final decision about acceptable terms and what decisions can be made. Other federal agencies will be involved if the act has national implications or involves a federal agency or national facility, such as a nuclear energy station.

The final phase is *resolution:* the hostage-takers surrender. If not, a decision is made about forceful intervention. If that occurs, the hostage-takers are either arrested or killed. The wounded are treated medically and the participants are debriefed.

How the Negotiator Can Handle His Role

The negotiator's behavior and efforts must be goal-directed. A goal may be selected, reached, and replaced by another goal. Most of these goals are short-term and steps in a long process which leads to a successful conclusion.

The negotiator's primary concern should be to work toward keeping the hostages alive.[8] He should bargain for an extended deadline. Food resources for the hostages and hostage-takers must be developed. He should strive to keep the hostage-takers on the phone for longer periods of time. Self-esteem of the negotiator and hostage-taker must be preserved if possible, as they are striking for a deal; the hostage-taker has the cards and must not be made to feel powerless. Powerlessness may cause the terrorists to resort to force or killing a hostage to prove power or esteem if the negotiator is challenging, threatening, or provocative.

The negotiator must strive to reduce the hostage-taker's anxiety. He can work toward keeping outside noise down by having police equipment and units approach the area quietly. He should talk in a low voice. The decisions should be clear and brief. His back-up should be limited to one other person so that the hostage-takers should not have to start over with each new negotiator. Any relationships the hostage-takers have with significant others, besides fellow terrorists, should be preserved and kept open, e.g., family members who might be used to reason with them, but not inflame them further.

The negotiator must not joke with the hostage-taker or try to humiliate him. One-up-manship is definitely tabu. At all times he must be respectful and cannot be thin-skinned so that anger or putdowns from the hostage-taker affect him. The most urgent thing to do is wait and try to buy more and more time. Not giving up something unless the hostage-taker does, too, is an important rule to follow. Avoiding phoney promises is absolutely essential because most hostage-takers, especially terrorists, will keep theirs. Ultimatums and time limits should not be made. The basic aim should be to achieve agreement and stall for time until that agreement occurs.

The negotiator needs to strive for a deal with as much intelligence information as possible. [8,9] He needs to know as much about the terrorist group, or the mentally disturbed person, or criminal, as possible. Some of this basic information he will have to listen for, and he should ask specific questions to bring out those facts. He should ask for an identification of the group or person. That information should be checked out by the police department or some intelligence gathering service. He should notice the quality of the hostage-taker's voice, his determination in regard to demands of the police or government, and how coherent or sensible his demands and thinking are. Notice if the hostage-taker sounds as though he feels others are plotting against him; if he sounds mentally ill, the negotiator should ask if voices threatening him or giving orders or directions have been heard. "Yes" answers would support the view that the hostage-taker might be suffering from a mental illness or schizophrenic condition.

The negotiator can ask about the health of the hostages, whether any have pain,

8. Maher, G.F.: *Hostage: A Police Approach to Contemporary Crisis*. Springfield, Illinois, 1977.
9. Crelinsten, R.D. & Szabo, D.: *Hostage-Taking*. Lexington.

or heart conditions, or are diabetic. He can have the hostage-taker ask hostages about these problems, or if any older hostages are having chest pains or if the younger women are pregnant. If the hostage-taker responds to requests for such information, it means he cares about people and might be less inclined to harm them, certainly not so easily or in cold blood.

Terrorists frequently demand to talk to the chief of the police department or some high government official. The negotiator must make it clear that there is no one else to whom the terrorists can talk. Just as the terrorist is the spokesman for his group, the same role has been assigned to the negotiator for his group or government. He can admit to his police identity but not his rank or full name.

The negotiator should be sincere, patient, and interested in being a good listener. This must be demonstrated, not merely stated by saying, "I'm a good listener." Along with interest in the hostage-holder, the negotiator should try to find out about any relatives who might be called to the scene and ask questions designed to bring out information concerning their relationship. Obviously, a relative who has been inflammatory and provocative does not belong at the scene.

The negotiator should use the same type of language as the hostage-taker. Obviously he may not be able to match an accent or a foreign language and an interpreter may be necessary as a supplementary resource or as a negotiator himself if he is a police officer. Along with using a similar vocabulary, the negotiator should be matched as to age and race, when possible. If the age gap is too great, the hostage-taker might see the negotiator as a parental figure and this might aggravate the situation and encourage unconscious rebellion against parental authority.

If the hostage-taker is on drugs, the negotiator must exercise greater patience, speak quietly, and wait. This approach helps the hostage-taker to remain calm until the drug wears off. Sometimes hostage-takers take an upper such as speed or amphetamines to stay awake to prevent being captured while asleep. If one takes too much, he may become paranoid, demanding, and be more belligerent than would otherwise be the case. Certainly, the negotiator should ask about drugs and whether the hostage-taker has been using them. If the answer is yes, he should find out what kind of drugs so that a medical consultant can offer advice about management.

The negotiator cannot promise release of the hostage-holder, at least in most police jurisdictions in the United States. The department which the negotiator works must also clarify and specify the limits against which he has to make decisions. Certainly, it is also traditionally held that no weapons be made available to the hostage-taker. The public needs to know that offenders will be held responsible and their criminality will not be encouraged by supplying them with weapons or by releasing them.

There are times when the negotiator can attempt some techniques of applying a squeeze on the hostage-takers. Such a squeeze has to be subtle and not in the form of open defiance.

For example, if they respond as though they are flushed with victory and are unified, and demand food, the negotiator can assure them food is on the way after taking orders but, before the food arrives, warn the hostage-takers that it was not possible to obtain eight sandwiches for the eight hostage-takers. Instead, the officer dispatched to get food didn't have enough money for eight. Perhaps the restaurant was too far away so that when he came back, the food was cold and the negotiator wanted to pass the information along so the hostage-takers would be prepared.

Such a technique accomplishes several things. It puts a dent in their feeling of victory and power. It can also cause some arguments among them about how to divide the food. Nothing fosters insecurity more than cold food, no lights, no water, and no heat. This lets the terrorists who sees himself as a soldier know he is in the foxhole!

The negotiator can handle terrorist complaints by saying that the department was caught by surprise, is not budgeted for such emergencies, and is doing the best it can until the Council or Board of Commissioners can appropriate enough money. He can point out that the police have to buy their food out of their own pockets. In the meantime, the negotiator is skillfully building frustration into the negotiation process and the hostage-holders feel the discomfort they will have to experience in order to move toward serious bargaining.

Qualifications and Training of the Negotiator
Maher[8] discusses the qualifications of a good negotiator. He must be a street-wise cop who feels comfortable talking with people. He must be more cerebral or brain-power oriented than body-action oriented, and thick-skinned enough to handle barbs, insults, and negative attitudes. He must be comfortable listening, saying "no" when reasonable and appropriate, and must also be able to question departmental decisions when their application is inappropriate. This assignment should be for volunteers only.

His only instruments are microphones or phones and, if the area is isolated, he might have to use a prep radio. He must know in advance what the departmental policy is about giving the hostage-takers a car. He needs to be informed about any intelligence information received by police or field investigators about the hostage-takers or hostages themselves.

He must be a good communicator and should prepare himself by taking courses which will enhance skills such as casework interviewing, taught in various schools of social work or psychology.

In addition, I have found it very useful to work with local actors playing the roles of the three basic types of hostage-takers and practice over the phone from room to room. Such calls should be taped and replayed for critique by the negotiator and the actors as well.

Various characteristics of hostage-takers have been discussed. What is known about terrorists is brought into focus by contrasting them with the criminal and emotionally disturbed types. Such information is vital for the negotiator to work out a deal with the hostage-takers. The negotiator must have special skills and understanding of his job because what he does and agrees to do can very materially affect the lives of his officers, the lives of the hostages, and even the hostage-takers themselves. He has to play for time, but reasonably, and make decisions which are in keeping with government and departmental policy.

Do's and Don't's of Hostage Negotiation
Carefully screen those who drop in with offers, with claims of expertise or of being a close friend or relative of the hostage-taker. Such people show up on every hostage-taking mission and seem to be motivated to help rather than in search of some reward.

If the hostage-taker wants to engage the negotiator in sharing a bottle (alcohol), it can sometimes be helpful. In general, the negotiator needs a clear head; I would therefore advise against drinking alcohol.

Usually, a hostage-taker undergoes a ceremony or ritual which is a pre-surrender behavior. He may want to fix himself up a bit, shower, shave, eat a sandwich, count money, and change clothes. All of this usually indicates that the negotiation has been successful. However, if the hostage-taker starts giving away presents to the hostages or others, beware. This very well might represent a pre-suicide ritual. Many suicidal persons give away personal property before they take their lives.

If the hostage-taker is taking methadone, the negotiator can give him some to keep him calm, providing a doctor is available for a medical assessment of the hostage-taker, even by phone. However, regarding heroin or other street drugs, a wiser policy would be to turn down such a request as being non-negotiable.

Some negotiators advise touching hands with the hostage-taker when surrender occurs, rather than slapping on handcuffs immediately. That is reassuring and represents human contact, but it may be risky. Some offenders are distant from others because of a tight "body buffer zone." (This zone is like air space would be to a country). They permit people to establish physical contact just so far. The negotiator must be sure he does not overwhelm the hostage-taker with more closeness than the offender can tolerate. It might otherwise cause some panic and bring about a retreat from surrender.

Some negotiators practice thought diversion or interruption by changing the subject and asking about the weather or some ball game or athletic event. The risk confronting the negotiator is that he might mistime the interruption when the hostage-taker is moving toward a decision to surrender. Also, if the hostage-taker is psychotic or schizophrenic, such a diversion might cause more panic and disorganization. A consultant psychiatrist could be helpful here.

As much intelligence material and information as possible should be gathered by police investigators and officers. Members of the family, co-workers and supervisors, as well as children should be consulted to assemble a profile for use by the negotiator.

If an alarm has been tripped off, it might be useful to permit it to continue ringing, as it might keep the hostage-takers off guard, especially when mentally ill or purely criminal hostage-takers are involved. On the other hand, this would not be useful when working with political or radical hostage-takers because they are too well disciplined to be bothered by an alarm.

If the hostage-taker is publicity prone, the negotiator can suggest surrender in time to make the next edition of the paper or television news. If the hostage-taker relies on a value system or political base for his actions, don't challenge him on theoretical or political grounds. Assure him you can accept the fact that his political beliefs are important to him.

Don't be afraid to engage the hostage-taker in small talk. It buys time (which helps keep the hostages alive), takes the rough edges off a frightened and upset hostage-taker, and builds a relationship of trust between the two parties.

Some humor can relieve pressure for all parties. On the other hand, it might be mistimed and irritate the hostage-taker, who may have no sense of humor; this is absolutely true of most politically motivated or terrorist hostage-takers. The latter persons take their work seriously.

Once the hostages are released, don't be afraid to let out some of your feelings. Who would not be grateful and relieved when everybody comes out alive? Not uncommonly, cops will cry when the tension eases. This is normal and helpful, providing it does not occur during the active negotiations. If crying does occur at the wrong time, the negotiator must be removed. If he starts to feel sorry for the hostage-takers, his unconscious feelings (called transference) might well cloud his judgment. The negotiator must remember he must perform a police function and not join the hostage-taker emotionally any more than he would side with any offender, and thus avoid performing his duty.

Let the hostage-taker talk himself out. Small talk may help. Letting him talk about how he acquired a gun for this crime is also important. Don't try to structure the interview or swing the dialogue to questions about the hostage-taking setting. He will know you are reaching for information in preparation for an assault. That option is inappropriate if negotiation is active or impossible.

If there is enough personnel, the negotiator should not participate in the arrest or read the Miranda warnings. Publicized court appearances may harm future negotiation efforts. Future hostage-takers might read of a negotiators court testimony and may want to shy away from making a deal which might be used against him in court.

Occasionally a member of the clergy can be allowed to talk with a hostage-taker for a brief time, especially if he knows the offender. On the other hand, if the hostage-taker seems to want final absolution in preparation for suicide, his presence should either be prohibited or he should be removed once that signal is given by the hostage-taker.

The negotiator must understand that no two cases are the same. He must also understand that a seemingly small detail might well lead to a resolution of the hostage siege, for example, sending in food or cigarettes or promising a chance to talk to an attorney to witness the surrender and details.

Snipers on the roof using Star scopes or some type of night-time illuminator must exercise care to cover up with a coat or blanket so that iridescent rays are not given off to alert the hostage-takers, who might otherwise see them through a window in the dark.

The negotiator must employ cool, subdued authority. He must never beg the hostage-taker to cooperate or release hostages. He must be credible when he assures the hostage-taker that he will not be shot or hurt if he surrenders. The hostage-taker is frightened of being hurt or killed and needs lots of reassurance.

Members of the media can help the negotiator by assuring a hostage-taker that he will not be harmed. This can be done over radio and television. However, if reporters or photographers start sneaking up to grab an interview or picture for purposes of sensationalism, they must be removed since they are not qualified for the role of negotiator.

If a show of force is going to be used, it should be done early and quickly, before the hostage-takers, especially in a jail or prison, can form groups.

Never permit a third party to be a negotiator. This refers to some champion of a cause like an attorney or militant leader. Their presence might be more inflammatory than helpful. This was seen with Kunstler and Bobby Seale at Attica.

Usually a hostage-taker can be taken at his word if he assures that he will not hurt anyone. This doesn't apply to the hostages but rather to contact with a negotiator or neutral person.

If a hostage-taker can be lulled into a false sense of security so that a hostage might be pulled out, so much the better. This can work when there are few hostages, and they can be grabbed when they are sent out for food or on some other errand.

The negotiator should be empowered to negotiate. His mission is solely to work for the release of the hostages. Conditions and demands or concessions should be transmitted from the hostage-taker to the government official in charge and then back again. If a governor or mayor is called in, the authority of the negotiator is displaced and his value will be destroyed.

In the background, the officials supervising the operation and making the ultimate decisions have a heavy responsibility in regard to what happens if the hostage-takers start killing their hostages. Most persons agree that the hostage-takers must be assaulted then and either killed or taken by force. It may mean that some hostages will also have to be injured or even killed. This cloud always hangs over the scene of a hostage-taking.

The success of a police operation in managing a hostage-taking incident depends upon many different policemen who take important roles, as well as the negotiator. Important to such success are the officers who keep the crowd away, the officer who fields questions from the press, keeps them posted, and also helps secure them in a safe area, away from the primary operation site. The special equipment squad, paramedics, and SWAT group all have specific roles and are under pressure until the emergency is over.

The traditional military intervention model approach is only one part of the management technique. The psychological approach of specialists such as the negotiator and operation supervisor are more valuable than ever. Furthermore, the need to share such information with other police agencies and within the same department when debriefing everyone connected with the operation facilitates working toward a more professional and effective method of management of the hostage-taker.

Summary and Conclusions
The hostage-taker, regardless of the classification he falls into, is a criminal who places the lives of innocent people in jeopardy. The executive and/or his family may become an unwitting victim of that same drama. Each type of hostage-taker rationalizes and justifies his mission, his actions and his purpose. He seeks affiliation with others of the same background and political persuasion, if he is a terrorist hostage-taker.

Regardless of type, all must be stopped and all must be negotiated with for the safe release of hostages. The people and the methods were discussed in this chapter.

Certainly the police and military are by no means the only ones who may be brought into the negotiation arena.

Executives are important to their companies and corporations. Security staff of those businesses need to appreciate what is involved in hostage-taking and negotiation. Knowledge of issues and aspects of this problem will reduce the period of confusion which appears early in the process of negotiations.

20

Survival from Hostage-Taking

We now come to the most fearful and upsetting part of threats against the executive, his staff and his family. This section deals with what to do if taken hostage. Basic survival from this type of danger is probably what you had in mind, when you picked up this book. If nothing else captures your attention, we hope that this chapter will serve as a practical guideline to survival from these types of experiences.

At this point, let us assume you have been taken hostage or have been kidnapped. It is not necessary to deal with the how this happened at this stage. We'll assume the following: a small group has picked you up at gunpoint, taken you completely by surprise, shoved you into a car or some type of vehicle, placed you in handcuffs or other restraints, covered you with an old blanket, and instructed you to lay still or you will be killed.

Your initial reaction will be disbelief. You'll think, "This can't be happening to me. Who are they? Why me? What is really happening? What will happen to me?" And, probably, "Why was I so stupid? My security man warned me about looking before I walked out the door. He told me his crew had spotted suspicious looking people standing around the front of my building. My God! What will my wife think? I didn't even discuss those threats our company had been receiving. Will I ever see my family again?" In the course of all these terrifying thoughts, the car is speeding through alleys, changing directions, and finally stopping so you can be transferred to another vehicle. No one says anything. No names have been mentioned and no reason for your abduction has been given.

Your mind is racing, filled with fears and recriminations for not having been more careful and interested in your own security. You're sweating, you have a terrible headache, your heart is pounding, and you suddenly become afraid that you might have a heart attack. "God! If I only had a cigarette, I could think more quickly. If I had only gone to the john before I left the building. I hope I don't wet my pants."

In your mind you find yourself reviewing the immediate circumstances preceding your abduction. You keep looking for those details you had not concentrated upon which might have served as a warning of impending danger. As you review those details you keep fighting a deepening sense of humiliation about your misconception of and indifference to security.

You feel like a smoker who has been ignoring the cancer scare ads only to be told you now have cancer. "OK Harry, don't believe them. Light up another just to show them they're wrong."

Nothing is said to you for about an hour. Then "OK, get out quickly. Do as we say or you will die!" They seem not the least bit concerned that you are in handcuffs and cannot leap out from underneath the blanket. They care not that you feel and act as if you are disoriented and can't seem to discover where your legs are or to command them to move. Your wrists are killing you as the cuffs are too tight and your hands are numb. The blindfold has been placed askew so that one corner of the cloth is cutting into your right upper eyelid. Nothing feels good. Nothing is right. For some crazy reason, you think, "This is no way to treat an executive. No staff would treat me this way. They help me with my coat and hold the door open for me until I'm ready to leave. My God! What's happening to me?"

Half dragged, pushed and stumbling, you climb some stairs, bump into a door-frame, and are propelled up some more stairs. Strange odors greet your nose. You're not sure they come from cooking or mustiness. Someone grabs you from behind and plunks you down on a chair. Another set of hands ties your cuffed arms behind you around the back of the chair. All is still. You hear some whispering. Familiar sounds are missing, like traffic noises, voices of passers-by, dogs barking, and horns honking. You feel like you've somehow climbed up into a cemetery, your own. You think, "Will anyone know? Will anyone care? Will anyone rescue me? What's it like to die? If I die, will anyone ever know what happened? What do they want of me? Im not a violent guy. I don't even watch violent television programs or read horror stories in the newspapers. At my most violent I swing a golf club or tennis racket. It makes no sense that this should be happening to me."

This scenario has not been made up. This is a scene based upon what hostages and kidnap victims have reported. It could happen to you.

During the initial phase of the hostage situation one will experience great insecurity, threat of bodily harm and even to life, and throughout may well feel a great loss of self-esteem. He may try to deny all the aspects of his emotional experience, may feel overwhelmed, and this may challenge the very foundation of how he has adapted and operated during his lifetime.

What can you expect of your mind and body if it happens?

From a mind/body standpoint, the initial reaction is excitement of the central nervous system. The pupils of the eyes are dilated, you're perspiring, your heart is beating fast, your stomach is growling or cramping, and you may feel a bowel movement suddenly coming on or you may be expelling a large amount of gas, your urine output will increase, you will feel very tense and uncomfortable, and you may find yourself crying. If this alarm persists, you can become rapidly dehydrated within a few days and your kidneys can shut down. If this happens, you can go into shock and your life may be in danger.

In the shock stage or reaction, you will feel some sense of derealization, "Is this really happening?" Your actions may be automatic and you will feel like a walking robot. Your captors may lead you around like a dog on a chain. On the other hand, some hysterical behavior may occur and you may be screaming, crying, and fear loss of control of yourself.

The third stage is counter shock. Your behavior will become controlled and you'll be able to size up alternatives more clearly. You will find yourself looking for resources of comfort and planning, i.e., food, water, talking with others who might have been abducted, a comfortable place to sleep and rest, and achieving some physical security.

The fourth stage is called energetics. Your adrenalin and other hormonal juices will be flowing and you'll become restless and hyperactive. You will become super-aware of all noises and stimuli within yourself.

The fifth and final stage is persistent exhaustion. In this stage you may find yourself feeling withdrawn from any interest, a process of extreme indifference to what is happening around you. You may want to escape into sleep as a way of coping with the situational stress of being a hostage or kidnap victim. This happened to one hostage in Columbia a few years ago when he sat in the corner of a room, his back to the wall, and before him was a line of unopened cartons of milk and plates of food. He talked to no one and was as indifferent to the happenings around him as one who had been hypnotized to tune out all stimuli from outside and within.

Throughout this mind/body stress phase additional factors may come into play. If you have a history of diabetes and heart failure or chest pain, various symptoms from such conditions may be aggravated and, if you lack normal medication to control any of these conditions you need to alert your captors to your condition. The same applies if you happen to be pregnant. If you are female you may find a period starting, even if you had just finished one before your abduction or had not had one for years because of menopause.

Some years ago Conrad Hassle of the FBI coined a term, the Stockholm Syndrome. This applied to the kinds of positive and even protective feelings some hostages develop toward their captor(s). This was based upon the action of a young female Swedish bank employee who, in 1974, engaged in sexual relations and fell in love with a bank robber who kept her hostage for several days. Following his capture she even berated the Prime Minister for his failure to understand her captors point of view.

Although the Stockholm Syndrome is rarely if ever seen, it can be an important means by which the hostage is kept alive. If nothing else it means that the hostage is not fighting the captor(s) and either they may develop some feelings toward the hostage or are less threatened by him from a security standpoint. This did not happen to hostages of the American Embassy in Iran and rarely happens in the terrorist type of hostage taking. It did happen to a newspaper editor, a Dutch ex-hostage, who, following his release from a train hostage-taking incident felt positive feelings for the hostage takers for more than a year. It does happen, and when it does, not out of sexual or romantic feelings as was the case in the Swedish bank incident, but because the hostage develops a dependency feeling for the hostage-taker who, under such circumstances, assumes the unconscious image of a parental figure. This image is one which to the hostage is providing for his needs, e.g., food, shelter, protection. The hostage may thus feel gratitude toward his captor during such a crisis. This sometimes happened among turncoats or those military prisoners of war who seemed to join the enemy during their captivity.

If the kidnap victim is a child, the kind of reaction which family members can expect is one of magical thinking. He will think in terms of omens. Various events might represent an omen of another kidnapping, e.g., sight of a car or bus like one involved in this kidnapping. Even the odor of gasoline fumes might activate old, painful memories of the kidnap event. To a lesser extent, the same type of subtle reminder might be involved with an adult victim.

In contrast to adult kidnap victims, children will have greater trouble describing their kidnappers. This occurred in one of the most famous cases where a group of 26 children were kidnapped in the Chowchilla school bus incident on July 15, 1976. All three abductors were described with great distortion by some, i.e., black rather than white, one with a peg leg who was chubby when no physically handicapped or obese kidnapper was involved, and one was described as a lady when none were involved. Obviously, such misperceptions confuse the police and frustrate not only the investigation and apprehension but also the prosecution of the offender.

Children do dream of the experience as do adults, neither of whom turn the event into some symbolic event. They relive the experience as it happened. Furthermore, both adults and children seem to show an unconscious acceptance of the reality of death with which they may have come close. The school bus children dreamt of the roof of the bus collapsing and adults dream of guns going off and guns being placed against their heads as did happen to hostages in Iran and various other European and South American settings.

Children may continue to play out the event of their kidnapping by re-enacting it. With other children or stuffed animals, depending upon their ages, they will switch roles to play the cast of characters involved in the kidnapping or hostage event. Despite their dreams and play activity, child victims do not experience flashbacks in the same way or to the same extent that adults do. However, children may become phobic about riding in a car, being in the dark, being near animals or anything which becomes a symbolic reminder of the crime. Adults fix on more realistic feared objects like strangers; being outside their home or office alone; being near people, even police officers, with firearms; or not being anywhere without some armed protection, alarm, security system, or measures.

Adults have a tendency to develop amnesia about the kidnapping, less so for a hostage situation, whereas children maintain a fresh recall for details, even distorted ones, for some time. In part, this depends upon the age of the child, sharp recall being altered in time if the child is younger than 10 years of age at the time of the crime.

Advice for Hostage or Kidnap Victims

　　1. Follow orders of the kidnappers or hostage-takers.

　　2. Maintain calm and control nervousness by concentrating, at times, on unrelated matters. If you have been taken hostage, keep yourself busy. Make yourself

work. In the Columbian hostage-taking the Israeli ambassador made work assignments for the group of hostages and began his own by cleaning toilets. Prisoners of war have tried to construct a suitable living arrangement. Search for pets like tree lizards or fowl to take care of. The hostages in Iran read; and one, Richard Queen, even organized the library at the embassy. Keeping busy drains off anxiety, stimulates optimism, and keeps your mind active and alert. It forces you to take your mind off yourself and your fears. It allows and encourages you to be productive even when held captive, either as a hostage or kidnap victim. Some captives turn to writing, even poetry. Why not? Just because you never tried it before? This is no escape; necessity is the mother of invention. You might learn something about yourself and your ability to be creative which you never had time or the interest to develop before. Moorehead Kennedy, one of the Iranian hostages, in a personal communication, stated that his son was a poor writer and hard to communicate with prior to the hostage event. As they corresponded, a talent for writing emerged for his son. Their communication became meaningful.

Concentrate on unrelated matters, such as business details, stories you've read or movies you've seen, design a house in your mind, or do some other mental activity which is unemotional and detached. Doing this will be like taking a badly needed "coffee break." You will feel some relief by concentrating on important as well as unimportant things.

3. Develop a dialogue with the kidnappers or hostage-takers and use languge which they can understand; make sure you listen and do not say things which will turn them against you.

4. When appropriate, subtly point out that you are worth more to them alive than dead in terms of ransom and the charges against them if they are caught. The kidnapper or hostage-taker is under stress, too. He wants to end it. By being cooperative and pointing out where realistic benefits like letting you live can help him, you are working toward a reduction of his stress. That will be helpful to you indirectly.

5. Don't use body language, such as glancing at the door or stairs, to suggest that you are really thinking about escape or capturing the kidnapper or hostage taker.

6. Without being obvious, observe all you can about your surroundings in the hideout; notice significant noises and sounds, such as church bells, traffic, train whistles, or airplanes which suggest a nearby airport; if you walk up or down steps, count them to yourself.

7. Subtly leave your fingerprints around your place of confinement and select out of the way places such as corners where walls meet, near baseboards, or in a corner of a window near where the moulding meets.

8. Pay attention to the conversation of the kidnappers or hostage-takers to catch names, employers, personal friends, places of residence, military service background, group or political headquarters, or other intelligence information.

9. If the police or military succeed in locating you and assault the place of confinement, drop to the floor, especially if shooting starts. When police or soldiers enter, raise your hands, identify yourself, and don't protest an initial arrest until identification can be made.

10. At all costs avoid threatening to identify your captors; make sure that they do not suspect you are memorizing things about them or displaying unusual interest in their papers or conversation.

11. Urge reasonable delays in any decisions or actions taken by your captors.

12. If you're an executive and accustomed to giving orders, stop making demands — it might save your life. Do not become sensitive about your captors not paying attention to your orders and demands.

13. Don't be afraid to show concern or fear or even tears — but do stay in control so that you don't become hysterical — remember, you will need the coolest head possible.

14. When under severe stress such as you may feel if you are kidnapped, you may find that you are putting out a lot of urine or may even develop diarrhea. If that happens, it will be all the more important that you drink as much fluid as is practical. By doing so, you will ensure good kidney function and fluid balance.

15. There is a danger of being killed or seriously injured if the hostage becomes physically aggressive toward the hostage-taker. Bolz[1], Livingstone[2], and Mullin[3] agree that overpowering captors is extremely risky. Luck may work when surprising one, but there are usually a minimum of five terrorists, and many have explosives and automatic weapons which if discharged at a high altitude aboard a plane can cause disastrous effects and all may go down with the plane. Fellow hostages may not know what you're trying to do and this will add danger and confusion to the situation. Bruce Lee, Sylvester Stallone, or Chuck Norris may be able to pull it off but they have the cooperation of the director, script writer, and actors to make the results work out. Strentz[4] discusses survivors and non-survivors and points out that among the survivors are those who control anger and do not engage in aggressive actions against the hostage-takers.

16. Controlling feelings, establishing a reasonable rapport with the hostage-takers, being able to blend into the background so as not to appear to be prominent and displaying an air of confidence are all additional coping skills which will serve the hostage well.

17. Trickery may strike some people as a good survival technique. To be successful, it has to involve someone who can act well, has a certain amount of luck and picks the right trick, one which will not either anger the hostage-

1. Bolz, F.A.: *How To Be a Hostage and Live*. Secaucus, New Jersey: Lyle Stuart, Inc., 1987.
2. Livingstone, N.C.: *The Complete Security Guide for Executives*. Lexington, Massachusetts: Lexington Books, 1989.
3. Mullin, W.C.: *Terrorist Organizations in the United States*. Springfield, Illinois: Charles C. Thomas, Publisher, 1988.
4. Strentz, T.: *A Hostage Psychological Survival Guide*. FBI Law Enforcement Bulletin, November, 1987.

taker or will work in the right way. If illness is chosen as the trick, the hostage-taker may feel the hostage can be eliminated as he is too weak and whose death will preserve an image of the hostage-taker as being ruthless, according to Frank Bolz.

18. Humor is a good survival technique for long-term captivity in a group of hostages. In the short term, it is poor as the hostage-takers are interested in instilling fear into the hostages to achieve control over them. They and any expert would find little to be funny about that. Joking to the hostage-taker may mean you are not taking him or them seriously and this situation invites physical abuse and/or death for the hostage. In long term situations, joking can be acceptable to the guard as well as providing relief from boredom. Having been a hostage myself, I can tell you that the gunmen in my experience were so frightened and so apprehensive about their authority and control being tested that I spent most of my time reassuring them I could accept their power and control, while a joke or humor would have blown the whole scenario. The stakes were high for me. I had three of my four children there and one gunmen held my then 18-month-old child under his arm with a revolver barrel shoved into his mouth. What's funny about that?

19. Intellectual game playing to embarrass the hostage-taker may invite retaliation. Captors can employ violence to cut you down to size and make your Ph.D. meaningless and laughable at the end of an AK-47. My feeling is that calm acceptance of the realtiy that the hostage-taker is in charge is the best avenue to follow. All challenge to their power should be discouraged if the hostage wants to survive. Once they feel they are in charge they will offer less challenge to the hostage and will make fewer physical assaults.

20. Eye contact should be direct in long-term hostage-taking situations as it shows respect and humanizes you. In short term situations, eye contact should be avoided to assure the hostage-takers you are not interested in identifying them, once freed.

21. Physical discomfort such as sleeping on the floor, or in dirt, not bathing or brushing teeth, or shaving should all be second place to survival. The hostage-takers may view Americans as soft and may provoke feelings of being spoiled by luxury to gain a sense of psychological advantage and control over you. Be prepared to establish a better sense of priorities than creature comfort.

22. Drink fluids when available and you will guard against dehydration. This will help keep you from becoming weak. Remember, you must think about preserving your strength! Eat, even if you are not hungry.

23. Remember, people will know you have been kidnapped or taken hostage. Hundreds and even thousands of others will be concerned about you and will be helping to find you and comfort your family. The police will be protecting your family while they're looking for you.

24. When you are freed, you will experience a tremendous release of feeling. You may either laugh or cry, as though a mighty dam has been turned loose. Doing

this will help. Another way you can be helped is through debriefing by the police and/or your security department. Talking about your experience and what you observed will help you in an even more substantial way — it will offer information about your experience and will give you a chance to share your feelings about what happened to you. The authorities will want to know as much as you feel free to share with them. It will help you and others who might become victims of a kidnapping.

Not infrequently, survival from a hostage or kidnap situation is not free of a short-term, at least, type of Post Traumatic Stress Reaction. That condition consists of possible loss of a sense of pleasure, including sexual feelings, humor, appetite, and attending movies. There may be nightmares and daytime recollections of the experience. Startling reactions and feeling hyper-alert may be experienced. Anger and irritability are common and social withdrawal to heal wounds is frequently seen. Anxiety may be increased or present to a more significant degree than had been the case. Depression, preoccupation with memories and fears can interfere with concentration. Tremors of the hands, drinking alcohol to calm down or blot out the feelings and sounds and sights of the recalled experience may rise to significant levels. Night sweats, paranoid thoughts about strangers or people with beards or those who in any way remind the hostage of the kidnapper or hostage-taker may bring back fears present during the ordeal. Depression and crying may occur. Physical symptoms may appear where none existed before. According to Symonds[5], a hostage goes through four phases of adjustment to his experience. In the first, he feels a sense of shock and disbelief that he has been victimized. In the second phase, a sense of reality sets in about what he had been through. In the third phase, he feels depressed because of his traumatic experience and equivalents of this feeling may be seen as well as, or instead of, i.e., apathy, anger, and irritability. Resoluation can occur in this phase and may involve a change in values about what is really important in life, may become obsessed with efforts to avoid the experience, and may feel a heightened sense of the second and third phases.

Rahe[6] views anxiety as a consequence of life stresses that are greater than a person's coping abilities. He comments on how people like those facing cardiac surgery may feel great anxiety before surgery. They tend to have the most difficulties in surgery. Similarly, for cancer patients receiving chemotherapy, anxiety may affect treatment outcome. If anxiety for either is controlled, the treatment outcome is improved.

25. Talking with others about your experience will help you understand what happened and assist you in gaining control of your feelings, especially if you have experienced either anxiety or depression. Not only are others genuinely concerned but they are also curious. They may want to know how you handled yourself so they can learn from you in the event they experience a similar fate.

5. Symonds, M.: The "Second Injury" to Victims. *Evaluation and Change*, Special Issue, 1980.
6. Rahe, R.H.: Anxiety and Physical Illness. *J. Clin Psychiatry*. 49(10, Suppl) 26-29, 1988.

Dealing with the Hostage after Release or Rescue
The police or military personnel will be the first to establish contact with the hostage. Fear, confusion and exhaustion may greet the officer and he should appreciate that asking for facts will not be the first way to proceed. The hostage may have been treated aggressively by the rescuing group and may have a fear of further injury. He must be calmed down, even before mental health or medical assistance is brought into play. Debriefing, to be meaningful, can best be done when the hostage has come down from his emotionally charged hostage-taking and rescue or release.

Debriefing should be done in a comfortable setting with soft chairs and possibly after a bath or shower and some warm and attractive food. Even prior to this there should be a homecoming celebration with family present or phone calls from them so he will feel he is free and back home.

Once his story has been told, in the initial stages he should be assured he handled himself well and has the respect of the interrogator.

Whatever attention he is given should be tapered down slowly so that after the news story has been exhausted he will not feel despair over a lack of recognition and attention.

The interrogator should try to involve the hostage in relating what he did to survive so that others might be prepared for such an experience and profit from his experience. He should be encouraged to ventilate feelings, even anger, at the police or military. Sometimes such anger comes out towards the police as they're fresh on the scene and available to drain off feelings. I recall breaking news of a death or homicide to citizens whose loved one was killed. They reacted by blaming the police for spending to them, unimportant time, on chasing traffic offenders and not preventing homicide, or, in this case, hostage-taking. A wise officer will not take such feelings or expressions personally.

Debriefings should be kept short. If more information is needed, another short session can be scheduled or requested. Hostages should be permitted to associate with one another. Group support is crucial at this point and contact with former hostages should be encouraged. In fact, a hostage support group is often helpful as each can appreciate what others have gone through.

The police and/or mental health professional should brief the families as they, too, have been victimized and require help to understand the needs of the hostage. They should vent their feelings and have someone serve as a resource for their problems as well.

Families of Hostage-Taking and Kidnapping Victims
Probably no story captured the interest of the plight of kidnap victim's families more than that of Charles Lindbergh and his wife in terms of the death of their son and the trial of the alleged kidnapper, murderer, and extortionist, Bruno Richard Hauptmann. Similarly, the world grew to know the survivors of the hostages of the American

Embassy in Iran. In contrast to other survivors or groups, they formed a group unto themselves, demanded contact with the State Department, held news conferences, and served as the organizing focus for a mass of American response to the hostages in terms of mail, special T-shirts, or other morale boosters. Unfortunately, such efforts are seldom seen for survivors or family members of kidnap victims.

The kidnapper creates tremendous pressure on the police as well as relatives of the victim. The police have to wait for the kidnap victim's family to be contacted for a ransom. The victim's family may not know who the perpetrator is, what kind of person or persons are involved, and whether they will keep the victim alive if demands are met.

Police must scan mail, tap phones, keep the members of the family under surveillance to wait for further contact by the kidnapper for both demands as well as instructions, and also for further information through tips.

Thus the police are placed under great stress and this may be further complicated for them and the family if the family distrusts or dislikes the police, decides to withhold important information, or becomes aggravated and impatient by the time that has passed since the kidnapping.

This is in marked contrast to a hostage situation where everybody feels greater trust for the police in a domestic situation and in an international hostage-taking feels the full weight of the government as well as world reaction behind efforts to free the hostages. Furthermore, others are involved, that is other victims, and some support is forthcoming from the family members whose loved ones and friends have been taken hostage.

The police, government, and news media can also exert an effect on what happens to the family. The police do not want to paint a bleak picture, yet want to avoid being overly optimistic. If the kidnap victim has been one of a series in which death has occurred, the family, police, and community have further pressure as the outcome is felt deeply and fear governs everyone. This was seen in the Atlanta, Georgia, and Oakland County, Michigan, child murders. If sexual abuse preceded the murders, then more fear and hopelessness is felt, especially if the victim has been a child. The police become frustrated, the family feels the same way, and the community feels impotent to stop the unknown murderer.

In a hostage situation the police or national governmental officials who are handling the crisis usually give out little information. Newspapers, radio, and television rush to the scene, to members of government negotiations teams, and to family members of the hostages. This situation has good and bad features. It may generate tip information, sympathy for the victims and their family, and insight for the hostage-taking group and its sponsors in terms of how the government, police or military may respond. Attitudes and hard lines can be read in the facial features and tone of voice of the government people interviewed. Hostage-takers have their own intelligence system and such information will help them determine how far they can press their demands.

On the other hand, it places an additional burden on the family as they see their own fear and emotional upset as they watch themselves on television, read their interviews and hear their words on radio. They may hear an edited version of what they said, or one which has been shortened and points they felt were important were lost in the version which was washed to meet the media needs. Many persons interviewed under such circumstances feel resentment toward the media as they feel they are more interested in the sensationalism and exploitation of personal tragedy than in being helpful. Some media persons are rather unscrupulous and even endanger a police or military operation because they want a personal interview with the hostage-takers, something highly prized by the hostage takers as they want theater and such news coverage adds extra benefits to the danger they have created for the hostages and they worry felt by their relatives and the government officials with whom they will be dealing. In such circumstances, the media seems not to care as they want the story, regardless of how they are being used by the hostage-takers. In all probability, it would be helpful to force the hostage-takers to negotiate if the media could move towards an agreement that no interviews of the hostage-takers would be sought until after their surrender. This might help reduce hostage-taking on an international basis as it would remove theater from the schedule of goals sought by such groups. The only message offered then would be that terrorists and hostage-takers end up being captured. That would be the key story.

Adding stress to the family and police or governmental authorities are those persons who call, acting as official spokesmen for the kidnappers or hostage-takers, and who make demands to obtain money by exploiting the situation. This happened in the Lindbergh kidnapping and almost every other one as well. The police, government, and family members have to be very careful not to let such callers stimulate hope and encourage private settlement without the police being informed. This also happened in the case of Timmy King, one of the Oakland County, Michigan, children who had been kidnapped and later killed. With all the tragedy felt by the King family, they also had to contend with some extortionists who complicated the investigation and gave initial hope to the family that all that was wanted was money rather than taking the life of their child.

If you are an executive whose family member or personal friend and company staff person has been kidnapped, you may find yourself to be all thumbs when instructions are given and you have to follow orders to take money to some drop site. As happened with the father of Barbara Mackle, ransom plans were complicated when he suddenly lost his sense of direction as to the location, one which he knew like the back of his hand otherwise.[7] He became confused concerning what was expected of him. He was to look for a light over the drop box which was perched on a sea wall ledge, and it had burned out. His thinking was rigid and he failed to conceptualize the location. Instead, he concentrated on the light bulb.

Some family members may complicate rescue operations and plans as their basic

---

7. Miller, G.: *83 Hours till Dawn.* Garden City, NY: Doubleday & Co., 1971.

dislike and distrust of police cause them to be demanding, insulting, and may even cause them to play games with the very resource which is trying to help them. Relatives and friends of the kidnap victims should feel fully committed to the idea that the only chance they have of recovering the loved one is to become a team player. As there is an outside chance that the kidnap victim might be killed, the family or governing board of a business must be alert to the fact that the closest relationship of cooperation with the police or appropriate government authorities is the best and possibly the only chance the kidnap victim has of being returned home safely.

For the family member whose loved one has been kidnapped, there is a similarity to the victim who might also be an executive role person. Both may be accustomed to giving orders and, in a kidnapping or terrorist abduction, orders have to be followed, both from the kidnapper or hostage taker as well as from the rescuer, the police, or the military.

If the kidnap victim is one of a series where sexual abuse of the kidnapped person in other cases has been practiced then fear, revulsion, and panic are natural outgrowths. Although it has been rare that a grown female victim has been raped during a kidnapping, it can occur. The number of children kidnapped when there has been no demand for a ransom, who have been sexually molested, homosexually and heterosexually, is high. Particularly when such a kidnapping involes a domestic kidnapper, one who has struck some times before, concern mounts and more pressure is brought to bear on the police to save the child and find the criminal.

General Considerations about Kidnappers

About 70% of kidnappers ask for payment within 30-minutes or less after the demand has been made. The demand varies, from small to almost fantastic amounts in the millions. If the person hearing the demand sees humor in the demand for an extreme sum of money, the kidnapper may be provoked into showing a greater level of the power his act reflects and he may either hurt the victim or kill him. One ear of the Getty heirs was sent to the family as proof of the seriousness of the kidnapper demands.

If the demand comes from a terrorist, the amount will be large: the target will be some bank or wealthy business or group of businessmen. Associated with this type of demand there may be additional ones to release prisoners and distribute food to the poor. If the demands are vague and the listener to those demands starts pressing for more details, the kidnapper may become more frustrated and vent his feelings on the victim.

Despite all that has been said before about the risk of death to the kidnap victim, there are important reasons for the kidnapper to keep his victim alive. If the victim is dead, the chances of getting money shrinks as most families want proof that the loved one is alive. The kidnapper may not want to buy more trouble than kidnapping carries, namely, murder, as well. And, the kidnapper may feel comfortable about extorting money but not taking a life. Of course, all of this thinking changes if the kidnapper or hostage-taker is severely mentally disturbed or is a terrorist who feels that homicide will soften the hard line of those against whom he is making demands for release of political prisoners, payment of a large ranson, or demanding release for escape.

Kidnapping and hostage-taking are serious crimes, ones which can be very life-threatening. There is no single victim as the family, friends, co-workers, and a whole nation may be affected emotionally. There are many insights that experts studying the problem have developed. There is no uniform set of guidelines or the "right way" of management which would satisfy all parties to the rescue efforts. However, what you have read here represents most of what experts would accept and what they have suggested.

Those who have or will experience this terrible type of crime need to prepare to learn how to survive, what to share with police so that more can be learned and how to survive so that others, if caught in the same net of fear, can benefit from your experience and survive in the best possible way psychologically.

In all these areas we have come a long way. However, were never satisfied with what we have learned or done. We need to keep our attention focused on those who kidnap or take hostages, and those who survive. History reveals that new directions are always taken by some who are reaching for the lost chord through these types of crimes. Both challenge the creative imagination of the terrorist and domestic criminal. In turn, both crimes challenge the imagination and skills of the police officer, soldier, and mental health specialist who have to deal with these problems.

21

Kidnapping, Kidnappers and Victims

Although kidnapping is not a new crime, it certainly has gained prominence since the Lindbergh kidnapping in the 1930s. Perhaps since that time most people assume that this crime involves the abduction of a child because the word literally means "kid" plus "naper", an old slang term for *thief*. However, recently the term *kidnapper* has certain political implications and meanings because it has been connected with some crimes committed by political terrorists throughout the world. Thus it is obvious that this term also applies to adults, children, the poor, the politically powerful, and the wealthy.

Despite a rather long history of kidnapping as a social phenomenon and crime, a search of psychiatric literature fails to reveal one single study of kidnappers as a group of or kidnapping as a type of behavior. How strange that for this crime of international proportions there is little recorded information save that of statistical reports about the incidence, information about the cost to the public, and newspaper accounts of kidnappings of influential persons in various countries.

The most exhaustive and carefully documented account of kidnapping, although primarily focusing on political or terrorism kidnapping, was the work of Caroline Moorehead.[1] Most of what follows in terms of historical information was taken from her work.

Moorehead says that few kidnap victims escape but most survive. Most are confined chained and hungry in the dark. Many have their ears plugged with wax or cotton to keep them from overhearing their captors, and most tell of feelings of loneliness, claustrophobia, boredom, marked terror, and have fantasies of being killed or totally abandoned. Few victims recover emotionally; most families of victims are left with permanent traumatic scars from the experience.

Most often the victims are middle-aged men chosen from the ranks of industry or are land owners, managers, or political figures, such as diplomats. During their confinement (ranging from days to months) they are mocked by their guards, especially the political victims, and many are abused. Many of the politically

---

1. Moorehead, C.: *Fortunes Hostages: A Study of Kidnapping in the World Today,* London: Hamish Hamilton, 1980.

kidnapped victims are forced to listen to political discussions about communist heroes while they squat or remain chained, sweating and feeling terrified.

Rarely do modern kidnappers torture their victims. Paul Getty, who lost an ear, was an exception.

Kidnapping tends to be seasonal. Spring and September seem to be popular among the terrorists who kidnap, and the winter months for European criminal gangs are most popular. Certain industrial concerns have been deliberately targeted. Fiat Corporation in Italy serving as the best example. Others can be found among automotive and oil company executives in South America. In 10 years, 1000 Fiat executives have been kidnapped and several lesser officials of that company have been assaulted and kneecapped. Several plants have been bombed by the Red Brigade.

Kidnapping was popular in history long before the word was first coined in 1688, at which time the London Gazette referred to John Dykes, who was convicted of kidnapping or enticing his majesty's subjects to function as servants on foreign plantations. In Greek mythology, for example, kidnappings were romantic. Jupiter, as a white bull, carried off Europa; Paris carried off Helen, the wife of Menaelaus; Poseidon swept away Amphitrite to be his wife, and Hades kidnapped Persephone as she was picking flowers in a meadow. These are but a few examples.

More examples of kidnapping can be found in the medieval period of history. People were kidnapped on whim, when money was needed, or just for safe conduct. Genghis Khan always took many wives and children from men he had conquered in foreign lands. He would send back the nicest and prettiest looking boys to his mother, Hoelun, as gifts to her.

In the Crusade era crusaders were prized catches for the kidnappers hired by the kings. Richard I was captured for that purpose in 1192 for Duke Leopold of Austria. He used him to make money — 100,000 silver marks. His brother John, however, and Philip of France offered large sums of money to keep Richard where he was, a kidnap victim.

Some kings sent substitute kidnap or hostage victims. Francois I sent his two sons in his place. Not every victim, however, was content to maintain hostage status. Cardinal Cesare Borgia escaped as a groom in Velletri, South of Rome, rather than wait for the good favor of his father, Pope Alexander VI, to be exchanged for his safe return. The plans of Emperor Charles VIII were foiled.

Kidnapping became so extensive that kings developed a plan to take kidnapped hostages with them on trips to prevent their own kidnapping. Others during the medieval period, however, were kidnap victims and could not rely on such measures for protection. Such persons were heiresses. The kidnapper usually was a rejected suitor and he made the father, king, or new husband pay for the return of his daughter or lady fair.

In this same period brigands and pirates used kidnapping to finance their lifestyles and add to their booty. Kidnap victims were picked up on the highways and seas. Among peasants, kidnapping of important persons was an act of heroism, not unlike modern cases of terrorist-inspired kidnapping in some countries or communities. In literary examples, Robin Hood played the role of the perfect noble kidnapper. Kidnapping in Italy and Sicily developed into such a problem that government troops were used to prevent kidnapping and chase those who got away with it. Travelers were warned to proceed only when armed. Algiers became a celebrated pirate city. The Corsairs and Barbary Coast pirates maintained a lucrative kidnapping practice.

Changes entered into this criminal activity, however, through the Moslems in the 10th century. They invented the formal machinery for negotiations for ransomed kidnap victims. These ransomers were known as Fakkak. Christian ransomers were known to work through the Most Holy Trinity for the Ransom of Captives. This organization received papal sanction in 1198. Others like some Jews and Christians acted as intermediaries for a fee. Renegade merchants joined in the intermediary business and a fee of about three percent was charged. The port captain might well charge 10% as a fee, however, for handling the shipment of goods through his port as part of the ranson payment. Sometimes rulers would demand payment of their ransom for their hostages before they would release the primary hostages. Some Redemptionist Fathers demanded month-long pilgrimages from the hostages, whom they then released through ransom negotiations. Other hostages were forced to promise not to swear, gamble, or cut their hair for a year.

Kidnapping was famous in China as well as on the European and African continents. Marco Polo felt that Chinese kidnappers were as important to the throne as the armies were to the rulers.

It was not long ago that modern-day government endorsement of kidnapping was seen in Nazi Germany. Babies were kidnapped from Danish and Norwegian mothers and transported back to the homes of Nazi wives and girlfriends. This was done under the Lebensborn Organization (life source), established in 1935 and thrown into operation in 1940. Assisting the SS men were the females of that order, the Brown Sisters. They scoured the concentration camps and schools and villages of occupied countries and were taught to offer a good prospect child some sweets on the road, question him gently about his origin, get his identification, check family records in the town halls, and abduct him for the SS project. Within months, 50,000 children were brought from the Hungarian Ukraine and 200,000 came from Poland. All organs of the children were measured and examined to ensure their addition to the German population would be valuable. Once accepted, they were given new names and parents, German of course. These children were primarily under six years of age. Those rejected at this final screening just disappeared. Older girls considered worthy of becoming mothers of children of the 'good race' were kept for breeding.

In New York in the 1870s, kidnapping in the form of Italian Slavery came to the attention of the police. Some of these had been sold by a father according to the padronis accused. The kidnappers were never convicted because the only witnesses appearing against them were the children themselves and such accusations occurred at a time in history when the testimony and rights of children were not given much legal support.

In the United States in 1932 dozens of children were seized and businessmen paid millions of dollars for their return. It became such a crime of public interest that when possible, citizens joined a posse to search for the children and even lynched some of the kidnappers. At the time of the Lindbergh child kidnapping, police estimated that more than 2,500 people had been kidnapped in a three-year period.

Almost everybody has learned about the Lindbergh case, especially those in law enforcement. Books have been written about Richard Bruno Hauptmann, the convicted kidnapper and killer. Views regarding his guilt or innocence have polarized citizens and professionals alike. The amount of scientific wood analysis which led to his conviction as well as the psychological profile, finding of extortion money in his garage, and the hundreds of witnesses have contributed to the detection and prosecution of this classic case. The fact that this case led to the famous kidnap law is another measure of its effect since the crime was committed in 1931.

This was not the first prominent case of child kidnapping. Blakely Coughlin, a 13-month old son of a Pennsylvania family, vanished from his cot on June 2, 1920. As in the Lindbergh case, the ladder was found near the nursery window. The kidnappers did not contact the frantic parents for a week. The letter demanded $6,000. Otherwise, the baby would be interred in a cell 10 feet underground to starve to death. A few weeks later the ransom rose to $12,000. The original ransom had been paid without fanfare or police involvement. This time the police were permitted to become involved. The kidnapper, August Pascal, was caught. The baby had long since been dead, having been drowned in the Schuykill River with a weight around his neck.

In that same period, the Ku Klux Klan employed kidnapping as a form of punishment for Jews and blacks. They tapped phones, flogged persons, burned homes and crosses on lawns, and harrassed their victims. Many of the kidnap victims were never seen again.

People in the city of Chicago felt the menace of kidnapping in 1924. Bobby Franks was kidnapped, killed by Leopold and Loeb, and the parents received a ransom demand by phone.

In the same city, Fred 'Killer Burke', who had participated in the St. Valentine's Day Massacre, entered the kidnapping field by kidnapping gamblers in Detroit. In six weeks he collected $1.3 million to finance his freelance execution business. Kidnapping increased among bootleggers and criminals in the underworld but kidnapping of children decreased when anti-kidnapping legislation provided the death penalty, life imprisonment, and stiff fines for kidnapping in almost all of the states. Members of organized crime knew their kidnap victims would not file a complaint with the police or call them in. They did not have to anticipate the legal penalty for kidnapping. However, once they ran out of rival gang members, they turned to kidnapping wealthy businessmen from the Midwest. These criminal kidnap gangs were ruthless, professional, and well organized. One of the members of such a group in Chicago was arrested and turned out to be a former Assistant States Attorney.

The death penalty portion of the kidnapping law in 1968 was found to be unconstitutional. However, from 1930 to 1962, 22 persons had been executed, and of them six had died under the federal kidnap law. During that period the FBI had become involved and only two cases were left unsolved on its books.

Kidnapping has not been solely an American crime problem. Probably, Nuoro in central Sardinia has been one of the kidnap capitals in the world since Tiberio came to conquer the island in 177 B.C. The shepherds have played the dual role of being part bandit and part survivor through kidnapping since that time. For the Nuorese, kidnapping is not even a crime. A person would rather serve a 15-year sentence than serve as a witness against a man who had actually committed a crime. More esteemed than criminal law there is the pact between kidnapper and victim. Such pacts in terms of ransom cannot be violated. This problem has persisted despite all efforts by government armies or police to stop the crime.

The shepherds turned to crime as they refused to become peasants. Following the enactment of the law of Enclosures in 1820, the peasants of the foothills were able to lay claim to land they planned to cultivate and declare private. Despite this move toward democracy, there were 1,000 murders a year for a total population of 500,000. Shepherds rode down the hills to rich estates, burning, killing, and setting fire to homes there. Brutality was frequently associated with their kidnappings. Despite repeated and continuous police efforts to stop kidnapping in Nuoro, the number of kidnapped persons continues to rise.

In Italy there has been a steady escalation of kidnappings since 1969. By 1975 there were more than 200 involving known cases. In 1975 alone there were 77 cases, all coming from the activities of the Mafia, the Sardinians, and theCalabrian Mafia. In Italy, representing a reversal of criminal values, children were seen as being more valued kidnap hostages. However, bodies began disappearing from cemeteries at about this time and some race horses like Wayne Eden, the most successful trotting horse of 1975, were taken from their stables. That horse had won a quarter of a million dollars for his Milanese owner.

Concern about kidnappings in Lombardy caused Pope Paul VI to declare that the ransom money would be damned.

Of the 334 kidnappings up to 1978, 54 persons were never returned. Of those kidnapped, the setting usually was Milan, the Italian kidnap capital. Milan ranks fourth in Europe in numbers of kidnappings, behind London, Paris, and Frankfurt.

The kidnap movement in South America arose from the terrorism movement which followed the rise of Castro as leader of Cuba in 1957, when he and his band of followers defeated the Cuban army. Several revolutionaries emerged following this event. One of the most important was Carlos Marighella, a 57-year old man from Brazil who had inherited his father's Communist philosophy and party membership. He was an urban guerrilla who produced major effects on countries all over the world because of his writings and deeds. In his Mini-Manual of the Urban Guerrilla[2] he wrote:

> "The principal task of the urban guerrilla is to distract, to wear out, to demoralize the militants, the military dictatorships and its repressive forces, and also to attack and destroy the wealth and property of the North Americans, the foreign managers and the Brazilian upper class.

> "Kidnapping is capturing and holding in a secret spot a police agent, a North American spy, a political personality, or a notorious enemy of the revolutionary movement.

> "Kidnapping is used to exchange or liberate imprisoned revolutionary comrades, or to force the suspension of torture in the jail cells of the military dictatorship.

> "The kidnapping of personalities who are known artists, sports figures, or are outstanding in some other field, but who have evidenced no political interest, can be a useful form of propaganda for the revolutionary and patriotic principles of the urban guerrilla, provided it occurs under special circumstances, and is handled so that the public sympathizes with it and accepts it.

> "The kidnapping of North American residents or visitors in Brazil constitutes a form of protest against the penetration and domination of United States imperialism in our country."

It may be no coincidence at all that "diplonapping" began in Brazil. Carlos was born and raised there. It soon spread to Uruguay, Argentina, Colombia, El Salvador, Guatemala, and Peru, all countries with dictatorial forms of government or with such leaders. In Uruguay, kidnapping was used commonly and between 1968 and 1973, 21 diplomats were kidnapped. This form of action was to become a speciality of the Tupamaros. They created peoples' prisons, small facilities where kidnap victims were kept until killed or released when suitable ransom or concessions from the government could be achieved. It was because of their kidnapping of an American, Dan Mitrone, a former Indiana police chief, that President Nixon developed a future policy of refusing to trade or make deals with rebels of any nation. The Tupamaros did not believe Nixon, found he meant what he said, and killed Mitrone, rationalizing that he was a CIA agent. This was untrue. The rebels lost more than they gained by executing this father of eight children.

---

2. Ibid., p. 102.

Although a small band of rebels, the Tupamaros eventually destroyed a once prosperous and flourishing democracy. Five years after they began kidnapping and performing other acts of terrorism, the military took over, unsuccessfully. Now the Tupamoros have thousands of supporters because of the repression of the military.

Kidnapping in Argentina began in 1972 and within two years 170 businessmen were kidnapped. The rebels learned that more ranson would be paid by business for its executives than for government officials. These activities were carried out by the Peoples' Revolutionary Army, the ERP. Businessmen were kidnapped to provide the financial base for kidnapping military figures so that the regime could be brought to its knees. Activities of the ERP influenced ordinary criminal circles as well as they exploited the political turmoil in Argentina by kidnapping for their own profit. The criminals did not always return their kidnapping victims after a ransom was paid. Murder for political reasons increased from 1973 when there had been 12 political deaths compared to 1,075 in 1975.

In Italy, the kidnapping of Moro, leader of the Christian Democratic Party, began the open declaration of war by the Red Brigade and helped to bring an end to the Christian Democrat-Communist Alliance. It also gave huge sympathy vote support for Moro's party. The members of the Red Brigade were tried and sentenced to imprisonment. Once again, like the kidnapping and murder of Mitrone, Moro's murder caused a tremendous loss of public support for the terrorist kidnappers. Yet without his death, the credibility of political kidnapping for the terrorists was lost.

In Germany, the Baader-Meinhof gang used kidnapping as a form of assault against the political system in control. It kidnapped Hanns-Martin Schleyer on September 5, 1977. Kidnapping of political figures had been progressive since it was employed by the gang in 1967 following the terroristic inspiration of a terrorist psychiatrist, Dr. Wolfgang Huber. Schleyer was taken to demand the release of imprisoned gang members. The government did not yield and he was killed. On February 16, 1978, anti-terroristic laws were passed.

Throughout history kidnapping has not been an impulsive act. This is more so in terms of politically inspired kidnapping. Kidnappings are planned with meticulous detail. The stage and victim have to be chosen with great care. This requires sponsoring capital and detailed preparation. Some plans like those constructed by ERP involve eight closely typed pages. People are required to carry out the kidnapping, others to guard the victim, others to handle the negotiations and managing acquisition of the ransom and turning over the victim, and still others to establish banking connections to launder the money. Those who make the arrangements have to acquire or rent safe houses in which to keep the victim.

In general, victims seldom escape. Those taken as political captives may return with stories of mental anguish but little torture or physical hardship. In the initial phase of the operation the victim may be thrown around like luggage, from one vehicle to another and from one safe house to another. He may be bound or handcuffed and eyes covered with various types of devices to prevent him from knowing who or what is involved in his journey. His captors may be very nervous and suspicious of everything until their goal is achieved.

If the kidnappers are political, they will be younger, will be seen sitting polishing guns, and engaging in political discussions. As the victims observe others from their place of confinement they may realize their physical condition is weakening from inactivity. Daydreaming may well provide some relief from their anxiety and growing weakness. They begin to feel like property that is being haggled over.

Much has been written about how kidnapping can be stopped. Aside from the kidnapping law in the United States which did indeed reduce kidnapping, especially that which led to homicide, the law has had little effect on political kidnapping. Caroline Moorehead wrote:

> "And yet, political kidnapping can be stopped. As the Rand study concludes: In all countries that have experienced a series of kidnappings by urban guerrilla organizations the critical factor for terminating that series appears to be mainly the capacity of the local security forces to destroy that organization and apprehend its members. Guerrilla groups can be prevented from taking hostages when there are no guerrilla groups left to take them. In fighting kidnapping it is the police and the army, and not the law, that has had most success.

Considering all kidnappers to be criminals makes it possible to refuse to negotiate with them, defuses the intensity, makes it a police, not a military problem, and keeps in check the over-response which might otherwise turn a democracy into a repressive government.

Creating problems for apprehending the kidnappers is the bond which is established between kidnappers and the families of victims. The police are seen by both as a source of interference; where the kidnappers knew of police involvement, the victim died. This obstacle must be overcome by the police because otherwise an emotional bond is established between kidnapper and victim; knowing this, other kidnappers realize the victim's family will want to turn money over to them. Despite this handicap, the police must maintain their commitment to fight kidnapping.

What kind of person is the kidnapper? What makes him turn to this type of crime? What can be done to identify him and establish prevention programs? What happens to the victims of kidnapping during the seizure? What advice can be offered to help prepare those likely to be victims so they can survive better psychologically? These questions and perhaps some others will be dealt with here.

Psychology of the Kidnapper

Most people would agree that power motivates the kidnapper. He is like a trumpeter reaching for high C or a prostitute searching for the "ultimate trick." Associated with his use of force is a game which includes certain props such as disguises, notes, phones, drop sites, weapons, etc. He also writes, directs, and acts in his own script.

He may be involved with a single partner or a group or simply act alone. The act of kidnapping permits and almost encourages a type of creative criminality. This crime is more complex and usually the kidnapper — in contrast to the simple abductor displays more intelligence when his plans are more complex.

Most kidnappers are males although Gary Steven Krist had his girl-friend dress as a boy as part of her disguise when they kidnapped Barbara Jane Mackle in a motel in Georgia in 1968. Some women have been involved in terrorist kidnappings, but generally men become more commonly involved in this crime. The reasons for more men in kidnapping are not clear. I would speculate that women in general experience a natural sense of power in terms of their social sexual role in our society. They know they are sought after as sexual objects even if all else fails. This strange power is appreciated at a very early age, regardless of cultural setting. On the other hand, most men have trouble locating the core of an inner sense of power. Apparently they need to seek out some proof of that power and so they strive for a macho image, a sense of business power, or power through sports or athletic prowess. Some turn to academic life for a sense of power and some turn to crime. For the male criminal, one crime which seems to offer a particular opportunity for achieving power is kidnapping. How kidnapping helps him achieve this need will be dealt with below.

What motivates the kidnapper, whether an individual or a member of a group, to kidnap another person?

Kidnapping may permit him to feel competitive instead of non-competitive. This was seen in the cases of many skyjackers who exercised and experienced great inner feelings of power over their victim(s), as well as over those who care about the victims, such as relatives, police, corporations, the community, and even a nation.

How does conflict about being competitive arise? Kidnappers such as Leopold and Loeb or the men who kidnapped children from a bus in California were sons of fathers who were unusually successful in business or a profession. Some sons of such men were not able to be competitive with their fathers and turned to a sensational bid for power, one which appeared to be quick and certain to capture the attention of the world. The kidnapper gains immediate recognition, assumes a fearful image in the community, and if caught, can bring disgrace to an otherwise successful father, and can sense a short-cut to power and prominence. Money is not the direct motive. This type of kidnapper has lived with wealth and knows he will continue to have it. Kidnapping, however, permits him to demand large sums of money, make a big "killing" in the symbolic sense, pull off a public crime with hoped-for anonymity, and to savor the victory of fantasied success in competition with his father.

Conflicts may be seen in another way as well. Some kidnappers abduct victims who were their love objects, such as girlfriends, estranged wives, or former wives.

---

3. McGuire, C. & Norton, C.: *Perfect Victim*. New York: Arbor House/William Morrow, 1988.

Sometimes the victims are fantasy objects, that is, persons who were unaware of and had no significant relationship with the kidnapper. In this type of kidnapping, there is a very clear-cut need on the part of the kidnapper to possess his victim, which can arise from either neurotic or psychotic disorders. He may seek out incarceration to enlist the sympathy of his victim.

An excellent example of the kidnapper who needs to achieve control of his victim is seen in the kidnapping of Colleen Stan by Cameron Hooker and his wife on May 19, 1977.[3] She was hitchhiking along the I-5 from Oregon to California to Westwood, California, to visit a friend, Linda. The Hookers picked her up. They were her third pick up since she left Eugene, Oregon. She paid little attention to a large wooden box next to her in the car. At a gas station at which the driver stopped she had a premonition to leave but did not heed her own second sense. A mile out of town the driver stopped, exited the car and opened the back door and pressed a knife to her head. The wooden box was placed over the head after she was handcuffed. A sleeping bag was placed over her body as she was put on the floor. She was in the dark. Although she did not know it at the time, she was taken to the Hooker home in Red Bluff, California, and became their prisoner and slave for the next seven years. During her captivity she was sexually assaulted, whipped while suspended from cuffs on her wrists to an overhanging pipe. When the blindford was removed she viewed a large photograph of a woman suspended in the same manner. Later she discovered that it was his wife whom he had treated similarly.

Cameron leapt at any opportunity to whip her in this fashion, either because she was not cooperative or not grateful enough for him giving her food.

On other occasions he fixed a broom handle behind her legs and dunked her while bound into a tub of water, almost drowning her. She was submerged and helpless. It taught her that she existed purely at his whim. Now he had given her life and hadn't killed her.

Shortly thereafter she became a slave to the Hookers. She did their work. While locked in a special room he had built outside the home, she shelled nuts for them and they were sold at some market. She was chained in her room and when not working her head was kept in the box.

On January 25, 1976, after 251 days of captivity, he gave her some reading material, "the S/M rage." With it he gave her an indenture or slave contract of sorts. Subsequently, he attached a collar around her neck. To encourage hopelessness about escape, he told her of "The Company" to which he belonged. Members were everywhere to prevent her escape and maintain total control of her. His control tecnhique was like Big Brother in Orwell's *1984*. She felt impelled to sign the slave contract.

It was after this that he removed her clothing and tied her to the marital bed and raped her while his wife had watched and left to retch throughout the procedure. His wife, pregnant at the time, had been ordered to engage in kissing foreplay with

Colleen before he raped her.

Adding to his efforts to dehumanize Colleen, he changed her name to K. Following the rape she was placed like an animal in a specially built compartment under Cameron's bed and spent her nights there, sometimes hearing and feeling the bed shaking motions of Cameron and his wife having intercourse.

When he interpreted K's actions as disobediance he burned her breasts with lighted matches.

His wife eventually achieved term and Cameron delivered his own daughter.

More punishment was constructed and rendered by Cameron. He designed a stretcher, securely fastened her to it and slowly turned the winch and kept her on this rack for 60 minutes at a time. Without realizing how far he had gone he almost completely cut off circulation to her hands. From that point on he limited his punishment of her to whippings, hanging and bondage. He forced a bottle of cheap wine into her mouth and made her guzzle it. Then, he forced her to have oral sex with his wife whom he had tied to their bed.

K came to accept that her lot in life was to be his slave. She worked hard to be a good one.

In 1980 Cameron let her out to go dancing with his wife. This was her first time away from their home since her kidnapping on May 19, 1977. He encouraged his wife to have affairs with men she met at the bar where they went to for dancing. It was at this time he permitted her to obtain employment outside the home. But, physical and sexual abuse continued regularly.

His confidence in gaining control was so great he took her for a visit for the day to her family. She said nothing of her kidnapping to them.

Eventually, Janice, Cameron's wife, told K that he had lied to her about the company and everything else to keep her his slave.

She assisted K in her escape on August 9, 1984. Subsequently, Cameron was convicted of kidnapping with a weapon and several counts of rape. On all counts he was sentenced to 104 years.

If a psychosis is involved, the choice of kidnap object may involve some erotomanic attachment, that is, a delusion of loving and being loved by the victim (who does not really know or want to have any contact with the kidnapper). The victim may have received phone calls, love letters, presents, and even threats of either being kidnapped or killed by the kidnapper, who may come out into the open or remain hidden to protect himself. For this type of kidnapper, the act of kidnapping as a form of violence makes having contact with the victim possible. Otherwise he shrinks from meaningful contact or efforts to assert himself to gain favorable attention from the victim.

It should be remembered that the victim may be a homosexual love object or a child. In the latter category, the kidnapper may be a woman who takes a baby to fulfill a wish to be a mother or a need to deprive a mother of her child because of resentment the kidnapper may have had toward a younger sister or brother in childhood. The kidnapper may have delusional fantasies that she is really taking care of an abandoned child rather than one she herself kidnapped. Or she may see the child as someone who really loves her and wants to live with her. In the latter case, she unconsciously denies her act of kidnapping.

The kidnapper who struggles with internal feelings of competition and wishes to be successful might also kidnap an employer or official of a company who had either fired him or perhaps turned him down for a loan. Perhaps the kidnap victim may have mistreated his parents or in some way been viewed by the kidnapper as inflicting dishonor on his family. In the latter case, the kidnapper avenges an early childhood grievance of a current political resentment on the basis that the victim represents an enemy within a political or economic system which as a terrorist he is fighting.

The kidnapper may experience psychotic fantasies in which he sees himself fulfilling a divine mission or avenging a delusionally perceived persecutory plan. He may kidnap to express the power of a religion or of God himself; he sees himself as being an agent of either divine idea. He may view kidnapping as a way of calling attention to a world problem, such as hunger or poverty, and may make kidnap demands as a power figure in a universal movement to feed the world, stop war, or end slaughter in war, or stop wastage in some particular energy conservation movement. It may be that this psychotic kidnapper feels he is avenging himself on some neighbor whom he delusionally sees as wiretapping his phone, spying on him, reading his mind or telling everyone about him. In the latter instance, the victim may be a child or spouse or the hated delusional object himself.

One neurotic disorder is obsessive compulsive neurosis, which involves behavior motivated by unconscious conflicts around impulses expressed in highly significant psychologically repetitive behavior. A kidnapper with this disorder might use kidnapping to control the victim. The victim might have a particular characteristic which serves as a common thread throughout the victim choices of the kidnapper, as well as his style of kidnapping and how he treats the victim. The victim might be a child, such as the children kidnapped and killed in Oakland County, Michigan between 1976 and 1977, who were all in the same age range, looked remarkably similar, wore similar winter clothing in the color blue, and in two cases, the children were wrapped after death in pieces of gold carpeting, were kidnapped in a similar manner, and were dropped to be found in a similar manner. Following their kidnapping, no effort was made to contact the family nor was ransom demanded.

In other crimes like the Correll and Henley murders in Houston, Texas, or those of Juan Corona in California, the victims all shared a cluster of similarities in terms of age range, sex, and other physical characteristics.

The obsessive compulsive kidnapper may not only treat the victim in a special or particular sexual manner, but also may deal with the body in a particular manner if there is a homicide. His victim may be mutilated, washed, dressed, or left undressed, or buried or left in full view. Each victim will be treated in an almost identical manner.

Ultimate power is obtained by the kidnapper who demands money and also kills a victim. This was true for Leopold and Loeb, the killers of Bobby Franks. Such a person soon assumes control of the hearts and minds of the families of the victim as well as the community, city, state, and even an entire nation.

Such crimes attract wide and searching media coverage. A police department will assign many men and women to investigate and possibly a Task Force or a special manhunt force will be created. Such a killer becomes a King Kong of criminals and when apprehended is the object of interest for a host of persons besides those involved with the homicide investigation and prosecution. Psychiatrists, writers, media persons, film makers, television special staff, and even politicians might use him and his crime as a way of establishing advancement of their careers. This criminal becomes a celebrity. His story rights may bring royalties which surpass what he had or would have earned in a lifetime had he not committed a "crime of the century." His prominence is a measure of the ultimate power he has achieved through his crime.

The relationship between kidnapping and homicide is an important one to understand. Having a victim under his domination gives the kidnapper the feeling of complete control over another person; if he keeps the victim in bondage, the kidnapper experiences a sense of omnipotence. It may also be his only way of getting a victim he can kill and mutilate. In contrast to the kidnapper who derives gratification from the act of kidnapping, for this criminal it might simply be a method of obtaining a victim he can mistreat in a way that fits his psychopathology.

Like Ian Brady, the Manchester child killer, he might want to kidnap, kill, and bury his victim in order to keep his criminal activities secret. On the other hand, he might want to use his crime(s) to get recognition from a world in which he had been otherwise unnoticed. He may keep news clippings and follow other media coverage in order to savor the recorded and demonstrated power he has achieved in controlling the life and death of his victims. Homicide in the context of kidnapping may offer him an opportunity to strike a blow at parents or spouse survivors. The victimization of a child by kidnapping and homicide says, "See, you are bad parents, you can't protect your child. I have replaced you and will deprive you of your child the way I was deprived of a parent when I was a child. You will suffer the way I suffered."

On the other hand, the kidnap victim may die — not as a natural outcome or plan of the kidnapping — but rather because he either panics or provokes the kidnapper into an act of homicide by screaming, becoming insulting, attempting to escape, or in some way challenging the power needs of the kidnapper. Similarly the families of the victim might inadvertently bring about the death of the loved one because they err in the way they attempt to deal with the kidnapper, i .e., not calling in the police or following directions of the investigating law enforcement agencies.

There is a different psychological dynamic for the political terrorist who kills. Not only does homicide provide this type of kidnapper an opportunity to gain publicity and also strike a blow against the economic or political system with which the victim is identified, the kidnapper is also able to rationalize that his act was not criminal homicide at all. He sees himself as a freedom fighter or hero involved in a military action against the enemy. In this way he prepares himself to write off the death of his victims without any pangs of conscience. He feels he has not acted against society, but rather has kidnapped and killed for the betterment of society, one which will be led by his political philosophy and system.

Willing Kidnap Victims
Ever since the Patty Hearst kidnapping, questions have been raised and suspicions have been entertained about whether she was really kidnapped and brainwashed or whether she was part of the plan from the beginning. Experts on either side of the issue claim to have evidence for their opinions. I'm not in a position to answer the question but point to it as an example of concern because there have been reports of persons who either confess or appear to be suspected of having cooperated with the kidnapper. Aside from the obvious publicity seekers who might even contrive a kidnap story or those who cooperate and plan the kidnapping as a means of obtaining a share in the extortion money, there are still others who might develop a form of the Stockholm Syndrome. This phenomenon has been discussed in the chapter on Hostage-Takers.

What may happen in kidnapping is that there has developed a meaningful relationship between kidnapper and victim, providing the kidnapper has not been physically or mentally abusive. Mixed in with a victim's deep emotional attachment to the kidnapper is a mixture of early dependency feelings such as a child feels for a caring parent, as well as feelings of relief and gratitude for being kept alive until rescue or payment of ransom. Although reports of such victim behavior are indeed rare, the police officer should be aware of this possibility. It may account for vague descriptions of what happened and a reluctance on the part of the victim to offer any testimony which might be damaging to the kidnapper. If this happens, it would be wise to obtain some psychiatric consultation to aid in the evaluation of such behavior.

Thus the police investigator must distinguish between a willing victim, one who has shared the kidnap plan and was consciously a participant, versus the unconscious grateful victim who identifies with his aggressor, feels grateful for his health and life, and is not even aware that his attitude toward the criminal — the kidnapper — is protective.

Psychological Problems Created Following a Kidnapping

Kidnapping occurs rapidly and may involve many factors, especially if it is an act of political terrorism rather than a psychologically motivated act. It catches the victim and those interested in him completely unaware. The victim and his family and friends as well as the police may not know who the enemy, in this case, the kidnapper(s), is.

Pressure on the family and friends on the victim as well as the police investigators may be increased because jurisdictional factors impair coordination of the investigation and capture plan. Under such circumstances, pooling information and establishing a surveillance at a number of possible kidnap sites may be impossible. This creates problems during the beginning and most crucial phase of the investigation. It might be a wise course of action for every community to have a special crimes type of Task Force on a standing basis to deal with special crimes such as kidnapping, child molesting, mass or serial homicide, and bank robbery, so that the initial phase problems are eliminated.

The police have the responsibility and are expected to develop a strategy of management to minimize the possibility of death to the victim. Unlike terrorism kidnapping, however, where the criminals announce their actions, the police cannot seal off the average kidnapper because they are blind to his actions. They have to wait for the family of the victim to be contacted and must scan mail, tap phones, and keep the home and family members under surveillance to wait for instructions or news of further demands of developments such as tip information. Strain is put on the police in this situation which is aggravated by stress felt by the family, and possibly even the whole community. Everyone expects quick answers and quick action from the police to save the life of the victim and bring the offender to justice.

Another pressure the police face is knowing how to deal with family members and friends of the victim, as well as others in the community. They must avoid painting a bleak picture, yet also avoid being overly optimistic. If the victim is one in a series of kidnappings, the pressure mounts because everyone knows that previous victims were killed. In such a circumstance, police officers and officials feel important, angry with the kidnapper, and may have trouble controlling their anger and sense of frustration at not being able to catch the criminal.

Plaguing any police management of a kidnap situation are the many persons who call families, corporations, or government agencies using the kidnap situation to make demands for ransom even though they have not been connected with the crime. This is a common occurrence and can confuse contact and negotiations with the real kidnapper(s). To counter this problem and control it, the police will have to assign a code name to the kidnapper so that all meaningful contact will be limited to the actual kidnappers: other efforts will have to be made to apprehend persons who are exploiting the kidnapping for their own financial or power gains.

Also hampering police investigation and capture management is the fact that many family members of victims have very responsible business or professional roles in the community, and may be more experienced at giving orders than receiving them; their own emotional turmoil makes cooperation with the police difficult and as time passes, they may resent the police for not finding their loved ones and capturing the criminals.

Some family members or friends may have a basic dislike of the police, may unconsciously enjoy playing games with the police, withhold evidence or information, and make critical and sarcastic remarks about the manner in which the police are functioning.

The relationship between the family member, corporation or government of which the victim is a member and the kidnappers, is different than in other forms of robbery. Here the kidnapper and ransom seeker and financial source victim (family, corporation, or government) do not have a face-to-face contact as in other robberies. The kidnapper tries to put distance between himself and his financial source victim. Using more than a simple mask or disguise, he seeks to conceal his identity except in a romantically motivated kidnapping, and prevents the financial source victim from having anything to observe which might aid the police in bringing about his capture.

If the victim has been sexually abused or if a series of kidnappings have involved such abuse, concern mounts about the potential treatment of the victim. Fear, revulsion, and panic are natural outgrowths of such possibilities and more pressure is placed on the police to capture the offender and save the victim from such abuse.

Lenore C. Terr conducted a psychiatric study of the 26 children of the Chowchilia school bus kidnapping on July 15, 1976. They had been kidnapped by three masked gunmen who had blocked the bus with a van. The children were confined in a buried truck trailer for 16 hours until two of the tallest boys escaped to freedom and dug out the rest of the entombed children. The children had disappeared for 27 hours before being liberated by the two boys, ages 10 and 14 years, who had climbed out of their truck trailer tomb.

Terr found that many of the children reflected about their traumatic event by thinking about some event which immediately preceded the kidnapping. They unconsciously drew a causal connection between that warning event and the kidnapping. Despite the lack of any rational connection, this over emotionally invested event turned into an omen, a magical type of warning seen in primitive thinking. Of course, when we think about any children, we have to see that much of their thinking is magical and primitive, especially when they are confronted with the frightening experience of being kidnapped. In that situation, anxiety is so great they return psychologically to earlier and more primitive ways of viewing their experience and coping with it.

All of them experienced fear of further trauma. Because of this, some were afraid to escape from their tomb or "hole." Some could not breathe when gasoline was placed in the tanks before their internment en route to the buried truck trailer. Later, anything which reminded them of trouble breathing because of the gasoline fumes brought about intensified fear of more danger; for one child such fear occurred 12 months later when riding in a new car and stopping for gasoline.

Eight of the children thought that some of the three kidnappers were either a black man or a chubby man with a peg leg, or a lady. Such misperceptions and problems with cognition would confuse the police, who used such information in an effort to apprehend the criminals.

Dreams of these children were specific to the event in terms of what actually happened. They did not generalize fears and turn the event into being chased by animals or some similar symbolic dream content. Furthermore, their dreams reflected an unconscious acceptance of their own mortality or death-proneness, i.e., dreams of the ceiling of the trailer collapsing, burying and killing them, or being bitten by a dog and dying while asleep, or the criminals killing the first and last child by shooting them.

Fourteen of the children continued to play out the experience 12 months after the event; others re-enacted the experience by treating other children as they had been treated or had seen others treated during the experience, i.e., slapping other children, putting playmates in closets in the dark or hiding when adults passed by who reminded them of the kidnappers.

Adult kidnap victims have reported flashbacks of their experience but this was not seen among the children. However, they did display fears in peculiar ways, for instance, some felt there was a fourth kidnapper who would return and take them away. Of the 26 children, 20 feared being kidnapped again. From these fears others developed, such as fear of automobiles, the dark, the wind, a mouse, a dog, the kitchen, and men with long hair. Each became a phobic object, that is, one which spoke for the traumatic event in total despite being an unconscious "piece" reminder of the event.

A painful finding was the childrens' fear of being kidnapped again. This fear represents the development of feelings of vulnerability. They also felt a distrust of the adult world and a need to be prepared for another overwhelming event, like being super cautious or always on guard. Unlike the experiences of adults, however, these children did not try to deny their kidnap experience. They failed to show amnesia for details of the event or haziness that adult kidnap victims frequently display.

Psyhological and Security Measures for Prevention of Kidnapping

There are many steps which can be taken to minimize the risk of being kidnapped. This final section is designed to offer a checklist-guideline for security agencies to program important high risk persons who might be subjects for kidnapping.

1. Maintain a low profile, prominence makes it easier for kidnappers to obtain information about where you work, live, what your lifestyle is, and your approximate income.

2. Avoid making public personal photographs, a listing of your club memberships, your address and phone numbers.

3. Keep any travel plans private; make sure that only trusted persons know your itinerary.

4. Avoid repetitive patterns, such as following the same route home or walking your dog at the same hour or parking your car in the same place or having personalized license plates.

5. Avoid traveling alone at night.

6. Park your car in a locked garage and remove signs which designate your name over parking space or your office.

7. Park only in well lit areas.

8. Install an alarm system in your car, (plus bullet-proof glass and heavy duty tires for high risk situations). Be sure your gas tank is never less than half full; always check for signs of illegal entries (hood not closed completely, windows and door locks forced open).

9. Check in your mirror as you drive to see if you are being followed. If walking, travel in a group.

10. If you see a road block, stop a safe distance away; if it appears suspicious, turn around and drive away rapidly.

11. Don't stop for strangers while you're driving for any reason; be suspicious if a pretty girl gives you a come-on along the road either as a hitchhiker or standing next to a stalled car with the hood up.

12. Make your own private travel arrangements.

13. Avoid openly identifying yourself on a trip.

14. Take your own lightweight lock on trips for use on windows and doors.

15. Register in a hotel under an assumed name and call your office daily.

16. Have your own identification code as well as a negative code of a few words so that if you are kidnapped, you can achieve some communications with your own security team or family member. In this way they will have a clue as to

how you're feeling and being treated. "I'm fine" might be used as a code for the opposite.

17. If you have a security service or advisor, have him make a tape of common sounds which you should hear to ensure you can identify them even when blindfolded or in a room away from any captors, i.e., clicking the hammer of a gun; locking and unlocking doors; boat, train, and factory whistles; airplanes and airport noises; police and fire engine sirens; footsteps on a hardwood floor, etc.

Kidnapping is a serious and life-endangering crime which affects not only the primary victim, but many other persons as well. Each of those person has his or her own unique type of psychological insights which offer better approaches to the police management of the kidnapping and can also promote better survival chances for the victim.

In addition, psychological factors about kidnappers must be observed and shared with police agencies to deal more effectively with the kidnapper and develop a dialogue with him in terms of hostage negotiations and working with him toward the release of the hostage as well as his own surrender.

Finally, psychological observations and insights are needed to assist the victim to survive, and the police and security agencies to develop effective kidnap prevention programs.

22

Bombs, Bombers and Bombing

Most governments and business executives think of bombers as presenting the very worst of dangers as their destructive work causes more loss of life and property than any other form of life endangering crime. This attitude is correct. Yet, most people view the bomber as being a person who is afraid of facing his victim. This is sometimes true but not always as the bomber knows what will happen when the charge is detonated, he runs the risk of being struck by flying debris. In addition, the police and photographers who rush to the scene may catch him if he lingers, admiring his own work.

The bomb is no destructive tool for a coward. Many are killed or seriously injured in the preparation of the bomb. This happened to some of the Weathermen terrorist group in New York in the 1970s when they blew away most of the brownstone house in which they were operating a bomb factory. This happened more recently in a French airport when an Armenian terrorist group was hauling in explosives in preparation for blowing up a Turkish plane in Summer, 1983. Many of these bombers were military heroes or at least brave soldiers and many today are determined young women who align themselves with a revolutionary cause.

What happens with bombing is that many innocents may fall victims of the explosion. Frequently, many non-military or political enemies may find themselves injured or killed in such lethal exercises.

In the United States during 1985 there were 2,226 bombing incidents resulting in 104 deaths and 477 injuries. Property damage from bombs that year was 26.5 million dollars.[1] During 1986 there were 2,432 bombings with 64 deaths, 373 injuries and 29.3 million dollars in damage to property.[1] In 1987 there were 2,228 bombing incidents, 57 deaths, 384 injuries and 45.6 million dollars in damage to property.

In Hartford, Connecticut, on August 16, 1983, a powerful bomb destroyed most of the home of Rabbi Solomon Krupka, the spiritual leader of Young Israel Synagogue. No one was injured in that blast but in two earlier incidents in the previous week at his synagogue, a fire destroyed most of the sanctuary and study hall. Another Jewish synagogue, Emanuel Congregation, was struck by fire the day

1. Bureau of Alcohol, Tobacco and Firearms, Explosive Incidents Report, 1987.

before a blast significantly injured the rabbi's home. Neither the rabbi nor either synagogue were involoved in political narrative or activities and no group claimed responsibility for the destruction which occurred. Despite the seeming anonymous nature of the damage several threatening phone calls had been received by members of both institutions some days before the actual damage.

Ironically, similar bomb blasts were reported within the same time frame in synagogues in Johannesburg, South Africa and in the Columbian city of Baranquilla. Despite the damage, no claims were made by extremist groups.

Types of Bombers
John M. MacDonald offers an excellent review of bombers.[2] All kinds of people have been arrested for this type of crime: priests, gangsters, police officers and criminals, brick layers and psychologists, normal and seriously mentally ill persons, men and women.

The Compulsive Bomber
This type of bomber is no different from others who kill or commit crimes because of envy, anger, revenge, power needs, attention, or to make some point politically or emotionally. Such motives are not always clearly seen in a bombing. However, for the bomber who explodes devices repeatedly there are some psychologically significant features which set him apart from other types of bombers.

This type of person is fascinated by bombs from childhood. In reviewing their lives you see how they started early enjoying seeing things explode. Some went into the military and were fascinated by demolitions or even war movies of explosions. They play around with explosive devices, frequently using ammunition filled with mercury to make them explode upon impact. As civilian occupations they may seek out construction work or handling demolitions in the oil fields or might seek out working for some local chemical company. They may find themselves entering some terrorist organization in order to find some philosophical justification for the life long fascination with explosives and blowing things up. As their inner drive for this type of dangerous excitement is so great, either threat of imprisonment or mutilation of fingers or other areas of anatomy does not seem to discourage such interest even when it has come close to being life endangering for themselves as well as others.

When this type of compulsive bomber develops a burning idea or plan of justification he acts out within the framework of an obsessive compulsive type of criminal or killer. An excellent example of this type of bomber was seen in the Mad Bomber case in New York whose capture did not occur for some 16 years from when he began his crimes in 1940, on November 16th. The bomb was not well made and was found on the window sill of Consolidated Edison Company, on West 64th St.

---

2. MacDonald, J.M.: *Bombers and Firesetters*. Springfield, Illinois: Charles C. Thomas, Publisher, 1977.

in Manhattan. It consisted of a brass pipe filled with gunpowder removed from rifle bullets. Wrapped around the bomb was a note, "Con Edison crooks, this is for you."

As it had not exploded the police wondered whether it had been a deliberate non-explosion to serve as a warning or whether it had not been made correctly.

In September, 1941 a second unexploded bomb was found 5 blocks from a branch of the same utility. Shortly afterwards, three months to be exact, the United States was at war. A letter was received by the New York Police Department with these words printed in capital letters, "I WILL MAKE NO MORE BOMB UNITS FOR THE DURATION OF THE WAR - MY PATRIOTIC FEELINGS HAVE MADE ME DECIDE THIS - LATER I WILL BRING THE CON EDISON TO JUSTICE - THEY WILL PAY FOR THEIR DASTARDLY DEEDS." It was signed "F.P." The company received 16 more letters signed in this manner from 1941-1946. The language used was similar. However, true to form, after the war, a third bomb was discovered on March 19, 1950. It had been placed in the lower level of Grand Central Station. Although longer than the previous bombs, it was the same or more skillfully made and included a flashlight battery and positive terminal.

The fourth bomb exploded in a telephone booth at a New York Public Library on April 24, 1950. A fifth exploded in a phone booth at Grand Central Station four months later and a sixth turned out to be a dud when found in the Con Ed office building phone booth. A seventh arrived by mail to the same office two weeks later and also turned out to be a dud. An eighth appeared at a movie theater, stuffed into the upholstery on the underside of a seat.

Before Christmas, 1950, the New York *Herald Tribune* received a block letter which read, "TO HERALD TRIBUNE EDITOR HAVE YOU NOTICED THE BOMBS IN YOUR CITY IF YOU ARE WORRIED, I AM SORRY AND ALSO IF ANYONE IS INJURED. BUT IT CANNOT BE HELPED FOR JUSTICE WILL BE SERVED. I AM NOT WELL, AND FOR THIS I WILL MAKE CON EDISON SORRY YES, THEY WILL REGRET THEIR DASTARDLY DEEDS I WILL BRING THEM BEFORE THE BAR OF JUSTICE PUBLIC OPINION WILL CONDEMN THEM FOR BEWARE, I WILL PLACE MORE UNITS UNDER THEATER SEATS IN THE NEAR FUTURE. F."

Of his first eight bombs, only two exploded. The next four in 1951 and 1952 all worked. One exploded in a subway locker, one in a phone booth and two under theater seats. The force of explosion was greater than the only other two. People were now being injured. In 1953 four more bombs exploded and four in 1954 with one being set off under a theater seat in Radio City Music Hall. Four persons were hurt, two of them seriously.

Six bombs were planted in 1955, two being found unexploded under theater seats. One exploded outside of Grand Central Station nearly killing a porter.

In 1956 more injuries occurred when he set off one in Macy's and another found by a guard in the RCA building exploded when he took this handy piece of pipe home to use for some plumbing purpose. In addition, in 1956, he stepped up his blocked lettered writings. In December, 1956, his most powerful bomb exploded in the Paramount Theater in Brooklyn, injuring three out of a total of six.

Through the skillful profiling by a psychiatrist, Dr. James Brussel,[3] the Mad Bomber was traced through employment records for Con Ed. His name was George Metesky whose signature, "F.P." he later explained meant "fair play." His obsession began as a result of a work injury on September 5, 1931 when he claimed hot gases had knocked him down at work, causing headaches and other symptoms. He remained off work and was dropped from the payroll. He sought revenge when his Workmans' Compensation claim was denied as it had been filed too long after the event and no tangible injuries could be demonstrated.

Besides such cases of an obsessional compulsive neurotic disorder, there are other types or causes of excitement for producing a bomber.

Power

Bombers, the compulsive ones, are excited by the strength of their bombs and the explosive force they produce. The flames produced as well as the noise are additional excitatory factors. The size of the crater produced or the magnitude of a stump blown out of the ground or the distance travelled by fragments is a turn on for this type of bomber. Although the bomber who finds explosions as a sexual turn on is not as common as seen among the arsonist, it does occur and more and more reports of this type reaction among bombers are being made.

Sadistic Factors

These factors are seen among those bombers whose childhood reflects cruelty to animals, the display of a vindictive tendency involving the nursing of grudges for a long time and great over-reactions toward any attempt to impose some restriction of freedom. Their imagined or real sense of injustice is always associated with a need to be violent and bombing appears as a dramatic way of showing violence. Many of them in childhood have shown cruelty toward their family as well.

Sometimes they deny violence and preach non-violence as they light the fuse of their bomb, so to speak. In this way they try to compensate for their sadistic tendencies.

Other Psychological Factors

For some persons bombing is an expression of masculinity or "being macho." Some see bombing as a means by which they can be associated with something very risky. For this type of person even carrying blasting caps in his pocket might excite fantasies of mastery over danger. Some are excited by their curiosity about the technology of mechanical things and reading about explosives is not enough. For

---

3. Brussel, J.A.: *Casebook of a Crime Psychiatrist.* New York: Grove Press, Inc., 1967.

this person the explosion is just a technological by-product of their work with explosives. For some, working on a bomb is being creative in a destructive manner and there is artistry and creativity involved in the manufacture of their particular explosive device.

Severe Psychopathology

For many, George Metesky was a psychotic type bomber, one who was delusional and megalomanical about his justification for setting off bombs, many of which hurt several people. Others fit the malformed structure of a sociopathic personality, one who is a misfit, a loser, an anti-social personality. They have never been able to make it in terms of reasonable social norms of responsible behavior. They're immature and egocentric and very impulsive. In addition, they're power oriented and have no regard for others, never work toward a clearly defined future and never feel for others or work to preserve the rights and health of others. They lie and manipulate and bombing for them is a way of demonstrating power to the world at large. One such person, Daniel E. O'Donnell, known to me, was running around with some friends in their early 20s also in 1981. They made a pipe bomb and threw it into the home of Synthia Steele, a black, in their neighborhood. On that May 4, 1981, she lost four fingers of her right hand when the bomb exploded in her home. O'Donnell had been convicted of also throwing the bomb. To hear his story when examined by a retained psychiatrist, it sounded like he had been victimized by everyone and had done nothing wrong. Like most sociopathic personalities, he and his friends felt no remorse.

The Political Bomber

The bomb is popular as a destructive device for assassination as it makes it possible for the assassin to plan the deed for a time when his chances for escape are better. He can enter an area, conceal his bomb in some location where his actions may go unnoticed, and he can exit without incidence. Increased security at vital defense points for political personalities and metal detector screening makes it almost impossible for assassins to rely on handguns or automatic weapons unless guards or the military turn on the political figures themselves as happened with Anwar Sadat or a political senate rival for President Marcos in the Phillipines on August 21, 1983. In fact, despite a cordon of guards wearing body armor, the assassin was able to move close enough to shoot his target in the head before he himself was killed by members of the military guard. He was able to move close enough to the target by wearing an airline's work coverall which made him appear like any other mechanic out to service the aircraft which had just landed.

On July 13, 1989, seven U.S. soldiers were injured outside a discotheque in the northern Honduran city of La Ceiba.[4] They were military police on convoy escort

---

4. 7 U.S. Soldiers Wounded in Honduras Bombing, *Los Angeles Times*, Friday, July 14, 1989, Part 1.

duty. It was the fourth serious attack on U.S. troops that year, the second bombing. In the bombings people were seriously injured. When the attack occurred they were a part of nine off duty soldiers, dressed in civilian clothes, and the bomb was hurled as they left the discotheque at 12:30 a.m.

This incident was similar to countless others like the bombing of a discotheque in West Germany when a soldier was killed and others were wounded a few years before the bombing in Honduras.

Adolph Hitler's "Wolf Lair" near Rastenburg in July, 1944, was defended by three eccentric circles of pill boxes and electrified wire. SS Guards armed with automatic machine guns lined the area. Despite this tight security, Colonel Claus von Stauffenberg was admitted without question. He was on army business and knew the password. In addition, he was above question because he had been a hero in combat against the British, having lost his left eye, right arm and two fingers from his left hand from an exploding landmine.

Before entering the meeting, he secluded himself in the washroom and opened his briefcase. With a pair of tongs he broke a glass phial of sulphuric acid which established contact with a wire which held back the time mechanism of a two pound bomb. He placed the briefcase bomb under the map table in the conference room six feet from where Hitler sat. Unfortunately a general recalled having moved the briefcase a little further away as it was underfoot. The bomber left the meeting on the pretense of making a phone call. Although injured, Hitler lived only to die at a later time in a bunker as the Russians were entering Berlin.

The Syndicate Bomber

The Al Capone era heralded in the use of bombers to enforce the gangster's rule. His bomb squad was headed by James "King of the Bombers" Belcastro. All enemies of the mob, i.e., police, politicians, rival gangs and businessmen who fought buying protection or the syndicate's wares, were targets of the bomb. Buildings and elections were bombed and revenge and extortion through explosives continued until Al Capone went to prison for 11 years on an income tax evasion conviction.

In 1975 government witnesses like Louis Bombacino were bombed after testifying against members of organized crime.

Fragging: The Army Bomber

This term dates back to the Viet Nam War when combat troops employed the fragmentation grenade to blow up unpopular sergeants and lieutenants. In Viet Nam between 1969-1972 there were almost 800 reported incidents against superior officers in combat and in 1971 there were 1.8 assaults with explosives per 1,000 troops. Booby trapped grenades were placed next to beds or in lockers. Grenades and Claymore mines were used. Superior officers who placed troops in especially high danger were the targets. Most of the reported incidents involved support groups rather than combat units.

Other Basic Motives for Bombing

Bomb threats are used for financial gain in terms of extortion, armed robbery with hoax threats usually, and for burglary where bombs and explosives are used to gain entry into buildings and especially bank vaults. At one time safe blowers were among the elite of criminals. Sometimes bombs are used to defraud insurance companies. Such an occurrence was noted in Sponge Rubber Products Company, a factory located in Connecticut on March 1, 1975. The factory was demolished but without loss of life. Twenty 50 gallon gasoline drums were placed around the plant, each drum containing 30 gallons of gasoline. Six to eight sticks of dynamite and blasting caps were attached to each drum and several thousand feet of detonating cord was used. A mechanical device set off the explosion which destroyed the plant.

Bombing for financial gain has been seen in the settlement of labor disputes as well. Police, non-union workers, labor leaders, strike breakers, company officials and buildings have been bombed. This was seen in the bombing of the Los Angeles Times building in 1910. Ten people were killed. The publisher, Harrison Gray Otis was known for his anti-union stands in his paper. He referred to union men as brutes, sluggers, rowdies, pinheads and anarchists.

Racial And Religious Disputes

The Ku Klux Klan has a history of use of explosives to intimidate non-racists leaders as well as defeating and killing racist and religious targets. School buses were bombed in Pontiac, Michigan in 1971 when a bussing controversy was in process in that city. John F. Kennedy's birthplace was bombed the day Boston schools reopened under an expanded desegregation plan in 1975. A black newspaper was bombed in 1974 in North Carolina by a man associated with the "Rights of White People" organization. Just prior to the conviction of its propaganda minister for that bombing, he had been acquitted of a synagogue bombing locally.

In 1974 when a fundamentalist group in West Virginia protested that the Kanawha County School System's textbooks were un-American and un-Christian, schools were dynamited as part of their protests and two men were shot. In Jerusalem, Israel, some orthodox Jews were jailed for bombing a sex boutique business. Their rationale was religious protest.

Avoidance of Punishment

The bombing of a car, home or business of a witness against a defendant in a forthcoming trial is a well known technique of intimidation. I was threatened in such a situation in 1974 when I testified in defense of a police officer who mistakenly killed a black person. This police officer had been associated with an undercover police unit which had been accused of killing innocent blacks in Detroit.

A cattleman and his wife were killed while inspecting their farm outside Weatherford, Oklahoma. The cattle farmer was scheduled to be a witness against the bomber in a local cattle theft trial. In Los Angeles three fire bombs struck the side of a home of a man who was scheduled to testify in an auto theft case.

In this category of reason for bombing, there may be an effort to conceal a crime of either homicide or burglary. Sometimes a burglar will detonate a gas stove to cover up his work.

Prison Escapes

Bombing used to accomplish escape has been known for years. All terrorist groups through Germany and Italy have used these techniques and the Irish Republican Army is as accomplished at this method of escape as any group. In 1974 nineteen prisoners, including leaders of the movement, bombed their way out of prison, one of the highest security prisons in Ireland. Guards were overpowered and sticks of dynamite were used to blast holes in the inner and outer prison walls.

In Dublin, in 1976, an IRA member posing as an American tourist, placed a knapsack filled with explosives against the jail wall next to a court house where terrorists were brought to trial. Prisoners escaped. Pipe bombs are occasionally found in prison and jail facilities. These devices are placed there for the same reason.

Revenge, Jealousy and Hatred

Defendants convicted of crimes, jilted lovers, disgruntled clients of attorneys and fired employees are the kinds of people who also may turn to bombing a person toward whom they feel resentment or hurt. The same applies to marital situations in which a jealous or enraged spouse may feel the need to show the magnitude of his hurt by bombing his spouse or her new boyfriend. Very few cases have been reported of a female bombing her husband or his lover.

Suicide

In Bavaria, a 55-year old man blew himself up. The only remains found were parts of his legs. In South Africa, a young man did the same thing and scrawled on the walls of his room, "All the kings horses won't be able to put Oliver back together again." In Mason County Jail in West Virginia, a young man forced his way into his wife's jail cell, was locked in with her and discharged his shotgun into a suitcase containing explosives.

The Terrorist Bomber

From the statistics in the introduction it should be clear that bombing is now an important part of terrorist activities, and the U.S. is becoming more of an attractive target in terms of citizens, visitors, businesses and now actual locations.

However, the terrorist bomber is not a totally modern event on the scene of history. In Paris, France, between 1892 and 1894, terrorists, then called anarchists, set off several bombs, killing nine and injuring many more. Those figures were significant then in light of limited technology. With modern weapons and bombs the figures would have been higher.

Revolutionary writers emphasize the value of violence. Fritz Fannon in his handbook for Black violence, *The Wretched of the Earth*, wrote, "Violence is a cleansing force. It frees the native from his inferiority complex and from his despair and inaction, it makes him fearless and restores self respect." He, like most political or revolutionary bombers, establish for themselves the image of being patriots, freedom fighters and revolutionaries. Others view them as being terrorists, criminals and truly dangerous people who defy democratic process and have no value for human life or the rights and property of others. They appear isolated from and insensitive to the suffering they cause to others, their political rivals as well as innocent countrymen.

No one would deny that explosions, noise from bombs and the extent of damage produced by them is frightening. This type of lethal and destructive device lends itself to terrorism as it has been defined almost everywhere. It is an action designed to produce terror resulting from violence and intimidation to achieve an end. Terrorists utilize anything which can achieve that end, i.e., bombing, arson, murder, assault, torture, kidnapping, armed robbery, extortion and threats to commit any of these acts in a community or country. These acts are planned and committed to induce fear. Obviously, threats in themselves are not sufficient.

The terrorist rationalizes his actions on the basis that he is challenging the unlawful or immoral power of his enemy, i.e., a government or business leader. What could create a better challenge to that assumed power of the adversary than the explosive power of a terrorist bomb. In this way the terrorist feels he has greater power and the explosion he creates demonstrates to others that he does have greater power.

When his bomb explodes it places anyone and everyone at risk, even the innocent as previously stated. When it explodes it conveys the old message associated with violence, "Right is Might."

This form of violence in terrorism is not mindless. It is an act which has objectives and some terrorists lose sight of the objectives as destruction seems more important. This has been observed in Northern Ireland where women and children have been slaughtered by both factions. It illustrates that no one is safe when terrorists are involved.

In the past, bombing has often achieved its objectives. Leaders and prisoners have been released by the target government. There have been changes in government policy. Sometimes a revolutionary manifesto has been published. These objectives have been achieved when moderate use of the bomb has been made. Of course, sometimes greater damage and loss of life is produced either by accident or design and sometimes there has been a miscalcuation in regard to explosive force or when a site may have more pedestrian traffic than anticipated. When these mishaps occur the community turns against the terrorists. Too much destruction and terror is counter productive, even for terrorists.

When terrorists blow up a military or police vehicle they aim their actions at the public. If enough of these incidents occur they hope to induce a feeling that the government cannot protect, causing mounting opposition to its leaders and policies. In order to keep this type of terrorist ball rolling, the terrorists try to warn of explosions as they do not want civilian casualties. However, such casualties are almost impossible to avoid. Bomb placement locations may change because of security and authorities cannot be warned in time. Sometimes the bombs may have defective timers and go off before scheduled. In Israel, transportation centers and hotels have been bombed to discourage visitors with economic loss for the government. Catholic-owned pubs in Northern Ireland have been attacked by the IRA for the same reason. Bombs have been used to intimidate witnesses against terrorist groups. Bombing makes news while rifle or machine gun assassination of a lone police officer or soldier is not even mentioned. Thus, the terrorist bomb is a publicity maker.

Persons are recruited for terrorist organizations because they possess certain qualities. They include women and children as well as young men, frequently, college students. Their personality qualities are described by terrorist leaders as being audacious, optimistic, adaptable, imaginative and inventive. Che Guevara wanted young men with all of these qualities. Grivas wanted men with boldness, resourcefulness, cunning and initiative, optimism, a strong constitution, sobriety and a resistance to hardship.

With their leaders they share a deep conviction to rid their land of foreign leadership, to overthrow a corrupt government or to obtain a better society. They are not necessarily sadistic or power hungry, but may have a drive to establish selfhood through their acts. However, some use rebellion against society as rebellion against their parents. Some react to early childhood experiences of harsh discipline in a private school. Some come from liberal parents. Their developmental style has been to indulge impulses rather than control them. Many are oriented to acheivement of immediate gratification. A school teacher may serve as a powerful influence at the campus level for recruitment into a revolutionary group. Some respond to the glamour of revolutionary life and movement. Some members are really bandits who profit from their rationalized revolutionary movement: Chink, from the Symbionese Liberation Army, is such an example. He was an armed robber turned revolutionary and as a terrorist revolutionary he continued robbing. These kinds of revolutionaries join the movement to fill their pockets with loot under the mantle of a political movement.

Most persons see revolutionaries as men, especially bombers. This has been proven to be wrong since terrorism struck such a forceful blow since the 1960s. Diane Oughton was killed by a bomb in a Weatherman bomb factory in New York. Hiro Nagata, the daughter of a Japanese businessman, participated in the torture of fourteen fellow members of the United Red Army group who had acted against the policies of their terrorist group. One of these victims had been pregnant when killed. Ulrike Meinhof was leader and co-founder of the Baader Meinhoff gang and Bernadine Dohorn was a leader of the Weather Underground.

By no means are children innocents these days. Homicide, vandalism, arson and other crimes like muggings are not the only areas in which the anti-social child functions. In the field of terrorism many children have crawled through sewers to implant land mines. They have shot at soldiers, aided in terrorist surveillance of victims or targets and have participated in armed robberies. Usually, a political leader or businessman is trusting of children and fails to protect himself from a child, especially one who is alone. Suddenly it is too late. The bomb goes off!

According to Jack Anderson, terrorist groups have a new bomb called the "invisible bomb." It is undetectable by known bomb searching techniques. Its presence was reported by a nervous member of a radical Palestinian terrorist group who contacted U.S. officials. The target would have been a Geneva hotel in Spring, 1983. Bomb dogs failed to find the bomb which was later, on a second check, found in a suitcase in the hotel room. The explosive had been molded into the cardboard of the suitcase. Its explosive power is greater than C-4, the so-called plastic explosive. It is powerful enough to blow up a seven story building. It had been made by an Arab living in Bagdad. It is suspected of being the bomb used to blow up the U.S. Embassy in Beirut. This lethal device has created considerable stir among intelligence and security agencies throughout the world. If found, the bomb maker will be eliminated.

Bombs and Bombing Methods

Bombs and explosive devices are not difficult to obtain. Mullin[5] discusses and describes various bomb devices. He points out a well known fact. Explosive devices can be manufactured on the streets and in shops from many materials, i.e., polyisobutylene, 1.6% motor oil and 5.3% of other substances. Gasoline, fertilizer, hand soap, steel wool, a soft drink cannister and hundreds of other substances can be utilized. Of course, the already made bombs like dynamite, nitroglycerine and C-4 are deadly and effective.

Explosives are either high or low types. The high type has a rapid rate of detonation and require no confinement like a container. It changes rapidly from a solid to liquid and then a gas. It causes a shattering shock. Forms of this type would be TNT, C-4 and fertilizer with ammonium nitrate.

5. Mullin, W.C.: *Terrorist Organizations in the United States*. Springfield, Illinois: Charles C. Thomas, Publisher, 1988.

Low explosives are slow burning and require some type of confinement. It goes from solid to liquid to gas more slowly. Examples of this form are black powder, the same chemical used in ammunition to ignite after the primer is struck in order to propel the bullet. Gun cotton, or nitrocellulose can be used for this type as well as a combination of compounds known as French Ammonal employs ammonium nitrate, stearic acid and aluminum powder.

Explosives have to be triggered by some initiator. Common ones are flame fuses, PETN placed in a candle and trip wires as seen in booby trapped devices. Electronic devices are used as well. They use heat or flame initiators. Clocks and watches are common for this type of initiator. One end of the wire is connected to the body of the clock and the other end is connected to the screw set in the crystal of the clock. A battery is connected to supply electrical current. The electrical circuit is completed when the hand reaches and touches the screw.

Chemical initiators are used by terrorist groups as well. A weed killer which contains potassium chlorate can activate the explosion. It can be used by filling a balloon dropped into a gasoline tank. The rubber balloon is eaten away by the gasoline and an explosion occurs.

Another form of detonator is a pressure type. The explosive is placed into a container with a plunger arrangement at the other end. Barometric changes can move the plunger downward, causing the explosion. A double switch arrangement may be used so that one switch arms the device and the second one detonates it.

Explosions cause fragmentation of steel or metal material as well as heavy wooden construction material and flying glass. Secondarily it causes a blast effect as the explosion causes sudden changes in air pressure. The faster the change from solid to liquid to gas, the greater the blast effects. The third effect of an explosive is the incendiary effect. Gasoline is destructive especially because of its powerful incendiary effect. That is seen in the use of Molotov Cocktails, explosive devices used by the Russians against the Germans in World War II. Whole tanks were burned up in this way. Grease was attached to the bottles containing gasoline and once the wick was ignited the bottle was thrown then stuck to the tank treads or main body of the tank.

Booby traps are effective as few persons suspect their presence until an explosion occurs. They can be placed inside candles, books, behind pictures, in cars, or hostages may explode when touched by liberators. There are two types: the Claymore Mine and trip wire devices. Once installed either of these devices or both may be used as primary and secondary devices to ensure that those who enter a room are going to be blown up. Even tertiary devices can be used and are usually placed on book shelves, countertops, light bulbs, cushions and drawers.

A not-so-funny example of a booby trap was seen in the movie *Lethal Weapon II*. An officer discovered one connected to the toilet seat which was set to explode when he removed himself from the toilet seat. Pressure of him sitting on the seat activated the bomb. If there had been secondary or tertiary devices many police officers would have been killed and injured.

As a tool of destruction and method of political or military warfare, the bomb is a formidable weapon. It takes a special kind of person to use it at all and also effectively. The bomber, a person who seeks a sense of power like a trumpeter trying to blow "High C", is a person whom we need to profile, identify and stop. Identifying him and the interests he represents is the best prevention. Tough laws and penalties for possession of explosives has totally failed to protect us. To the potential target the best defense is vigil, intelligence information and the early identification of the bomber himself. That means that intelligence, professionally trained security personnel and unrelenting awareness are the best defenses for those of us who are likely to become targets of the bomber.

Kobetz and Cooper[6] point out that not all bombing is clandestine. Some bombs are thrown in public places. For the terrorist, if objectives are not achieved through other means, bombing is the way for them to go. Whether innocent life is lost means little to the frustrated terrorist who seeks the world stage of political theater.

Most of us who work in the field of security and counter terrorism believe that the most significant terrorist threat against the United States and our citizens will involve bombings. The loss of hundreds of Marines in Beirut a few years ago and the explosion of the Pan Am flight 103 plane after take off from England in December, 1988, illustrate the point. Occasionally, there are firearms' assassinations like that of Lt. Colonel Nick Rowe, my former commander is Special Forces, Project Sere, who was gunned down in the Philippines by a terrorist group on April 20, 1989 but bombing is used for multiple deaths.

For the past 10 years at least, many like Kobetz and Cooper have mentioned the possibility of the use of nuclear weapons against the free world in the near future. The reader may remember that the Israelis a few years ago bombed a Libyan nuclear plant, one whose products could have fallen into the hands of terrorists like other weapons and money from Kadafi have done over the years.

Bombing is economical and produces great public reaction. Yet, it has been employed relatively infrequently. Perhaps that is due to the fact that it runs the risk of great negative publicity if there are too many victims. Thus, hostage-taking and assassination seem more popular as a terrorist device. Moreover, bombing produces such maiming and loss of life that it takes a particular mind or personality to undertake such a means of reaching for the headlines among terrorists.

Prevention of bombing requires specialized and particular forms of security for the private corporation as well as government agency and location involved, whether in this country or overseas. When a bomb threat occurs it requires a calm, useful and experienced person or staff to make decisions about plans and disposi-

6. Kobetz, R. W. & Cooper, H.H.A.: *Target Terrorism: Providing Protective Services*. Gaithersburg, Md.: Bureau of Operations and Research, International Association of Chiefs of Police, 1978.

tion. However, an effective security officer or staff must make those important plans and decisions in advance of the threat. Such plans will be presented elsewhere in this book.

Christopher Dobson and Ronald Payne[7] discuss bombs and terrorists and point out that while law enforcement and even the military try to choke off the supply of explosives, there are supplier groups within a country that make them available to the terrorist groups, who also work with neighboring groups in other countries to buy or borrow bombs for their political purpose. They steal them from the military, and use them against public and private targets. The third source of bombs comes from chemical fertilizer used in gardening. Like the Irish Republican Army, they make bombs by mixing garden chemicals with diesel fluid which can be detonated with gun cotton and a couple of sticks of gelignite. Electrical fuses are used more commonly as they want something to allow their own safe escape. In Europe, Russian made rockets are aimed at cars of military figures like the RPG-7 fired at the armored Mercedes of United States General Frederick P. Kroesen in Heidelberg on September 15, 1981.

Over 200 pounds of explosives may be used in a car bomb, or a 100-pound bomb may be buried under the pavement or road surface and be detonated at a distance like the one which missed United States General Alexander Haig in 1979 when he was the Supreme Commander of NATO forces in Europe. A letter bomb may involve only a few ounces of explosive which can kill if it is held close to the body while it is being opened. Radio controlled bombs are becoming more popular but counter-terrorist forces can send out radio signals and blow up the terrorists en route to their lethal mission.

Booby traps are especially important for the executive to know about as one can be planted in a regular smoking pipe and when lighted it can blow off the head of the smoker. Booby traps can be detonated by striking a trip wire while walking into a darkened room. A land mine can be planted under a loose board and opening a door can pull a cord to detonate such a bomb.

Secondary fuses can explode a bomb if the primary one fails to work. They act as a fail safe device.

Bomb Security

The single most effective protection against explosives and the terrible injuries and deaths they can cause is prevention. Livingstone[8] outlines measures against bombs.

First and foremost access control of both the outer and inner perimeter of a home, office or vehicle must be achieved. This involves the use of fences, lights, motion sensors, guard patrols and video cameras.

7. Dobson, C. & Payne, R.: *The Terrorists: Their Weapons, Leaders and Tactics*. New York: Facts on File, Inc., 1982.
8. Livingstone, N.C.: *The Complete Security Guide for Executives*. Lexington, Mass: Lexington Books, 1989.

All vehicles entering a business area should be inspected for bombs, especially in a high risk area like a foreign country where bombings and terrorism are serious problems. Speed bumps will slow down a vehicle and may also detonate a vehicle containing explosives. Pop up barriers and tire puncturing devices will offer protection.

To counter blast damage, the executive can ensure that trash is not permitted to collect because of incendiaries and flying debris from explosions. Windows should protect against bombs being tossed in. Grenade screens or even decorative gratings could thwart a thrown bomb or grenade. Physical searches of the facilities as well as purses, brief cases, and lunch buckets, should be done on a continuing basis and X-Ray searches are excellent as an adjunct to this type of search.

The loading dock needs protection as large packages are brought into the building through this entry. Delivery vehicles should be kept under surveillance.

Other preventive steps in a building to prevent easy access to bombs should be the addition of a grille to cover opening to air conditioning and heating ducts, inspection of rest rooms regularly, locking stairwells and having security check on them regularly, installations of sprinklers, use of closed circuit television, designating certain areas as critical zones and frequent briefings of staff regarding bomb threats and attacks. Evacuation drills should be held.

Mail should be screened for letter bombs. Warning signs are no address on the envelope or the address is obscured and not recognizable. Letters may be clipped out of magazines or newspapers to make up the address label information. A clay or putty feeling may be from explosives contained inside. The parcel may feel too heavy for its size. The paper may contain greasy patches from the sweating of explosives inside. Wire may be felt through the envelope. The hairspring trip mechanism may be seen and resemble a small coin. The package may have the smell of almonds or marzipan, a form of almond paste.

If a bomb is discovered or suspected, the police should be notified at once and no effort should be made to touch the suspected bomb. The area should be quietly and promptly evacuated.

If the letter contains a bomb threat only, it should be handled with plastic baggies to avoid finger print contamination and placed into a plastic bag.

Most bomb threats are made by phone. The person answering the phone should attempt to pay attention and make notes about demands, the groups making them if possible, the quality of voice and type accent and noting the time and place of the bomb which is alleged to be exploded. Most bomb threats are read as they are prepared in advance. Efforts to engage the threatener in conversation should be made but are seldom successful. Notation of background noises should be made.

When an evacuation procedure occurs, someone in authority must order it. BOMB THREATS SHOULD NEVER BE TAKEN LIGHTLY! Avoid panic and request people to leave the area without mentioning the reason as being a bomb. That would cause a stampede. Windows and doors should be left open to reduce damage from blast effect. Evacuate people to an open area. Terrorist infiltrators should be searched for. The Fire Department should be notified first and someone familiar with the area involved should participate in the search as he is familiar with the area, can obtain drawings and has keys with which to open doors. Be mindful that a bomb hoax may be used and by having a plan and orderly manner of dealing with the threat, the employees will more likely feel reassured that the company or facility is a safe place in which to work.

Bomb searches require a detailed and well thought out plan. Search patterns and areas should be broken up into small areas so intense search can be accomplished. A grid method should be useful here.

Alarms should be turned off and the move through the facility by the search team should be slow and methodical. Searchers should not bunch up in the event there is an explosion. Tables should be checked on the under side, the same applies to suspended ceilings, elevator shafts and the like. Walkie talkies should be turned off. A bomb suppression blanket should be handy so it can be carefully draped over a bomb if found.

Before a speaking event or public event, it is useful to have the area checked by bomb sniffing dogs. The stage, orchestra pit, press area, area above the stage from which scenery and decorations are dropped and moved, the dressing rooms, seats and entrances and exits should be checked as well. Any delivery of material to the facility should be checked.

Aircraft should be searched like a vehicle as discussed in the vehicle section.

Conclusion

This chapter and the media in general seems to deal with bombings as if their use by terrorists is exclusive. That is not the case, certainly in the United States. A few years ago a bombing occurred and seemed to involve a dispute about certain documents in the Mormon Church which had been sold as authentic. Planned Parenthood offices have been fire bombed and in my opinion it is only a matter of time before we read about abortion clinics receiving the same treatment by political groups who oppose their operation and aims.

Aside from political groups and terrorists, the executive and his board needs to be aware of the disgruntled employee who is either fired or is aggrieved because of some work injury, failure to be promoted or who has been harrassed on the job. An explosive or semi-automatic weapon offers the user a feeling of great power when employment or economic injustice produces a feeling of powerlessness within real or imagined victims. Thus, the need for the executive to pay attention to the way in which employees are handled and terminated is important and Gavin de Becker in his chapter highlights the problems to be found with this type of employee and the methods by which termination of them may be handled more effectively.

When the executive travels or is assigned to an overseas division his devotion to and interest in his security should heighten because he is in a strange land where he is the foreigner, one ignorant of the culture, politics of the country and the natives who may work for his corporation. His status as a security risk escalates several fold and his need for a reliable and specially trained security staff and advisor increases in the same way. With his family living with him, his needs increase even more and if the police agency is small or primitive he will need more than spears or revolvers in their armory to offer safety for him and his family. If he developed a security attitude while living and working in the United States he will be better prepared to extend the same view when he moved abroad.

23

Written Threats and Fan Letters: Psycholinguistic Analysis

In July, 1989, a rising star and actress, Rebecca Schaefer was killed as she answered the door of her home. A young man, later captured in Tucson, Arizona, had killed her, after having written to her for purposes of his own delusional structure, felt the need to end her life. He had written to her and apparently developed an erotomanic or love delusion type psychotic fantasy about the very woman he killed.

When I was a Deputy Sheriff with the Lane County Sheriff's Department in Detroit, Michigan, serving on a child killer task force in Oakland County, I was involved as a person to be interviewed by all forms of the media. I was the recipient of two telephone death threats plus several written notes, one of which was considered to be a very serious death threat from a man in Lafayette, Louisiana who was visiting Detroit. His quest was to get me to arrange an appearance for him on a popular ABC news show on Channel 7. As that was impossible, he then became very angry with me, threatening to kill me if I did not comply with his wishes.

At that particular time of the investigation I was used by the Task Force to promote interest in the investigation of the four killings, to solicit tip information and to follow leads, many times on an undercover basis concerning the deaths. I was considered to be at risk and had surveillance teams with machine guns outside my home during the night time hours and was followed continuously throughout the day as were members of my family and members of the surveillance team.

Although I was a psychiatrist and investigator I was still considered to be a celebrity because of the almost daily and certainly weekly appearances in the newspaper and the press. All of these media appearances and interviews were cleared through the Commander of the Task Force and the topics of these contacts were approved by that Commander. In an undated newspaper article by Lisa Fay Kaplan, she commented that stalkers are "all kinds of people where the lines between reality and imaginary social worlds are somewhat skewed. . . . For lots of people who focus on the public figure, that focus is the only anchor that holds their lives together."

The letter writer and stalker of a celebrity is a person who is frequently psychotic, usually suffering from paranoid schizophrenia. It is apparent that they yearn for recognition and the power which the life and style of a celebrity or an important person offers them by way of fantasy. It is as though by having contact with the celebrity, they hope to either merge with that celebrity and become like him or her or achieve a sense of power and prestige which their life up to that point had failed to bring them. In some sense their behavior seems to suggest and confirm the popular notion, it's not so much who you are but who you know. To apply that basic concept to an understanding of the stalker and letter writer would be to overlook the serious psychopathology involved and the possible great risk which lies in waiting for the celebrity.

His mission for his own aggrandizement is messianic. Contact with the star or an important dignitary is an achievement of recognition which carries the stalker beyond his wildest imagination.

He affronts the person to whom he corresponds by offering his love, guidance, ideas for becoming successful even though frequently the stalker is unemployed, his wrath in the event that the celebrity does not follow his directions and grant his wishes. DeBecker, in his analysis of more than 2,900 stalkers and written communications by them, developed some profile sketches of the stalker. He is most often a single, white, male, between 28 and 32 years of age, with an excessive interest in television and the movies.

As will be shown here, stalkers are not limited to persons with a psychopathologic interest in celebrities. My experience has involved plain people, ones who have threatened lesser known people like police officers as well as persons of the grandeur and reputation of Madonna.

Park Dietz, M.D., an expert interviewed by Lisa Kaplan, felt the central point for the stalker is his need to assume the identity of another person, as I stated. Mark David Chapman signed out of work on his last day with the name, "John Lennon."

Quoting Robert Ressler, Special Agent with the FBI and Criminologist with the Behavioral Sciences Unit, Lisa Kaplan indicated that he feels that stalkers latch on to celebrities because they are unable to handle a real relationship. It is well known that they have a poor track record in handling women or men and that in order to accomplish a relationship, an individual has to have a firm grip on reality and has to be responsible and be gainfully employed.

Most victims have achieved a level of fame and fortune as well as physical attractiveness and popularity, all the attributes which are missing in the stalker. The attraction is not limited to fame or beauty, however, because plain people can elicit the same level of devotion. Ressler feels that such stalkers tend to rationalize their love for the ideal person, with whom they attempt to communicate, as being pure. They want a perfect union, the type of relationship of a love object they have never known even as a child at home. They over invest and romanticize this union and I feel this forms the basis for the erotomanic attachment.

One thing that makes entertainers so popular as targets is because if they sing or are involved with romantic dialogue, the stalker seems to feel the singer or actress is making a special communication to them through their art form. It is the performer whom the stalker feels is extending an invitation to be contacted by him.

According to Lisa Kaplan, Park Dietz feels that about 10% of all letter writers will make some effort to contact the celebrity. What both Dietz and deBecker fail to note because their work brings them into contact with truly important people, is that the same phenomena involves a host of little people to whom the same link of erotomatic attachment may be made. In the mind of the average person the situation which looms up as one of the most easily recalled illustrations of the phenomena of the stalker and the celebrity is the Clint Eastwood movie in which a fan develops a homicidal interest in the person she has fantasies of having an affair with.

DeBecker and those of us in the security field in general, point out that public figures may well forfeit rights. In order to prevent encounters with persons who might be dangerous or disruptive, the individuals who pose this type of threat have to be identified. Otherwise, they may engage in stalking, trespass or lying in wait for the person who is the object of their delusional concerns.

Types of Stalkers and Letter Writers

In my experience there are six types of stalkers and letter writers that can be classified. I feel that we should start with the most simple form and work up to the greatest security risk for the principal being protected or who should be protected.

1. "The Fan."

This stalker and letter writer is someone who yearns for contact with the celebrity but feels the need primarily to share his or her admiration for the star. A response in terms of a personal note, autograph, photograph or the like is enough to satisfy this star-hungry correspondent. There are times when the fan will stalk the star or the important person in search of an autograph as the star leaves a restaurant or theater. This type of person frequently takes a bus tour around Hollywood to the homes of the stars and never seems to get enough of his or her favorite star in terms of not only patronizing their movies, plays or concerts but also feels a need to see them once again.

2. "The Erotomanic Worshipper."

This is an individual that goes beyond simple adoration of the star or celebrity and expresses feelings of love and romance. He may speak of undying love, a wish to marry or live happily ever after with the star. This may involve the thinking and actions of a true romantic type of fan who carries to a more personal level with the star or it may begin to show the early signs of a psychotic merger with the star in terms of seeing the star as a vital part to the stalker or letter writer's life.

3. "The Controller."

Type three involves a stalker or letter writer who carries it beyond the level of romantic attachment and begins to show an aggresive need and quest to control the life of the star. This individual frequently wants to take control of their future as a special kind of agent even though his own track record of achievement in reality is very poor. In his correspondence with the celebrity he expresses a fantasized concept of power through control of that celebrity, a sense of power that obviously he has never achieved in any real way in his own life.

4. "Violent Threatener."

This individual has begun to react to the celebrity or star's failure to not only correspond with him, but grant his wishes to come true in terms of either romance or the need to control. The celebrity's rejection of him as the letter writer defines it, produces such narcissistic injury that he begins to feel powerless in being able to achieve any fulfillment of his basic fantasy toward the celebrity. As a consequence of his growing feeling of impotence in the sense of power, he then tries to recover his loss of self esteem by threatening violence or reprisal towards the star. In this sense he engages in a form of emotional extortion and this makes him somewhat analogous to the terrorist making demands. In some respects this may is very much like a terrorist hostage taker. The only difference being, of course, he doesn't have the hostage in this particular case.

5. "The Death Threatener."

This type involves an individual who seeks to employ the ultimate form of power, death, by pronouncing a death sentence against the star. This would be comparable to the Shiite Muslims in Lebanon who threatened to kill Colonol Higgins and possibly Terry Waite as a threat to Israel's refusal to release the Shiite religious leader they had kidnapped a few days before.

This type, the death threatener, should be taken very seriously because he has reached a point where in all probability he has devised a plan and if not that, the intent to take the life of the celebrity or star. This of course, makes him extremely dangerous.

6. "The Killer."

This man has passed through the previous stages and has reached a point where reality testing has become very impaired in most cases and where he is prepared to make the celebrity pay the ultimate price, namely, losing his life. This is a person who feels justified in this unholy mission because he had given warning to the celebrity and feels that he has been as fair as he possibly could be.

This individual, not withstanding his psychopathology and mental illness, will engage in a stalking process regarding his prey, the celebrity. He may hire a private detective agency as was done in the case of the assassin of Rebecca Schaffer, the movie star. He may take a tour of the studio, attend a concert or political rally as Arthur Bremer had done in connection with both President Nixon and Presidential candidate Governor George Wallace.

He had made a decision about the weapon to be used and taken steps to obtain such a weapon. He devises his own plan to accomplish his execution of the celebrity who by this time he views as being the wrong doer, the one who destroyed his fantasy for power.

The security agent whose task it is to analyze these threats, should keep well in mind that if a given body of letters shows progression from type 1 through 5, then type 6 is just around the corner. He also should keep in mind that there are more people who are not celebrities who are recipients of these types of threats. The difference is that they are not prominent, they lack the funds frequently to hire private security, and they don't make the newspapers because their story is not as much of a priority as that involving a celebrity or important political figure or community leader. What I am saying here is that the security advisor should not limit his perspective to prominent people only. The same would apply to a police agency where citizens come in with correspondence of this type. As a Sheriff's Deputy with the Wayne County Sheriff's Department and as a forensic psychiatrist, I have had ample opportunity to read letters of this type.

Let's take a look at some examples of various types of stalkers and threateners. I would want to advise the reader to view my classification system as one in which there may be an overlap of one type of another, but at least one predominates over the others. As in the case in all efforts to classify behavior, we cannot always isolate an absolutely pure type remarkably and completely distinct from any other type within the classification system.

Case I

A wealthy, elderly couple received a mailgram with the following information:

"This letter is to inform you that your grandson, Adam, has a terrible, devastating addiction to crack. His habit is getting more and more addicting, yet, it is also getting more and more expensive. Adam is getting to a point where he has to reluctantly agree to take part in high risk crimes that yield high profits which include burglarizing, stealing from gamblers, smuggling Mexicans over the California border. With every close call Adam has destined to die of an overdose or be murdered. Do you care about Adam? You have to believe me, Adam does have a terrible drug problem. Why are you so scared of him? Get him help. The more you keep welcoming him in your house you are just letting him do it more. Remember when he stole your jewelry five years ago? He took it to the pawn shop over on Main Street and pawned it for drug money. Why did you let him get away with that? How could you love someone as bad as Adam as you both are very high class conservatives and prosperous people to have such a low life, good for nothing sleezebag, cold hearted bully for a grandson. If I were both of you, I would disown him or have him committed ten years in the County Jail. Please get him some help soon before it is too late. Adam thinks that when you both are dead he is going to inherit all your money. He is going to spend it on drugs. Please do yourself a favor whatever you do don't bequeath or endow all of that money to Adam, your grandson, because it will go to waste. Adam once stated that when you both are deceased that he is going to fence all of your material possessions for drug money. There are three things that are very important in Adam's life and those are drugs, money and sex. Adam is a very sick, twisted demented person and he needs help. Please see that he gets it or he'll end up in jail. Somebody will murder him or he will die of an overdose. Please get that through your heads. Sincerely yours, Jane Meadows."

The signature on the mailgram was a manufactured name. In reviewing the correspondence I noted that it alleged drug use, theft and predicted death twice and recommended jail for the alleged illegal activity of their grandson.

I felt the letter did not involve a death threat against the grandson or grandparents. It seemed to me to be a revenge motivated communication of harrassment, designed to terrify and create suspicion on the part of the family involved. There did not seem to be any personal risk of danger being directed toward members of the family. I cautioned that such a prospect might be forthcoming in terms of future contact by the perpetrator.

By way of background this family had received at least one phone call from an Hispanic accented woman whose communication followed the lines of the mail-gram but focused on knowing where the lady of the house kept her jewelry and acknowledging that the grandfather had a cane and knowing where it was kept. Notwithstanding the suggestion that the perpetrators had intimate knowledge of the home and family of these grandparents there had been no record of disloyal or fired employees, break-ins of the home, trouble with neighbors or relatives or with romantic connections of Adam or any other member of the family. There was no history of extra-marital relations with bitter feelings and there had been no problems with service people who had come to the home. Shopkeepers also had not posed a problem. There had been no public knowledge of the true address of his family as the phone was unlisted and the address was a post office box.

Thus, I suspected someone who had inside information would be some person of Hispanic identity who was either in the employ of the family or who had a relative, under 30 years of age, who might have been innocently informed of things by a member of the household staff or some unsuspecting employee in the normal course of conversation away from the job.

I suggested that employees be investigated and questioned carefully about family members, that they be permitted to hear the taped interview to enhance voice identification and be encouraged to cooperate in the security effort on behalf of the employer. Further I urged that all communication, written or verbal, be analyzed through the forensic section of West Coast Detectives, which I direct. I pointed out that an on-going effort had to be made to evaluate any further communication to see if the risk assessment changes.

Case II
In November, 1988, I performed a forensic psychiatric examination on a woman who had been an employee of the Post Office in a small community in California. In the course of her employment she had fallen and suffered a back injury. Her claim against the government was one which involved the development of psychiatric damages and problems as a result of her pain.

I submitted a report in which I excluded myself as an expert regarding whether or not she had a back injury, but did indicate that a review of her history showed that she had had not only a pre-existing psychiatric illness, but also a history of hospital treatment several years before her accident.

In April, 1989, I received two letters, approximately 2-1/2 weeks apart. Her first letter read as follows:

"Dr. Danto:

When I saw you in November I thought you would listen and tell the truth about me and my emotional condition. But I was naive. I should have known better than to believe you and tell you things that you turned around to your own and the Labor Departments advantage. Well, now I have anger directed at you instead of myself. A lot of rage is in here waiting for the right moment. I never stated that I wasn't on medication until 5/88. I have been on medication for years. I never hid that from you. There is a statement in your report that is not true. You state that I have a good recall for short term memory. That isn't true. I have increasingly less short term memory than at any time in my past. (Such a symptom, even assuming that it were valid, would not be connected with her back pain.) Ever since I had my accident, I have feelings that someone is watching me at all times. I feel that I have no privacy. I feel like someone has wired my house for anything I might say. I never had these thoughts before my injury. When you state that there is no evidence of a psychiatric disability at this time. (Sentence incomplete.) While I have been on medication for many years, but until the accident and resulting stressers placed on it by the pain staying or getting worse, I have not had to ever increase my medication to the point it is now. Most of my short term memory is gone. I have even been having blackouts, or freak-outs in which I find I am functioning, but in a state where I don't remember. Phone calls I don't remember, letters I wrote and don't remember, almost a whole day gone recently in which my husband says I acted ok, but none of which I remember. Now the latest, which is driving places, and not remembering how I got home. This is getting to really be traumatic to me. My psychiatrist is changing my medicines. The stress of living like this is killing me. There is no way you can in all honesty state that none of this comes from the stress of the injury. You state that there is no psychiatric disability. You are — well — you are wrong. I am at the point where my rage against you might come to fruition. I think you are scum. You should not consider yourself a doctor, trying to help them. All you are concered about is your money and the pocket. Even at the detriment of others. Well, you may have to pay some day. I'd start looking over your shoulder, and think that I might be out there waiting for the moment."

This letter was followed by another dated 4/24/89.

"Dr. Danto:

Thought you wouldn't hear from me again. I just wanted you to know that no one has the power to stop whatever I do. And if that means concerning you, you better think about it. Your deplorable examination was farcicle. You asked me many questions, and then you turn against me and tell me there is nothing wrong with me. (The point was not that she was free of psychiatric diagnosis, but rather there was no cause or connection between the injury and her psychiatric condition). Of course there is nothing the matter with me. Its all you. And you will pay. Do you remember who I am? If you do, who cares, I certainly don't. I know everyone is looking at me all the time. I can feel their eyes upon me, and its all your fault. (This ia frankly paranoid thinking and expresses ideas of persecution.) You told so many lies about me, that I have everything over you. I am going to make you squirm and feel like a bug that you are. A bug that can be squashed whenever I want to. I am so full of anger for you, that you watch out. I am at a point where I am ready to do something. I am not all talk. I will act, and act against you. I know where you work, and I will be waiting sometime, and you won't know when,

THINK ABOUT IT."

From this communication it is quite apparent that we are dealing with a person who is extremely angry at being questioned about what she considers to be a causal connection between her work injury and her psychiatric condition. She is unable to accept the reality of the fact that she had been ill for a number of years and that the feelings and symptoms of which she complains are not causally connected with her accident, or the injuries. In her threats to me she attempts to balance her own fears that people are following her, causing her to peer over her shoulder for some unidentified enemy, by trying to put me into a similar situation where I have to view her as an enemy the way she views the world as her enemy.

As one can see comparing the two letters, there had been an escalation and aggravation and intensification of feeling and it had gone from a basic complaint with resentment to one of a very clearly stated death threat, her statement that I could be squashed like a bug. One also sees the paranoid level of coping with the loss of power, namely in persuading me to do her bidding, and trying to offset it by holding the power of life or death over my head. This is an example of what I referred to when I talked about the inability of such a person to cope with narcissistic injury and the feelings of powerlessness to make the world conform to the fantasized wish and to have things go her way.

Case III

A young corrections officer at a county jail in a midwestern city was contacted by her aging parents with whom she did not live. Her parents turned over some letters which had been left with them by a black male. The corrections officer and her family are white.

This letter was followed by several others, some sixteen in all. It would be unnecessary or impossible at this juncture to duplicate all of the cards and letters that she received. Thus, some suitable and illustrative examples will be chosen to illustrate the point.

"Dear Ruth,

Dig the confession. You know at times I was the worst enemy to women, girls, female and tried in so many ways. Did destroy females from the earth as a man I was the man of steel or the strongest in ruling and dominating. I was the 'king of love.' I won in every war and fight over girls. None no matter how pure or decent. They were could feed me in no sex contest and none could defeat me in breaking hearts. I was colder and I never had to go to a girl. Every girl I loved for some magical reason and every how I thought it was thats the way it was. So I was saying if I loved the girl she loved me. If the girl was beautiful so far so was I. (This is an excellent example of merger with the love object.) I never really had no loss, of course some girls wasn't up to the standards so I couldn't love them because they do and would do things that I could never get low enough or things I wouldn't think of doing. Religion calls it sin and that expressions says, sin, they'll never be forgiven for. My expression (meaning impression) they're weak, to weak to exist very long."

"Well baby if you don't want me to go out hustling so much I won't, maby, youll want me to stay home and guard the house. If you want me to drive you to work and pick you up I will or do you use a shoff department car? (At this point he is asking for intelligence information so that he can know whether or not she may be armed or how to identify her location if he's keeping the department under surveillance.) Maybe you will have enough money so that I won't have to go out gitting things so much. I want some cats to have and I can find good milke in dumpsters so they'll grow strong and I'll find good meats and stuff eatable as the stuff inside some stores. I done wore about 10 or 9 bicks (bicycles) since I been out. Am in good shape for you, do you still like to ride bicks? My ankles and curves are super. Ok, let's work out or bicks sometime. (Bike sometime). I want your hips and thighs and ass to be super girl or perfectly perfect. If you're not going to haft to be the one on top and working or if you keep up your shape you can pump under me al the time, ok I'll just lay BACK without working sometime without complex." (This is a direct description of sexual fantasies toward her in terms of having intercourse.)

"Ok lets go back into that war."

"Ok girls ain't never won nothing from me in sex. You want to try? I challenge you. A Leo never turns down a challenge so let's get it on. Just seeing you a few times and once I seen you again. Now I can't forget you. You are in my mind days and nights and now you're taking over my dreams. (It is apparent at this point he not only wants to be taken over by her but he wants to merge with her and he is involved with obsessive thinking and compulsive behavior in terms of letter writing to deal with his obsessions). I haven't been able to forget you since love at first sight. So I feel quilty for some reason to want to build the rest of my life with you. Maby you think its reckless of me always thinking of a little girl and I've never kissed good. Well I can't and I'll be thinking about you the rest of my life, so do something for me. Do you think of me. Did you. Maybe you can patch me up by telling me you was in college when I was looking for you and that you didn't know I wanted to go steady with you. Don't lie. Did you think of me? If not I might surrender to you, but you might be more highly than I understand and I don't know you may not want to rule me. It's hard to do since I am very 'strong that' so it may be to much work and strain on you to DoMinate me the way I have been thinking about you all the time. I want to be slapped and taken, I want to be the positive quine (kind) knowing shes got me rapped (wrapped) around her finger and knowing she's everything. You have a love slave in a way, that's what you need isn't it, some gody (goody) you can be at east with, somebody you know and you want to be uncompterble (uncomfortable). You can live free and relaxed rulling (ruling) me like I ain't nothin but something you fuck and I'll obay (obey) you al the time."

"The sun is hot and so am I." (He drew a picture of a sun.)

"I've always tried to be the strongest in sex and love but if you've got the beauty to hold or take over my thoughts. By just a glympse at you so I know you have the power to dominate and rull. I'm sure your supreme command is irestable. The true virtue is for man to rule but it's gitting to be the true virtue for girls and women to rule. Maybe you'll be gitting the best dick ok I don't want to use those words so pussy me. Dick so you will be getting the purest stronger most faithful royal pussy in the world. I got some and lots mo'es so you'll be gitting the most. I got beauty marks so I'll have facuak an Indian ink blue marks on some of the mo'es. Ok I can do it better and longer than anyone but you so get of (off) this crazy blue golden snake. I'm sure I love to be on you and in you better than anything. On you in you ok and my tung (tongue) in your mouth is the greatest and the best thing I ever was and ever will be. I love you so much I can see everything you do. I might be walking through your walk soon, now if I'm expected the expected one, the twilight zone may carry me through."

And he continues on and on repetitiously showing the same kinds of meandering thoughts with loose associations.

In his most recent letter of 7/9/89 he began writing about his phone number and location, telling her that he had some cats for her.

Then he states, "now I've did alot of fighting and I don't want to do, I don't like fighting unless you are cornered like a rat and I had the right to kill those punk bitches when they broke in to kill me. And I almost did but I dropped my knife when I grabbed the pipe away from the one who got throw the door and then the one with the bass Ball bat jumped through the window. So I almost got both of them but they were outside with pistols. They would have killed me if I wouldn't have got up and jumped out the window. They tried to kill me with a knife like I said they stole all my close (clothes) and food. Really they stole $100 worth of things and my paintings are unlimited in value."

Further on in the letter he makes this statement which shows his poor grasp of symbolism and reality when he wrote, "so you got to live your own miserable life now. Though you hate me, my hatred is stronger and you may get killed cause your image is to beautiful to be a, you know what, especially since laws are the weakness and downfall of reality." It is very apparent in this statement that he very clearly sees laws and limit setting as impairments to his control and he feels that all that is important to him is discharging and gratifying his wishes.

Right after he makes a threat against her which would definitely move him from type 3 with a wish to control her life to type 4, he states as if nothing had been said before, "well baby, after this page that's it." (It was not it he continued to write several more pages.) "Ok I guess I'll send you some pictures. Later on why shouldn't I give you the freedom to go and git fucked and knocked up. Let me do the fucking and knocking you down, ok?" (It should be important to note that he really on the surface had intended to say to refer to getting knocked up as a way of chracterizing pregnancy. However, his aggressive impulses dominated in this communication and ran away with him and it came out as knocking her down. This again is an ominous message in such a communciation.) "If it was anybody else, they would just want you to lay on the, at night holding on to your ass, not me, and al I wanta do is lay on you al night while you got your amrs raped (its interesting that it comes out raped and it also is a misspelling of the word wrapped) around my back and shoulders, pulling me deeper and closer and further in you body with my tung and lips on yours ok? And my eyes looking straight down into yours. I know I'm getting no where so after fighting all those niggers and now those pigs and don't want to fight you so leave me alone."

This becomes an important passage to understand because it represents a cross current of a number of feelings, sexual and aggressive, and so he describes what he would like to do with her it seems that he really is setting up a situation where he becomes sexually aroused and may actually have masturbated after this passage because then he goes into another passager as though all of the sexual significance and feeling is gone and he refers back to how he fought with some blacks.

One thing that is important about a letter like this is that it does not mean somebody sat down and continued to write the letter without end until it was completed. I feel he gave himself some sexual gratification in a sexual way before he went on to then express anger because his sexual fantasy obviously was not real and would not be brought to fruition.

He concluded this note by saying, "I apealed (appealed) my ssi decision but I don't have a lawyer so fuck it."

"So now you've got make me work with a broken head and back."

"I guess you would be mad with me alot if I lived with you and not working."

"I guess I'd be fucking you and you would get mader and mader (madder) and you would start trying to dominate me like your the one fucking."

"So if you would try to do that, I would go find a job. I got a cherry and dont want to be fucked."

"I would rather live over that way. Do you know where is a house and an apartment I can rent."

In my review of the material I corresponded with the investigating detective and pointed out that he was a man who was a poor speller who either has done a lot of fighting, has been violent or has had violent fantasies. Throughout these fantasies he showed control by stating that he dropped the knife even though he could have killed "those punks."

Throughout his writings, I felt, there was a significant amount of fragmentation of thoughts and confusion, i.e., "if you aren't going steady with me, are you?" "Who are you? I don't even know you?" I felt there was identity and object confusion for the girl to whom he had been writing and felt it was apparent that she is a psychotic transference object for another person, possibly his mother. His thoughts and ideas fragment and run from cats, to going steady, to violence, to work, to travel, all within the same paragraph. He seemed to think of her all the time and this reflects the intensity of his obsessive thinking about her. I felt that his thinking was disconnected, i.e. "you may get killed because your image is too beautiful to be a, you know what, especially since the laws are the weakness and downfall of society." This is a typical rambling speech of a schizophrenic person with a strong paranoid cluster of symptoms. Her paranoid power concerns are seen in this statement but also in other letters, "though you hate me, my hatred is stronger."

His need to possess her was seen in his statement, "why would I give you your freedom to get fucked and knocked up. Let me do the fucking and knocking you down." This is an important slip as he goes from sex to pregnancy to assault. He refers as armed "raped" and means wrapped and in this sentence was an unconscious message, his sex, the fusion of sex and aggression.

He wrote in another letter of hitting a man thirty times with a pipe, bragging that he weighed 135 pounds and the other man 280 pounds. This too I felt might be a fantasy rather than an actual encounter. Then he fragmented badly, searches for some identity by stating that he will become a great singer, mentioning pieces of other identities like being Black, Jewish, Russian, etc. I felt this man really did not know who he was.

As I've already commented, each letter seemed to contain sexual references along with many drawings of sexual activities showing oral, anal and genital sex. I felt that he seemed to get so worked up in his writing that it sounded like he was preparing to masturbate. Along with sexual things he would like to do to her he also added, "blood is dripping from my feet, blood is dripping out of your dick." It is quite apparent that there is a lot of sexual confusion as he gets worked up emotionally. This is another example of a merger, an effort to identify with her and merge with her where he even gets to take on some of the sexual qualities of her sexuality and he sees her as taking on his sexual characteristics. It's almost as if he has an oceanic feeling of wanting to merge with the mother and practically back to the womb and this is a hallmark sign of a highly regressed psychotic individual.

Aggression was prominent throughout all of his writings. He refers to beating a man to death, "ass fucking, biting your ass and tits" and his perversion is seen in licking off her nasal snot, licking her ass, eating her pussy, having her punish him and other times his slapping her is punishment but in this area he backs off quickly by saying that if she doesn't want to he will not. His sado-masochistic fantasies keep him running into more pages of writing.

I felt the death implication was seen in his writing, "You don't have a life to live no more." His sexual confusion was seen in his statement, "My house, my hole, my life, my womb. ...." Another death implication warns, "don't desire somebody else" and that he "can destroy her in a heartbeat if anybody desires her."

His writings were filled with the use of an eye, a large eye, which is a paranoid kind of symbolism as though he's watching her. He also expressed ambivalent feelings about possessing her and being possessed by her and this was seen in this statement, "You fuck. I'll obey at all times. You'll have the power to dominate, to rule." Another ominous note was, "the more you hurt, the better I feel."

There was some homosexual material, a reference as seen in his writings when he stated, "I've never been fucked by a woman or a girl." His sexual urges display a very deep longing, almost an oral need to be fed by a maternal figure.

I felt there were other ominous notes in his writings concerning the fact that he had contacted her parents, knows that her mother has her phone number as she called in his presence to ask her daughter whether or not she wanted to talk to this man. He also knew that she had a blue truck. I felt some concern about the possibility that he could take her parents as hostage or torture or hold the mother hostage until he teases her daughters phone number from her as well as her address.

On the positive side of his letter I felt, "I don't kill except in self defense." The question is of course, how does he define self defense? I felt that in his twisted mind he might feel the need to kill in self defense when it is a definite offensive action, killing her, i.e., to save himself from being destroyed because she will not answer his pleas to marry him. He states that he will not kill her but then asks if she carries a gun. I would be concerned about that. A second time he mentions beating her to death if she flirts with another man. I wondered what would happen if he learned from some source that she is either married or had a boyfriend. Would that justify him, in his own mind, that he should kill her? I think so. He wrote, "I don't want to hurt you unless you hurt me." If rejection by her is hurtful as he sees it, then he may feel a paranoid justification to hurt her.

I felt that this man suffers from a schizophrenic reaction, chronic paranoid type. I feel that he is very dangerous at the class 3 and 4 level but was not an immediate threat to a homicide to the corrections officer. I felt that if he was able to locate her and could force her into being his sexual slave and could fulfill the extent and range of his sado-masochistic fantasies, that this would be a possibility and thus would pose a serious security risk for her, even though it didn't involve her life directly. This was very clearly the case when Cameron Hooker and his wife kidnapped and tortured Colleen Stan, in California, for a seven year period of time and kept her prisoner in a special compartment under their bed.[2]

I felt that this man was close to a loss of control and would try to track her down through her jail assignment or reach her through her parents. I felt he was the hunter in search of prey.

Psychodynamically, I felt he was a man who was unconsciously frightened of women. I see him as feeling that they are more powerful than him as they can grant love and sex, can control and punish and have attraction he feels he does not have. He talks of himself as a man with a banged head and a bad back who can't even qualify for social security disability and has to beg the corrections officer to write, to be his girl and wife. I feel in fantasy at least, he turns to violence to make himself feel powerful, to offset the deep underlying fear of women he feels.

Case IV

Early in 1989 an unemployed young man, under the age of thirty, wrote several letters to a female newscaster. Much of his correspondence concerned her and fantasies that he had about the well known entertainer Madonna.

A sample of some of his correspondence to the newscaster, whom he wanted to

2. McGuire, C. & Norton, C.: *Perfect Victim*. New York: Arbor House/William Morrow, 1988.

use for her own attraction plus the go between role he wanted to have between her and the movie star, will be presented. It's not possible to cover all of the correspondence, but to offer the reader a sample so that the psychodynamics and intent can be established.

"Dear Mable,

Maybe the next time I'll try to phone you. I still want to see you. I think you and I could make the most of our worlds if we just got to be around each other. The thing is, one look at what we are doing would make us the best of friends in the world (physically and morally.) Another is me and you are the only two people that will and were made meant to be together. Phoning seems it would hurt our first impression. You know the only thing that I am learning to do is think of why you married Gabe and what your new plans are. You know there's a girl that worked at a restaurant in Anaheim with me. Actually she works in the front offices and I worked in the labor shops but I just have a feeling the story how Gabe caught you is catching up to me. Too scary for me. Just know who I am and how I feel. Don't let me catch me getting to know those rumors unless involved people."

"I got laid off and now nothing interesting my way. Try to get a hold of me and I'll drop everything for you to give my listen. I like what you're involved with, what you look like and what you seem to be. I lived the most interesting life but seems unintelligent unless I have a way of knowing what you would advise me to do about my near future. I'm losing how to feel what you think."

In this communication it is apparent that he is unemployed, is troubled about the fact that she is married, and that he lacks the opportunity of having a relationship with someone so highly desirable.

In another letter he said, "can't be your secretary or something. You seem like a sister to me. Who does all of your real friendly stuff for you. I've seen alot of bad things before but you know I don't see what any of those things could be a part of your life. Kind of funny there are things about you no one seems to be interested but I'm keeping quiet, maybe a great start huh?"

In another letter he states, "I'm ready to lose my apartment, any forseeable job, my family never stuck together so I'm on my own and my mom helps but says she's half disabled and I'm taking move twenty times. Ive never had a long distance money to save the phone numbers. I got under ten days of whatever it is I do to keep things going for myself. I don't see how you fit in to any of this except the phone call. (He gave his phone number.) I don't think you understand Polly Atkins (this guy's name for another female newscaster) as well as I do and Boris Joines (a morning show host)."

This was a chatty type of letter in which he reports his failures but it's obvious that there is no strong psychological undercurrent.

However, in another letter he wrote in the following way:

"Why do I have reactions from Madonna? It's not nerves, I wrote down situations of my reactions in my other letter."

"That Friday night it turned into obsession, love and hate, at that time she thought

I hated her. She didn't think anything that night, and there was no feeling on my face and I was nervous. I don't hate her, I'm very fond of her. I wouldn't hurt her. I feel happy inside. Radiant. I read in the newspaper last week something about love, It has a relaxing affect on my body, the heart, that reminds me of the time I saw a picture of her in the newspaper with a hat on from Shanghai Surprise. The way I felt mellow inside and had a warm feeling in my heart. I don't hate her. How would you feel if somebody wrote songs about you and left you neglected?"

"That night it was turned into obsession. That part when a fan's voice is saying, I loved her the first time I saw her."

"I didn't love her the first time I saw her. I just liked her. I didn't realize my feelings. It was too late. I didn't notice my feelings. I don't know when I began to feel this way. It wasn't an instant crush."

"I like others like Sheena Easton, Jacilyn Smith, I just like them, that's all, I don't love them. I know better than to be hooked on Madonna. I don't daydream about her. I'm awake. I never saw this coming. I didn't know it was going to turn out like this."

"I don't understand how this is all in my head. The way these things started happening somebody else noticed it first. My friend saying it seemed like every time I came over that song about San Pedro is on. The way it happened again and again. My friend didn't know about me and my feelings at the time. I know it sounds strange but somebody else noticed it at first."

He continues in this manner and then reports a conversation he had with a friend about Madonna,

"I told him about those two earthquakes and he told me they shouldn't have happened because of Madonna. Sam said they did happen on those two mornings. They could have happened any other morning. That tremor in February 88 was an aftershock from that October 1, 87 quake. Instead of that Thursday morning it could have happened another time. The world doesn't revolve around me. My brother says it happens because I think about it. But I wasn't thinking about it. When I got that TV Guide and saw Shanghai Surpprise for 8:00 a.m. that Tuesday morning, I just skipped passed it. No thought or mention of seeing it. I just skipped passed it."

"... I want to forget my past. One of the first letters I sent at Warner Brothers Records in Burbank, I said how the songs from Who's That Girl are about me. That was January, 88. A Saturday night at that time, between 10:30 and 11:00. I had this feeling in my face. She found out about my letter and I felt it."

"Then in late February, A Marilyn Martin song came out, 'Possessive Love.' It was co-written by Madonna."

"When I heard it, I had a bad feeling it was about me. I held too tight."

"I felt sorry and hopeless inside. At that time she was in New York. I sent a letter explaining why I was holding too tight. I sent that letter, my face felt tired and my cheekbones were hurting with an ache. That Possessive Love video was being shown on until and then it wasn't on any more."

In all, the subject of this investigation had written thirteen letters to the celebrity newscaster about Madonna as well as his feelings about her.

My analysis of the written communication which refers to information not revealed in the sample of correspondence shown suggests a man who seemed to write when the impulse hit him. The impulse might make itself known by a feeling in his face which he interpreted as a telepathic communication from the celebrated with whom he yearns to have contact. There was no date, time of the week or month which seemed to fit a pattern. He struck me as being an impulse driven person who yearns for recognition from someone in power and feels insecure about himself and seeks recognition from the rich and famous. He adores the idea of seeing his name in print, as evidenced by a printed letter and response from "what your dream means" article with an interpretation from Dr. Morris.

Of interest to me was the fact that more than six times he assured the reader that he is not dangerous to Madonna and has no sexual interest or fantasies about her; yet, he also repeated the story about her having an affair with her body guard. I sense that he harbors intense sexual fantasies which were dominated by his wish to see her as a maternal figure, giving him unending nuture. He seemed to be afraid of being sexual and operates at a fairly childish and infantile level of psychosexual function.

I felt there were at least latent schizophrenic illness signs in his writings and his use of his face as a telepathic confirmation of Madonnas awareness of him. This is a typical schizophrenic reality distortion. In addition, he seemed to suffer from an obsessive compulsive disorder. This was seen in his unending obsessions about her and then the female newscaster as well as his compulsion to write letters and make them aware of his presence, interest and magic powers in making him seem important despite his own lack of success as measured by job layoffs.

In one note he commented about the beginning of a feeling of a love hate obsession. This to me was an ominous sign. It was quickly followed by a denial of wanting to hurt her. Why did he have to mention that? He is angry over her failure or refusal to give him recognition. The basic narcissistic personality he displayed was reflected in his feelings that the world revolves around him, the songs are about him and Madonna has a need to communicate with him. In order to deal with the painful reality that none of this is true he has to imagine a telepathic communication. Many references to real life are made by this man but such statements do not offset the fact that all of his productions are sheer fantasy. His reference of the ice turning into the image of a cross mentioned in one of the letters is a sign of schizophrenic thinking with decompensation. Frost assumed the shape of a cross in the same letter. Again in the same letter he discussed feeling the pain of another. This represents a hysterical identification with that person, showing poor ego boundaries and a defective sense of self which he could not separate from the boundaries of another person with whom he invests his erotomanic or love delusion feelings.

In another letter he expressed resentment over being ignored "because I'm not somebody famous." What concerned me is what he was willing to do to get recognized. Would he use violence or kidnapping to achieve that status? That is a risk that preventive protection must consider for this man, I felt. This is seen in the same letter when he asks, "why do you already have to be popular? My reactions have to mean something."

I felt that impotency was suggested in the same letter on the second page when he wrote, "I don't have those kinds of urges. I am ready to take an oath on the Bible, to a priest."

Dr. Morris, the columnist to whom he wrote, suggested that Madonna represents sexuality, excitement, rebellion as well as virginity and motherhood. I would agree but felt that she also represents power, the power of a maternal woman and how by contrast he feels so weak as a male. For a person with these kinds of feelings, violence offers a feeling of having a competitive edge. For him, it seems there is a wish to possess her, control her, and run her life. This would thus qualify him for a rating of 4 on the scale of 6.

In another letter he searched for what is real and wrote, "why do I have reactions? This isn't a movie, this is real life, I feel her feeling, what does it mean?"

I did not see him as constituting an immediate threat in terms of either violence or homicide. It seems in his letters he was falling apart and might try to do something to gain attention by crashing the security barrier at a studio or tracking her if he succeeds in locating her address. I recommended that he be permitted to write freely, thus enabling monitoring to be established of his thinking, but would not recommend any kind of response by way of a letter from her or anybody. Once he gains that type of concession, like many of the letter writers, he would be able to gain some confidence out of the recognition and press for contact or some other concession. I felt that contact with a celebrity made him feel important and powerful. This feeds his fantasy life and will keep him at bay unless or until actual contact becomes more important. In the event that would happen, I felt he would communicate his thoughts and wishes to achieve that end before he acts.

I urged more opportunity to analyze the correspondence as it emerges in the future. I felt he was mentally ill and was cracking and his behavior and thoughts were becoming more regressed as were his ego defenses which appeared to be wearing thin. This type of mental deterioration portends irrational behavior at some level but there was nothing to point in the direction of danger to either celebrity.

Case V

For a number of years a self styled minister had attended a local church in a mid-size California community. In 1982, his wife passed away and this parishioner donated an engraved plaque to the church as a memorial to his wife. However, it was church policy not to receive gifts with memorials written on them and he was advised of this and could direct the offering to a certain activity of the church. It was suggested that he could make an appropriate donation for hand bells for their hand bell choir and that this would be greatly appreciated. The parishioner donated $1,000 for purchase of an additional octave of hand bells.

Subsequently, the parishioner began dating a woman in the church. Although she was advised not to marry this man, they were indeed married, but six months later the woman had the marriage annulled. It was at this point that he began to engage in letter writing. He wrote to almost anybody who was connected with the church. His correspondence consists of a hodge-podge of incoherent and unrelated, rambling thoughts.

In his letters he wrote about his childhood and how his father had accused him of wasting money. He wrote about his lack of sexual fulfillment and how in reference to his frist wife who had died, a doctor had instructed him that he had to have 52 orgasms a year. He indicated that that wife was not fulfilling for him. He began raising sexual questions about another woman to whom he had been married before the deceased wife. He made reference to the fact that he did not want to "pat a man's ass" and that many wives do not want their husbands to pat other peoples' behinds.

Throughout his correspondence he expressed feelings of being rejected even by his Sunday School class and that he was rejected by his pastor as well as his former wife.

Soon the correspondence began to express the view that "the system" was against him.

In one letter he wrote of his minister, "Jake Smith has been anointed a prophet of the inner-mix Gospel of Jesus Christ, best known to me in the words of Ethan Allen open in the name of Jehovah and the Continental Congress of the United States of America or Jake Smith is dead."

In another letter he wrote, "don't die, Jake, you have balls. Get it up. What is it? Your riffle or your gun."

In another letter he wrote, "Lord Jesus, take Jake Smith home or through Mrs. Jones." In another undated letter he stated, "Damn it, Jake, rejected me they rejected her. Are you evil Jake? I hope not, because I don't really want to go to jail in it already in myself."

He began to act out in church and on one Sunday when the body guard of the minister was gone, he approached the minister, touched him aggressively in the chest and began to recite various passages from scriptures.

In a letter to his former divorced wife, he wrote, "when you told me not to believe Christy about you chocking her adoptive mom, you finally admitted that Christy was not telling the truth when you tried to chock me."

When a fourth grade girl was found masturbating in church, and this raised questions about sexual molestation, the parishioner wrote, "blank is a younger you with an M.A. in education, some much easier to teach than you everything goes in sex. Why question? You are thirty years with not able to masturbate as early as many others, therefore, able to keep an erection longer than most."

In a letter to Jake he said, ". . . am I blind? No I'm minded. Why. The rejections. Who Jake, a Jesus Christ rapid! No one, who do you reject just as much as me? When the convention was wallowing, yes. Why? The dome. It's meant old but the absence of good pets definition and stain is powerful. Why is Jake brilliant? He is a Norman Vincent Peale disciple, Disciple of Religious Science. Who do you reject. 8, 9, 10,

11, 12th graders. Where's Milly? You rejected her father. When do I want glory. In my casket. I like George Saunders' butt. Who rejected me for years, rejected me. Why? He thought I'd steal his church. I don't have time to steal his church. I did not reject your church. Jake, your church rejected me. Why? I am not a pariah. If there is only the Christian everyone on earth your stories Jake, the cow, Pat says it is a autumn joke used.

You admitted you twisted it. Why? Because you have a tiger by the tail . . ."

I don't think it takes a psychiatrist to figure that this is a man showing a great deal of degeneration in this thinking and decompensating, reaching a point where he is unable to think out his thoughts logically. He is feeling very rejected, blames the minister of his church, and shows a wandering and bringing together of ideas without any particular sense to them.

I have the feeling since he was critical of his father and that his minister, Jake, offered him an opportunity to retaliate, based on the letters and information that I had obtained. I was called upon by the attorney for the church to testify as to an opinion concerning whether or not this man seemed to be unstable and was creating a sufficient disturbance within the church that a restraining order should be issued. I gave testimony and filed a report so that a restraining order was issued against this man's further participation in the church.

Shortly after my testimony in April, 1988, I received a letter from him.

"Dear Dr. Danto:

Because of the gossip you listened to on the telephone and in an hour long conference with the attorney and the law offices of the attorney, you have mal-practiced in describing me a mentally disturbed paranoid schicophrenic who should be institutionalized to not actuate a death threat against Jake Smith similar to that actuated by John Hinkley actuated against President Ronald Reagan. What you determined leading to that actuality was delivering of a court small claim's claim and order by Dr. and Mrs. Green while I watched. The Reverand and I met in the Center for Enlightenment she founded in 1986 just before I entered the hospital. I was subconsciously grinding my dentures. The doctor suggested I try Xanax. I did a week and then checked in to another hospital. The Reverand Little, the valedictorianof our high school, herself apsychiatrist or an attorney, the mother of law students, herself a psychiatrist or an attorney, did her brilliant uneducated salesman father think a woman had any worth in the professions. I wasnt eating right and I was tickling why I checked into the hospital. The hospital thought I might be atartive diskynesic because the medications and took me off them. I still tick because of the resolution of life's stresses you have aggravated in your ignorance, Dr. Danto. I went to the college hospital to read what I could of you material most of which is printed and not published. Because of your grant from Wayne State University in the Federal Government you found during I think three months summer periods Blacks with unregistered guns and Whites with registered guns were homiciding and commiting suicide probably because of societal economics forces were out of manufacture had been transported to Japan. Through this you met the Vita Society and Suicide Prevention. The society from LA transferring to Detroit, Michigan, with you editing the material that stopped coming to the UCLA medical library last decade, I think. Because you are not an evangelical protestant, Dr. Danto, you know next to nothing about fundamentalism evangelicism, neo-evangelicalism and liberalism. The church of Fullerton is a highly fundamentalist church which calls itself evangelical which it is not. The radio pastor, the church having no senior pastor, will not call spades spades because of the effect upon giving. I am a graduate of the seminary which second president, the school only having three, called spades, spades in his book is the three part series discussing fundamentalism, evangelicalism, and liberalism. His book, A Case for Orthodoxy, was detrimental to giving in those days in the seminary."

His letter continued to ramble about things that were totally disconnected and reviewed his failures in the Navy to achieve the rank of commander, his wife's death and his desceased wife's family background. Each area of information he offered was a jumbled mass of thoughts that continued to collide with one another.

This man did not at any time make a direct threat toward anybody. What was interesting in three or four letters was his rather consistent reference to a study I did on firearm violence and death. Here is an example of the way he dealt with this problem:

". . . They would rather read the bull shit Dr. Danto endorses . . . enclosed "

"I'm back in court again in six months . . ."

"Why were people in Detroit dying by registered and unregistered guns in the study the physician is 'milking' for too much."

He also had made a reference to "riffle" in another letter which was a misspelling of the word rifle.

I felt that this man was extremely disturbed mentally, filled with erupting and conflicting ideas and each sentence was an odyssey in indistinguishable separate clauses, sometimes numbering fourteen or fifteen. I felt that he had the capacity to be dangerous but that in the absence of real threats I would not have classified him more than a disturbed letter writer whose thoughts were rambling and fragmented and who was seeking attention for whatever cause he felt justified his actions.

I recommended to the security committee of the church that he indeed was a man to be watched because of his instability but that he did not pose an immediate threat to the minister.

Case VI

A businessman received a communication and turned it over to a security company which then contacted me.

The message read:

"Mr. J,

YOU ARE KEEPING COMPANY WITH SOMEONE ELSES GIRLFRIEND AND HE IS NOT TOO HAPPY ABOUT IT. JANE FISH WILL BE TAKING A TRIP SOON SHE WILL NOT BE RETURNING. DO NOT EXPECT HER, OR TRY TO GO WITH HER, OR YOU WON'T RETURN EITHER. THAT IS AN EASY PROMISE AND YOU ARE PLAYING OUT OF YOUR LEAGUE.

THIS IS YOUR FIRST, LAST AND ONLY WRITTEN WARNING. THE PHONE TAPS HAVE BEEN REMOVED BUT YOUR MOVEMENTS HAVE BEEN WATCHED AND RECORDED, SO DON'T GET IN THE WAY."

There was no other information to go on and the security agency would not discuss any of the personal factors of their client's social relationships or the like.

I did have access to a second document which consisted of printed messages taken obviously from a magazine with key words to make up the message which had been chosen to communicate.

Glued on the top of the page was, "there are no simple answers, but you can find happiness." Then below that, "to error is human" and below that in large letters perhaps an inch and a half tall was the word, "MOVE."

I felt that the writer of both documents was the same person, one who might be a secretary or works in an advertising agency. The pasted letter was made in the form of key-lining and the typed letter appeared as if the person has written an advertisement in want ad style.

It was obvious that there was a threat since the primary message was for the recipient of this letter to stop dating a certain woman. However, it was not a direct threat of homicide but a hope that the man would stop doing what was so offensive to the writer. This did not mean that he or she could not kill Mr. J. What it did mean was that the writer was trying to avoid that necessity and manipulate him away from the other woman successfully.

I speculated that the writer could be a boyfriend of the writer but, although this was a possibility, the note had a distinct female quality and I sensed that the writer was a woman who had been shoved aside by a new woman in the life of Mr. J. I felt that this woman could be found in his own office in light of the information I had received.

I suggested that the suspect be polygraphed and furthermore if this was inconclusive, then I would be happy to follow it up with a Brevital interview.[3] Brevital sodium in a 1% solution acts much in the nature of Amytol except that it has the advantage of avoiding any prolonged sedative effect. It is a safely administered drug which I have used in some 500 different examinations and it has the advantage of being safe except for those who may have cardiopulminary disease, liver disease or allergies to various kinds of medication. The drug is given intravenous and the whole procedure is recorded or videotaped from beginning to end so that whoever views the tape will be able to know exactly what was said and what happened.

The mechanism of action for Sodium Brevital interviews is that the chemical serves as a hypnotic agent which paralyzes the sensory portion of the mind, and makes for spontaneous responses to questions. This is in keeping with the World War II use of Scopolamine, a similar drug by the Germans which led to the name Truth Serum for this procedure.

---

3. Danto, B.L.: The Use of Brevital Sodium in Police Investigation. *Police Chief.* 66 (5) : pp. 53, May, 1979.

Case VII

This case concerns a 25 year old deputy from a rural sheriff's department in the midwest. He had received five or six very brief notes, each arriving on a Tuesday in which his life was threatened. Investigating detectives contacted me for assistance in some psycholinguistic analysis of the notes. The writings were half in hand writing and half in lettered writing. [Samples of the writings are not available for publication because they are part of a sheriff's department investigational file, thus this is being offered in an anecdotal manner.]

The lines were simply written and concerned simply stated death threats and statements of anger, written more as if the writer was attempting to ventilate feelings of anger rather than actually make a very determined death threat.

Each letter was hand delivered to me after its arrival and after it had been checked for latent prints. Of interest was the fact that it was postmarked in a town which was 60 miles away from where the letter was received. We knew that mail deposited in front of a drug store in this town was taken to this other city where it was processed by the post office and then returned to the same town. There was one other drop box which was delivered directly within the town. This helped us locate a possible drop box for the letter.

One note in particular that was delivered to me for analysis was different from other letters to the extent that it made allusions to a powerful revenge the letter writer would carry out against the officer to whom the notes were addressed. By the way, all notes were delivered to the Sheriff's Department where he was employed.

The letter struck me that this was an escalation of aggressive feeling and I somehow envisioned that the letter writer might very seriously consider delivering a bomb and I expected the next communication to be a box with a bomb.

As fate would have it, the next communication on the following Tuesday was a box with a bomb.

However, this was not a lethal bomb but a toy bomb consisting of a 7-Up soda pop can with Kleenex stuffed on the inside in the form of wadding.

This suggested a playful prank on the part of the writer and also suggested that the writer was a young person, possibly even a child.

Because I felt the letters were placed in a drop box in front of the drug store I then proceeded to investigate another lead in the case. The deputy's wife was a full time worker at the drug store and recalled that a woman whom her husband used to date was extremely angry over the fact that he had married his current wife rather than her. I then obtained samples of the suspect employee's handwriting; these were easily obtained from inventory sheets that she had handled at the store. The combination of writing and printing seemed almost identical to the notes. We thought we had our letter writer.

However, the police department with the postal inspector established an observation post at a store across from the letter box drop. The investigating detective wisely suspected the letters were dropped on Sunday, taken by the postal employees to the town some 60 miles away, processed, stamped and assigned for delivery back to the town where the letter had been dropped and delivered on Tuesday.

On a particular Sunday, the detective and the postal inspector arranged that each time somebody dropped a letter in the drop box they would then cross the street, examine the letter to see if it was addressed to the officer, and then put a thin sheet of tissue paper on top so that the next drop would then land on a clean surface.

At about 2:00 in the afternoon on that Sunday, a church school bus stopped in front of the box and the minister descended from the bus and deposited a letter in the drop box. After the church bus left, the detective and postal inspector crossed the street, and low and behold, there was another letter addressed to the Sheriff's deputy.

Further investigation revealed that the minister deposited the letter for one of the young adult mentally retarded parishioners on the bus. He was, with his peers, being brought back from the church to the community placement where he and his peers lived.

The young man, in his late twenties, when confronted, admitted that he was the letter writer and then revealed his reason for threatening the life of the deputy. He had been on the church bus some months before and had thrown a rock at a patrol car that was passing the church bus. This patrol car was driven by the officer he had threatened. The officer pulled the bus over, ascended into it and admonished the passengers that it was dangerous to throw rocks at cars and that anyone damaging government property could be arrested.

The bus driver reported the incident and the letter writer then was brought to the Sheriff's Department by the bus driver and was forced to apologize to the police officer in front of the Sheriff.

Apparently he felt very humiliated and sought revenge.

This incident had occurred some eight months prior to the delivery of the threatening letters.

The case was solved and the young man was moved back to an institutional placement from his community placement.

Conclusion

The stalker and letter writer have been discussed in terms of what they do as well as the kinds of clinical psychiatric and emotional problems that seem to be associated with the activity. It is apparent that most are very disturbed, particularly those who want to merge with celebrities or who express very possessive feelings about the stars or other subjects they stalk and threaten. Five different types of letter writer-stalkers were discussed, each progressing to a more serious level of risk. The sixth type is the person who has initiated a plan of action to actually kill the object of his stalking and communication.

A great deal more has to be learned about this type of individual who threatens and sometimes takes the lives of people. It is important that those of us who are engaged in analytic work let the results of our work be known so that we can perfect the art of analysis. In this way perpetrators will be prevented from carrying out their sick plans and lives will be saved through prevention and apprehension of such persons.